The Gospel of Matthew

Question by Question

Also in this series

THE BOOK OF GENESIS: Question by Question

by William T. Miller, SJ

The Gospel of Matthew

Question by Question

John F. O'Grady

Paulist Press
New York/Mahwah, NJ

Cover and book design by Lynn Else

Library of Congress Cataloging-in-Publication Data

O'Grady, John F.
    The Gospel of Matthew : question by question / John F. O'Grady.
        p. cm.
    Includes bibliographical references.
    ISBN 978-0-8091-4440-2 (alk. paper)
    1. Bible. N.T. Matthew—Textbooks. I. Title.
    BS2576.O37 2007
    226.20071—dc22

                                                              2006037683

Published by Paulist Press
997 Macarthur Boulevard
Mahwah, New Jersey 07430

www.paulistpress.com

Printed and bound in the
United States of America

Contents

Contents

Contents

"...so shall my word be that goes forth from my mouth;
it shall not return to me empty."
Isaiah 55:11

For students and friends who by their encouragement compel
me to relate the word of God to ordinary living.

Especially:

Mrs. Mallory (Mary) Horton
Neta Kolasa
Angela and Micajah Pickett
Marta and Ignacio Prado
Lurana Snow

Introduction

I have always liked the Gospel of John. Most of my professional and personal interest has centered on this gospel. My least favorite gospel has always been Matthew. I decided I wanted to do this commentary on Matthew for three reasons. It would offer more of a challenge for me and I would learn more about this unfavorite gospel. Also, for more than thirty years I have been associated with St. Matthew's Parish in Voorheesville, New York. It is about time I learned more about the patron saint of this wonderful parish.

Over the course of writing this commentary I have come to appreciate Matthew. I always thought it was too "custodial." I read into this gospel what I thought the author was saying and trying to do with his community. How wrong I was!

Matthew more than any other gospel is well structured. It gives evidence of an organized and hierarchical Christian community. The author tried to be a centrist, holding on to the old and being open to the new. Unlike many centrists, he succeeded. His mixed community of Jewish Christians and Gentile Christians paved the way for the Catholic Church as many know it today.

I believe that Matthew wrote his gospel in Antioch. Many think he wrote it somewhere in Palestine. Antioch seems the better choice precisely because of the history of Antioch at the end of the first century and the beginning of the second century. The letters of Ignatius of Antioch demonstrate a well-organized church with a monarchical episcopacy. I believe such a Christian community was the natural outcome from the community of Matthew.

Today many question the hierarchical and institutional church for its failures to deal effectively with church problems, especially the use and abuse of power and the failure to protect the young. Matthew has much to say to church leaders today as well as members of the church who hold different opinions on serious matters. This old document speaks to issues today both in the church and in society.

While writing this book I was surprised how much I actually knew about this gospel. Over the years I have taught the Synoptic Gospels on undergraduate and graduate levels. Evidently I learned more from this teaching and from the students who wrote papers than I had realized.

The dedication to people who like how I teach and how I preach means much to me. Like every human being I need encouragement. Over the years I have been blessed and encouraged in my teaching by good students who learned and grew in the love of the word of God. Some have become lifelong friends.

I enjoy preaching and do my best to relate the word of God to the daily life of ordinary people. The people mentioned in the dedication support and encourage my preaching. Since they have told me I preach well, I am compelled to become a better preacher. "One hand washes the other." They help me and I help them.

The terrible hurricane season of 2004 in Florida was the time period when this book was written. One time I evacuated and took with me a laptop computer with some disks, my Bible, and a few books, not knowing if I would ever see my apartment and my library again. Miami was spared major damage but not the rest of Florida. Both apartment and library remain intact.

Matthew believes in divine providence. God has a plan and even the cruel death of Jesus makes some sense in this ultimate plan. I do not always like or understand why so many bad things happen to good people. Matthew says that ultimately meaning in life comes from people taking care of each other. People did that with Hurricane Andrew in 1992 and people did the same in the terrible hurricane season of 2004. Even prejudices broke down. Slowly Florida returns to a lovely place in this world. Much beauty surrounds me and many good people here have become part of my life. I have often seen the Beatitudes in action.

This gospel comes from yesterday, almost two thousand years ago. It lives on in the church today, especially in the Catholic Church. Originally I had thought Matthew was too much of yesterday. I have learned Matthew has worn well and fits very well today.

Miami Shores, Florida
Feast of St. Matthew, September 21, 2004

"How To Use"— Reading Guide for Individuals and Study Groups

This book may be read either individually or in a group as a way to study the Gospel of Matthew. It is especially designed for adult Bible study groups to use over the course of several weeks with fifty-six sections encompassing the twenty-eight chapters of this gospel.

The following may be helpful ways to make use of this book:

1. A study group should attend to the practical details as to frequency of meetings, when and where they will take place, length of time for each session, and how many sections per meeting will work well for the group.

2. It would be easier if the same English translation of the Bible is used by all group participants. The NAB (New American Bible) is generally used by Roman Catholics and is the translation familiar to most because of its liturgical use. The NRSV (New Revised Standard Version) is often cited by scholars. Using the same text is a helpful basis for common reading, reflection, and discussion.

3. A group meeting should include reading aloud Scripture passages, praying in common, and discussing ways for practical applications of the Bible to daily life. The Introduction, Questions, and Conclusion in each section of this book are primarily designed for this purpose.

4. Decide on how group leadership will operate. Will one individual be responsible as a group leader for preparing each session, or will the leadership rotate from session to session? The one leading the group needs to prepare prior to the meeting session.

5. Referring to the Answers section after group members have shared their own personal responses will probably work best. It might be helpful to read them over, see what they offer in comparison to what the group response has been, and return to reviewing them the following week.

6. This book is not an academic textbook but a study guide of 339 different questions to help individuals and groups who use it to learn more about the Gospel of Matthew, engage in a personal dialogue of their own experience of faith, and grow spiritually as twenty-first-century disciples of Jesus Christ.

7. The study of Scripture is very rewarding. Contemporary analyses and insights from biblical scholarship may be troubling and confusing to some since previous understandings and beliefs may be challenged. However, as St. Jerome, who is responsible for translating the Bible into the Latin Vulgate edition, noted: *"Not knowing the Scriptures is to be ignorant of Christ."*

Questions

THE ORIGINS OF JESUS, 1:1—2:23

Section One: The Beginnings, 1:1–17

Introduction

The Gospel of Matthew usually begins with the translation "the book *[biblos]* of the genealogy *[genesis]* of Jesus." Matthew alone refers to the gospel as a "book." *Genesis* can also be translated as "birth-record" or "origin" or "existence" to bring this section in relationship to verse 18, "the birth *[genesis]* of Jesus Christ" (some ancient manuscripts have only "Christ" or "the Messiah"). In the Greek version (LXX) of Genesis twice the author used *biblos geneseos* (Gen 2:4 and 5:1) to summarize the preceding creation account and to list the descendents of Abraham. Matthew intends to present not just the origins of Jesus in this gospel but the whole life and meaning of Jesus. Every reader easily sees this as the first section of the gospel.

The reference to Abraham roots Jesus in the beginning of the Israelite tradition and the "son of David" relates Jesus to the royal Jewish line. Also, since in Abraham all nations will be blessed (Gen 17:5; 22:17–18), Jesus has something to say to all peoples (Gentiles), and since he is a descendent of David, he will speak to Jews. Both Jews and Gentiles made up the audience of the gospel.

The genealogy follows a pattern set in Ruth 4:18–22, bringing Jesus in line with the ancestors, Abraham, Isaac, and Jacob. Unlike the usual genealogies, this one includes four women: Tamar (Gen 38), Rahab (Josh 2), Ruth (Ruth 1—4), and the wife of Uriah

3

(Bathsheba) (2 Sam 11—12). The first part of the genealogy seems to follow Ruth 4:18–22, while the second part (from David to the Babylonian Exile) seems to follow 1 Chronicles 3:5, 10–17.

The final verse of the section brings the origins of Jesus through Joseph. Other ancient manuscripts add a reference to Mary as virgin to exclude any possibility of accepting Joseph as the physical father of Jesus and to bring this verse in line with verse 18 and following.

The ancient world frequently used numbers to symbolize aspects of life. Unfortunately, no one completely understands their use of numbers. At the time of Jesus, Jewish apocalyptic literature tended to divide history into neat sections of sevens. By using this imagery Matthew shows that God has been moving human history with precision to the time of Jesus as the Messiah. From Abraham to David there are fourteen names, and from David to the Exile there are fourteen generations, although it seems that several generations have been omitted to create the fourteen. From the Exile to Jesus there are thirteen generations, unless one includes the followers of the Messiah as another generation. Some liken fourteen to the numerical value of the name David—d = 4, v = 6, d = 4 = 14. Others see fourteen as a multiple of seven, which also is a significant number.

Questions

1. Why bother with a genealogy for Jesus? Why is it different from the genealogy in Luke?

2. Most people do not realize that Abraham was not an Israelite or Jew. Does it help to include both Jews and Gentiles in the genealogy?

3. Relating Jesus to Abraham, Isaac, and Jacob, the patriarchs, would appeal to Jews. What might this mean to Gentiles, especially today?

4. Why do you think Matthew included women? What do you think the four women have in common after reading about them in the Old Testament?

5. Why do people still think of magic in terms of certain numbers?

Conclusion

This first section sets the tone for the entire book. Matthew's community consisted of both Jewish and Gentile converts to Christianity. By referring Jesus to Abraham, Matthew acknowledges that Jesus will bless all nations. By emphasizing his royal descent from David, Matthew roots Jesus in the best of Jewish traditions.

Genealogies give support for legitimacy and even inheritance. Jesus inherited not only a bloodline but a line of faith going back to Abraham. Some of the names can be found in the Old Testament, but other names from the Old Testament are omitted. This genealogy differs considerably from Luke's, and the belief that Luke traces the lineage of Jesus through Mary has little or no foundation. Matthew probably used a genealogy prevalent at the time.

The inclusion of women adds to the theology of Matthew. All are part of Christianity: men and women, saints and sinners, Jews and Gentiles. Each woman has a shady past and perhaps since Jesus was born within the nine-month period from the time Joseph and Mary lived together, some might have thought that Mary also had a shady past. Three of the women are Gentiles and the fourth married a Gentile. Evidently God writes straight with crooked lines.

This opening section gives us a glimpse of the entire gospel. Matthew traces the story of Jesus back to the story of Israel by his frequent use of Old Testament quotations. He renews belief in the coming of the Messiah as the descendent of David, thus fulfilling all of the hopes and expectations of the people of Israel. Jesus continues what God began in Abraham through Isaac, Jacob, the patriarchs, and kings. But now the promises made to Israel will be offered to all nations in Jesus. Something will remain but something new has happened in the coming of Jesus.

Section Two:
The Birth of the Messiah, 1:18–25

Introduction

If the first section of the gospel told readers who the Messiah was, son of Abraham and son of David, the second section tells how. Here Matthew repeats the word *genesis,* binding the two sections together. Some manuscripts say "Jesus the Christ." In all probability the original just said "Christ" or "the Messiah" or "the Anointed One."

The passage makes clear the marriage to Joseph had not been consummated before Mary became pregnant. In the end when Joseph gives Jesus his name, he becomes the legal father of Jesus although not the physical father. All is accomplished through the Holy Spirit.

Joseph, being just, faced a dilemma. Deuteronomy 22:23–27 stipulates that an engaged woman found pregnant should be returned to her father's house and stoned to death. Joseph does not follow this law, but rather intends to put Mary through the divorce procedure.

In a dream Joseph learns of the divine origin of her pregnancy. Jesus will be Son of God as well as son of David. Joseph then takes Mary as his wife and gives his son the name of Jesus, or Jeshua in Hebrew, which means "God helps" or "God saves."

Matthew's use of a fulfillment formula by referring to the Old Testament will continue throughout the gospel, maintaining a continuity between Christianity and Judaism.

Matthew then quotes the Greek version (LXX) of Isaiah, which changed *alma* (young woman) to *parthenos* (virgin). Originally the birth of a prince gave the people of Israel hope for the future.

Now this birth will give the whole world hope for the future. Actually, Matthew's quote differs from both the Hebrew and Greek texts of the quotation from Isaiah. Perhaps Matthew changed the text to "they will call" to relate the passage to "people" in verse 21: "he will save his people from their sins."

The Hebrew title Emmanuel is explained with the phrase "God with us" to support the divinity of Jesus and to assure the followers of Jesus that in truth he will be God with them to the end of days (Matt 28:20).

"He did not know her" euphemistically refers to sexual relations. Matthew emphasizes Mary was a virgin in the conception and birth. He makes no claim to her perpetual virginity.

By giving Jesus his name, Joseph established the legal and Davidic origin of Jesus. Joseph assumes his role as guardian and will protect the holy family until they return to Nazareth after their sojourn in Egypt. Joseph will not appear anywhere else in the Gospel of Matthew.

Questions

6. Matthew makes an early claim that Jesus is a divine Son of God. Why is this important?

7. The marriage had not been consummated. Would it make a difference if Joseph was the physical father of Jesus?

8. A just man does not follow the Law. How can he be just?

9. What is more important: physical virginity or its theological meaning in the origin of Jesus?

10. God helps or saves through Jesus. How?

11. Why was the Old Testament important for Matthew?

12. Is Jesus still with his followers? How?

Conclusion

In the time of Jesus engagement had legal consequences. The minimum age for males was thirteen and for females was twelve.

It seems that with Mary and Joseph the betrothal took place and they were awaiting the marriage ceremony. When he discovers Mary is pregnant, Joseph had a choice between following the law of Deuteronomy or simply going through the divorce procedure. Or perhaps Matthew, a gospel known for its emphasis on law, knew that in some cases laws do not oblige. For whatever reason, Joseph decided not to demand the observance of Deuteronomy.

Joseph in the Old Testament Book of Genesis also had dreams. Joseph in the New Testament has a dream and as a result takes Mary to be his wife. The announcement of the angel follows a typical Old Testament pattern seen in the birth of Isaac (Gen 17:19), Solomon (1 Chr 22:9–10), and the child to be born of the young woman in Isaiah 7:14–17.

This section contains the first fulfillment quotation so common in Matthew. Although most of the quotations from the Old Testament in Matthew do not conform to either the Hebrew or Greek text, usually an idea or a word from the text prompts Matthew to make application to Jesus. Perhaps some early Christians familiar with the Old Testament combed the texts to find any possible applications to Jesus and compiled a collection of such texts. Matthew may then have used this collection in the composition of his gospel.

The central meaning of this section focuses on Jesus as the divine Son of God. Unlike Acts, which sees divinity associated with the resurrection (Acts 2:36), and Mark, who associates divinity with the baptism (Mark 1:11), Matthew claims Jesus is the divine Son of God from conception.

Certain Jewish Talmudic texts claim that Jesus was fathered by a Roman soldier and thus was an illegitimate son of Mary. Matthew counters this with his description of the virginal conception through the power of the Holy Spirit. Others see the charge of illegitimacy arising from the Christian belief in virginal conception rather than the other way around. The meaning does not imply that the Holy Spirit is Mary's sexual partner, but that the conception of the child is God's initiative and not through ordinary human means. Theologically virginal conception supports the belief that Jesus is the gift of God to the human race.

Throughout the gospel Jesus will maintain a unique bond with God unlike all other human-divine relationships.

When Joseph gives Jesus his name he not only assumes legal paternity but also reveals the mission that God gave to the Son: salvation from sins. Throughout the gospel Matthew uses the name Jesus some eighty times, calling attention to this divinely given mission.

Jesus is the Christ, the Anointed One, the Davidic Messiah fulfilling the hopes of Israel. Jesus is the divine Son of God, conceived through the power of the Holy Spirit and bearing the name Emmanuel, God with us, not just for Jews but for all nations and for all times and places.

The arrangement of this scene with its Christian faith foundation precludes an assumption of an accurate historical scene. The section contains both theology and faith. Both Matthew and Luke have received Christian memories of the origin of Jesus and each has crafted these memories into stories, with Matthew emphasizing Joseph and dreams and an angel and Luke emphasizing Mary and an annunciation by an angel. As is true for all the books of the Bible, readers should pay attention to the story and its meaning without attempting to solve the historical questions surrounding the story.

Section Three:
The Magi and Egypt,
2:1–23

Introduction

Like Luke, Matthew situated Jesus in time and in place: the reign of Herod (40–44 BC) and Bethlehem, a town five miles south of Jerusalem. Bethlehem was the ancestral town of David and in the time of Jesus a backwater town. Herod, famous for his construction, was more renowned for his cruelty.

Magi were astrologers. The Bible does not tell us where they came from. As Magi they sound like Persians; as astrologers they sound like Babylonians; with their gifts they might have come from Arabia. As Gentiles they interpreted the stars to ascertain major historical events. They sought the king of the Jews, the title of Herod, and so he and his court would interpret the question as one challenging his own position.

Since Magi would have interpreted a new star as the sign of the birth of an important figure, they intended to discover whose birth was heralded and went to Jerusalem. Over the centuries many have tried to explain the star as a new star, a supernova, a comet, or the juxtaposition of planets. Since this is a birth story, perhaps the origin lies more in Numbers 24 than in a planetary phenomenon. "A star shall come forth out of Jacob" (Num 24:17). Only in verse 9 does the star actually guide the Magi.

The Greek word for paying homage connotes submission to or even adoration of a higher authority. Matthew places the term on the lips of Herod in 2:8 and uses it again when the Magi find the child in verse 11. Since the word can also be used to denote the proper relationship of humans to God, Matthew may be pressing

10

the image of Jesus as divine and worthy of worship. The evangelist will use the word frequently throughout the gospel.

The chief priests and scribes offer their expertise, and Matthew includes his second fulfillment quotation. The quotation actually seems to be a combination of Micah 5:1–2 and 2 Samuel 5:2 with Matthew's own addition, "by no means." In the time of Jesus people commonly thought of Bethlehem as the birthplace of the Messiah (John 7:42).

The house in verse 11 has caused some concern over the years since the popular image is that of Jesus and his parents living in a stable or even a cave. Or perhaps some time has passed and they found a house in Bethlehem in which to live. Eventually, they end up in Nazareth. Matthew explains how they got there after Egypt as Joseph sought relative security for his family (2:19–23).

The Bible does not mention the number of Magi but many presume there were three because of the gifts. The notion of the gifts as well as the idea of "kings" may come from Psalm 72:10 and Isaiah 60:6. Matthew probably added myrrh to the gold and incense to signify the death of the Messiah.

Instructed by an angel in a dream, the Magi do not return to Jerusalem but go back to their country by a different route. Joseph, fearing Herod, takes his family to Jerusalem. In Exodus an evil king tries to destroy Moses and kills newborn boys. Herod does the same thing.

The fulfillment quotation from Hosea 11:1 links Jesus to Egypt and divine sonship. Matthew also adds a quotation from Jeremiah 31:15 associating the slaughter of the innocents to the weeping of Rachel.

Eventually, the holy family returns to Israel, to the security of Galilee in Nazareth. "He will be called a Nazarean" appears to be an Old Testament quotation although no such quote even remotely can be found in the Old Testament. The word connotes three meanings: he is from Nazareth, or the word comes from *nazir,* meaning "one devoted to God;" or the word is from the Hebrew *neser,* meaning "root," to imply the root of Jesse or David.

Questions

13. What part of the story of the Magi do people find so appealing?

14. Did Matthew have a purpose in joining Gentiles to Jews and contrasting the Magi with Herod and the religious leaders in Jerusalem?

15. Years later, when people had a knowledge of Jesus as the divine Messiah, might they have remembered some unusual heavenly phenomenon and then associated it with the birth of Jesus?

16. Why the references to the Old Testament?

17. Is there some historical confusion when comparing the birth stories of Jesus in Luke and in Matthew?

18. Great people in history often face obstacles in their youth. Is this history or anthropology?

19. Relating Jesus to Moses both helps and hinders. Why?

Conclusion

The first chapter of Matthew focused on who and how. The second chapter centers on where: the East, Jerusalem, Bethlehem, Egypt, and Nazareth. At the centers are Bethlehem and Jerusalem. The quotations that Matthew used seem to have been created from Old Testament ideas and his own interpretation.

For centuries Christians have joined the story of Matthew and the Magi to the shepherds of Luke to create the Christmas story. For many Christians everything was accepted as historical fact even if some had trouble harmonizing Matthew and Luke. Then for a period of interpretation some denied all history to any of the stories of the birth of Jesus. Today most will try to decide the meaning without ever having any hope of separating out what might be the historical nucleus of the origins of Jesus.

Matthew likens the birth and ministry of Jesus to that of Moses. In Exodus the Pharaoh, the wicked king of the Egyptians, decrees that Moses and all Jewish males be killed (Exod 1:16, 22). Moses is saved. Later Moses flees Egypt; he returns to Egypt after he is told that "the ones seeking your life are dead" (Exod 4:19). Jesus seems to have had a parallel experience, only he flees to Egypt but then goes to Galilee.

If Matthew used the Old Testament to create or add to the stories of the birth of Jesus, he may have also focused on Numbers 22—24, making Balaam the model for the Magi. The pagan prophet prophesies good for Israel rather than evil, climaxing his prophecies with the assertion: "A star shall come forth out of Jacob and a scepter shall raise out of Israel." Philo, the Jewish philosopher-historian, refers to Balaam as a *magos*.

Throughout the chapter Matthew draws his readers to the Old Testament and in particular to Moses. He wishes to maintain the connection between Jesus and the whole Israelite tradition. All the places mentioned have a biblical foundation to support the itinerary of Jesus done under the divine plan.

The Magi come from the East and represent Gentiles who come to believe in Jesus as the divine Messiah and Son of God. This fits in with the close of Matthew, when Jesus commands his disciples to make disciples of all nations (Matt 28:19). Here in contrast to the religious leaders and Herod, Gentiles worship Jesus, prefiguring the Gentiles in Matthew's own community.

The typology of Moses/Jesus relates Jesus to the whole history of Israel. The reference to myrrh and the slaughter of the innocents points forward to the passion and death of Jesus caused by an evil king (Pilate). The fulfillment of the divine plan becomes evident in the Old Testament quotations. The Magi point to the universality of the teaching of Jesus, which includes all nations.

The Beginnings of the Mission of Jesus, 3:1—4:25

Section Four: John the Baptist and the Baptism of Jesus, 3:1–17

Introduction

Throughout the Bible, "in those days" refers to a new period. Matthew goes from the infancy of Jesus to his adulthood and abruptly introduces John the Baptist. Unlike Luke, the first gospel does not include John in the early life of Jesus. He appears in the desert like an Old Testament prophet dressed in garb similar to Elijah's (2 Kgs 1:8) because John will be the new Elijah, announcing the coming of the Messiah. He ate what was available in the desert region and was probably more concerned with ritual purity than any effort at asceticism.

The wilderness is the area east of Jerusalem close to the Dead Sea where the Qumran community and other religious Jewish movements had their settlements. The desert in the history of Israel was the place of intimacy with God, associated with prayer and success and also temptation. Jesus came from Galilee, which would tie in with the infancy narratives, but now moves closer to Jerusalem to begin his ministry.

To repent means to rethink and then act differently. Matthew explains the need for repentance, or rethinking, since the king-

15

dom of heaven is near. The gospel uses "kingdom of heaven" rather than "kingdom of God" or "reign of God," but all three expressions convey the same idea. People should change their way of living for soon the power and presence of God will be recognized by all and judgment will fall upon those who refuse to change their way of living.

The quotation from Isaiah (40:3) refers to the return of those in exile to Jerusalem around 540 BC. In the gospel the voice is John the Baptist and the Lord is the coming of Jesus the Messiah.

John baptized in the Jordan, ritualizing the decision to rethink how one was living in preparation for the coming of God's presence. Many came for baptism: the sincere and the curious and even evidently some vipers, symbolizing evil people. Pharisees and Sadducees and vipers would represent those in opposition to John, to Jesus, and even to the Matthean community, including perhaps some of its own members.

All must demonstrate that they had truly rethought their lives by bearing fruit. The mere observance of rituals, whether in the Temple or the baptism by John, will not preserve someone from the wrath of God. Only good deeds will bring God's favor. The image of Israel as a tree that bears fruit was a frequent image of the Old Testament (Isa 17:6; Jer 12:2; Ezek 17:8–9). The reference to the ax might be seen as an additional warning: bear fruit, or be cut down.

Claiming to be children of Abraham will not protect those who do not repent. The reference to children and stones is a play on words in Aramaic. The idea seems to be that God is not limited by natural processes. This may refer to the inclusion of Gentiles, especially in the Matthean community.

John contrasts his baptism with water with Jesus' baptism in the Spirit. Baptism for repentance points to the eschaton, while baptism in the Spirit means the eschaton, the last days, are here. Throughout, Matthew presents Jesus as superior to John, bringing the reign of God to earth through the power of the Spirit.

Jeremiah used the image of the winnowing fork. The farmer would throw the grain and chaff into the air; the lighter chaff would blow away, while the good grain would fall to the ground to be saved. The same will be true through the power of the

Spirit, separating those who have repented from those who refuse to change their way of living.

Jesus came to John to be baptized. The dialogue between John and Jesus appears only in Matthew and supports the superiority of Jesus over John as well as the question of repentance. Surely Jesus does not need to repent. "Fulfilling all righteousness" probably refers to the decision of Jesus to live according to the demands of John's baptism. Righteousness, *dikaiosyne*, appears frequently in Matthew, signifying a divine attribute, God's fidelity to Israel, and then the proper response of Israel to God, fulfilling obedience to God in moral integrity. Jesus will personify both God's fidelity to people who repent and the proper response of the individual to God.

The heavens opened show a new relationship between God and humanity through Jesus. The Spirit descended dove-like, which may evoke a remembrance of the Spirit in Genesis and a new creation (Gen 1:2). Whether this is a private experience of Jesus remains unclear. Comparing all three versions of the baptism of Jesus by John in the Synoptic Gospels seems to imply that it was a public event in some instances and at other times a private experience. The reference to "This is my beloved son…" rather than "You are my beloved Son…" (Mark 1:11) seems to imply a public manifestation of Jesus to the crowds.

The opening of the heavens, the Holy Spirit, and the voice all support the claim that Matthew will reinforce throughout the gospel: Jesus is God's Son. Son, beloved, well pleased are all Old Testament ideas explaining who Jesus is and that what he will do will please God.

Questions

20. A prophet points out the presence and absence of God in life. Why is John a prophet? Is Jesus a prophet?

21. Repentance means rethinking, changing one's mind, and doing things differently. How often must a person do this?

22. Rituals express something else. What does the ritual of baptism mean? Is the ritual the same for Jesus and everyone else?

23. Actions follow values and beliefs. What does this mean after a ritual baptism?

24. Religious leaders should not just "talk the talk" but "walk the walk." What are you thoughts?

25. Jesus is superior to John. Why would Matthew stress this point?

26. The Holy Spirit creates anew. What is new in the baptism of Jesus?

Conclusion

Both Jesus and John have the same teaching. "Repent, for the kingdom of heaven is at hand" (Matt 3:2), declares John. Jesus says in 4:17, "Repent, for the kingdom of heaven is at hand." Both proclaim justice (*dikaiosyne*) toward others and piety toward God. John ends the Old Testament prophecy and Jesus begins the New Testament prophecy with clear continuity. Matthew presents John as Elijah preparing for the Messiah. Each evangelist shows some relationship between Jesus and John, but once Jesus begins his ministry John leaves the scene. He has fulfilled his role. At the time of Matthew some still thought that John was the Messiah. Making Jesus superior to John in every instance counteracted such a belief. Whether John or even Jesus was a part of the Essene community at Qumran in the desert near the Dead Sea remains unknown. Perhaps yes, perhaps no. Both John and Jesus were prophets since they both pointed out the presence or absence of God in the lives of those who listened to them. Both were connected with a deserted place, and both proclaimed a personal relationship to God. The Essenes also were prophetic, lived in the desert, and wanted a personal relationship with God.

John declared that God was absent from the lives of many, including the Pharisees and Sadducees. These religious leaders should not think that just going through a ritual will save them from judgment or being children of Abraham will prevent God's judgment on them. They should not waste any valuable time since God is near. This is the first encounter with the groups that will be opponents of Jesus in his ministry.

Probably the Pharisees were the chief opponents of the Matthean community after the destruction of the Temple in AD 70. The Pharisees were the "separate ones" who withdrew to observe Torah according to their own interpretation and considered themselves superior to ordinary Jewish believers. Sadducees were descendents of the priestly class, rivaling the Pharisees for power and political and religious dominance. Matthew seems to imply that the message of John has particular relevance for these religious leaders. He uses the image of vipers in 12:34 and 23:33 again against the Pharisees. In 21:25, 32, Matthew says that the leaders did not believe John. It seems Matthew points out their hypocrisy in dealing both with John and with Jesus. If they believed properly, they would act properly. This theme will persist throughout the gospel. All religious leaders have a greater obligation to ensure their actions follow their beliefs and values.

Ritual washing characterized almost all religious traditions. The Bible prescribed washings for the priests before (Lev 16:4) and after (Lev 16:24) offering sacrifices. The Qumran community had frequent ritual washings. Rabbinic sources also refer to proselyte baptism in which a Gentile underwent immersion to separate himself from other Gentiles. But John administered his baptism only once and in preparation for the kingdom of God. He emphasizes moral purity and repentance, not just ritual purity.

Matthew identifies Jesus as the one who comes after John. In the gospel, Jesus will preach and teach and live as the final prophet announcing judgment for all. He completes what John began. John has played his role and now Jesus takes over.

Matthew had the Gospel of Mark as one of his sources. He took the simple account of the baptism of Jesus and introduced the dialogue to explain why John baptized Jesus. Of all of the historical events of the life of Jesus, his baptism by John seems most clear. Certainly early Christians would not have invented the story precisely because such a baptism submits Jesus to John's authority. Matthew needed to explain why and show the superiority of Jesus over John.

The baptism declares the identity of Jesus before he begins his ministry. Jesus is God's Son and God is pleased with his ministry. Now Jesus can begin his ministry, having made evident his relationship to God. Jesus is Son, he is beloved, and in him God is pleased.

Section Five:
The Desert and the
Temptations, 4:1–11

Introduction

The desert might cause people to think of the uninhabited place east of Jerusalem, but it seems the desert is more theological than geographical. Israel wandered in the desert for forty years. During that period God took care of them and they acknowledged their commitment to God. In the same desert the people of Israel failed. Testing manifests fidelity or failure. God tests human fidelity. No one can test God's fidelity since God always remains faithful.

Forty was one of those special numbers in the Old Testament and may refer to the forty years of Israel wandering in the desert, or the forty-day fast of Moses (Deut 9:18), or the fast of Elijah (1 Kgs 19:8). Both Moses and Elijah appear to Jesus in his transfiguration (Matt 17:3).

Matthew uses the word *diabolos*; the word is usually translated as "devil" but in fact means the "slanderer" or the "accuser" or the "tempter." In the New Testament no appreciable difference exists between *diabolos* and *satanas*. Satan is also called the strong one in Matthew 12:29 and the evil one in Matthew 13:19. When Peter attempts to dissuade Jesus from his passion, Jesus calls Peter "Satan." Rather than use the word *devil*, it seems best to use the word *tempter*. Twice the tempter wants to know what kind of Son of God Jesus is. The tempter first does not ask Jesus for a miracle since they are alone. Rather, the temptation mirrors the situation of Israel when they were hungry. They were not satisfied with God's food, manna, but wanted earthly food. Would Jesus do likewise? Jesus responds with a quotation from

21

Deuteronomy 8:3. He knows the word of God is the true source for life. Jesus does not fail the first test.

The holy city is Jerusalem and the pinnacle of the Temple is a prominent point. Perhaps Psalm 91 supplies the Old Testament foundation for the reckless action that the tempter proposes to Jesus. Using Psalm 91 as a background, the tempter asks Jesus to verify the validity of the promised divine protection. Jesus again quotes from Deuteronomy (6:16). The place is Massah (Exod 17:1–7), and Jesus will not attempt to test God as did the people of Israel in the desert.

Finally, the tempter invites Jesus to view all the kingdoms of the world with their power and glory. The tempter wants worship, the same word used by the Magi when they encounter Jesus in Bethlehem and the same word used in reference to the risen Lord in Matthew 28:17. Jesus refuses. He will worship God alone. The tempter leaves, for Jesus has passed the test. Fittingly, angels come and minister to him.

Questions

27. Is the devil the tempter or is life?

28. Moses was the lawgiver and Elijah was the prophet. Why does Jesus follow their example in fasting?

29. Both the tempter and Jesus quote the Old Testament. Who wins?

30. Throwing oneself from the pinnacle of the Temple clearly is foolish. But should people not trust in the love and protection of God?

31. Power and wealth are continual temptations. People still worship them. How can the worship of God help to overcome these temptations?

32. Matthew seems to be forever relating Jesus to the history of Israel. For what purpose?

33. No one was present other than Jesus and the tempter. Do you think Jesus told his disciples about what happened?

34. Are the temptations of Jesus not only the temptations of Israel but temptations that all humans face?

Conclusion

The Epistle to the Hebrews says that Jesus was "tempted in every way as we are, yet without sin" (Heb 4:15). Israel failed in the desert; everyone fails as frequently, but Jesus as God's Son passed every test.

Each time Jesus quotes Deuteronomy and in a rabbinic argument Jesus wins since his quotes are superior to those of the tempter. Luke has the same temptations but in a different order. Luke has the final temptation occur in the Temple in Jerusalem.

Either Jesus told his disciples or an early Christian scribe or teacher gathered the material from the experience of the people of Israel in the desert as well as the teachings on Jesus on these very human temptations. Deuteronomy not only supplies the quotations that Jesus used but also contains the key words *son* and *test*.

Since both Matthew and Luke contain the temptations, most ascribe the episode to the unknown source of both gospels called "Q," the first letter of the German word for source, *Quelle*. Some think that Luke changed the order of temptations because of his fondness for Jerusalem. Luke's order also seems more logical: miracle worker, power seeker, tempter of God. Others think Matthew changed the order to bring the events in line with Exodus: Exodus 16, manna; Exodus 17, water at Massah; and Exodus 32, the golden calf. No one really knows whether Jesus told the story to his disciples and in what order, or whether the temptations are a compilation of some of the teachings of Jesus along with some ideas from the Old Testament and the history of Israel.

Matthew used the temptations to connect the divine sonship of Jesus, already made evident in the first three chapters, with the experience of Israel, also God's son, in the desert. Some will see Jesus as the "new Israel." Later, others will see Jesus as the "new Moses." Without claiming either of these titles for Jesus (in the Sermon on the Mount he seems more than Israel and Moses), this passage connects Jesus to the history of Israel. Jesus accepts the testing by God, which will be present throughout his life, but he will not try to tempt God.

The temptations also have meaning for the early church and for the contemporary church. Bread may symbolize pleasure. Jesus does not condemn pleasure but says pleasure is not everything: "Not on bread alone..." People must accept responsibility for their actions. Throwing oneself off a high place will bring death. Do not blame God for such foolishness. People tend to blame others as well as God instead of accepting personal responsibility. Finally, people still worship power and wealth. Jesus knew that people like influence and glory and honor and wealth. He told his followers to look for these in the right place by worshiping God. In 25:40 he says: "As you did it to one of these, the least of my brethren, you did it to me." Taking care of people in need brings honor and glory and position and power and, sometimes, even wealth.

Section Six:
Ministry in Galilee,
4:12–25

Introduction

When Jesus begins his ministry John had been handed over. The word *paredothae* has been translated as "arrested," "put in prison," or "handed over." The last translation seems preferable. The word will become prominent in the passion of Jesus. Just as John was handed over to his enemies and to his fate, so will Jesus be handed over. Just as John died, so will Jesus die. Matthew relates the tragic events in the end of the life of John in 14:1–12. Since John was handed over to Herod Antipas, who ruled over Galilee, it seems strange that Jesus "withdrew" to Galilee. Nevertheless, his ministry begins in Galilee of the Gentiles.

The northern region of Israel had more Gentiles than the southern region around Jerusalem. This goes back to the conquest of the northern tribes by the Assyrians around 732 BC. At the beginning of the ministry of Jesus, just as he had the Magi present at Jesus' birth, Matthew includes some reference to the Gentiles. Capernaum in Galilee seems to have been the home base for the ministry of Jesus in the north and not Nazareth. Preachers at that period often moved from town to town much like the early circuit preachers in the United States. They gathered followers and some followers continued with the preachers as they moved from one place to another. They also had a home base to which they returned for rest and regrouping.

Matthew has another of his fulfillment quotations from the Old Testament from Isaiah. Again, the emphasis is on the territory of the tribes of Zebulun and Naphtali, in the north in the land of the Gentiles. He loosely adapts the quotation from Isaiah to apply to the nations in darkness that will see the light of the teachings of Jesus. Here Jesus teaches as did John: repent, change your way of thinking and living, the reign of heaven, the reign of God, is at hand. All will see God's power and judgment, including the Gentiles. Matthew does not forget the Jews since Jesus also teaches in the synagogues.

The Sea of Galilee, also called the Lake of Tiberius or the Sea of Gennesaret, lies in the middle of Galilee about thirty-two miles around and, at its widest place, eight miles across. The Jordan River flows into it and out of it. Here Jesus calls his first disciples.

Jesus calls two brothers, fishermen, Peter and Andrew. Some may think these disciples were poor and illiterate men, but in fact they owned their own boat and the necessary equipment. One need not conclude they were destitute or completely uneducated. They were smart enough to be owners. They left a stable and secure way of living to become fishers of men, a mission to join and continue the mission of Jesus. Since they followed immediately, Matthew acknowledges the charismatic character of Jesus to attract disciples.

James and John soon follow. They too were fishermen and worked with their father. They too give up a secure way of living and follow the charismatic Jesus. These two along with Peter will form an inner circle of the Twelve. James should not be identified with James, son of Alphaeus, or James, the brother of the Lord. Three different people are named James.

Jesus preaches in all of Galilee (an exaggeration to encourage "all nations" in Matt 28:19?). Jesus teaches and preaches the good news of God's victory over evil, sin, and death. He performs miracles of healing, freeing people from any evil forces: those under the influence of the moon (a more accurate translation); epileptics; those paralyzed; and anyone suffering from any malady, physical or psychological. Jesus ministered in the Roman province of Syria, which included all of Palestine, and the ten Greek cities of the Decapolis. No one was excluded from the powerful ministry of Jesus' teaching and healing.

Questions

35. John and Jesus faced powerful opposition. Why?

36. The ministry of Jesus begins in the north, in the land of the Gentiles. Why?

37. The Jews considered Gentiles inferior to them because of the Gentiles' paganism. How would this affect the community of Matthew, composed of Jewish Christians and Gentile Christians?

38. Why is the Sea of Galilee still attractive to followers of Jesus?

39. What are your thoughts on the earliest followers of Jesus, fishermen?

40. Why would Jesus have an inner circle of friends?

41. Jesus preaches the good news, the victory of God over evil, sin, and death. Is this true?

Conclusion

The fulfillment quotation from Isaiah founds the ministry of Jesus in Galilee on the will of God. God wanted the Son to begin to preach to those who "sat in darkness." Jesus obliges and follows God's will. The same will be true for the early preachers after the resurrection: they preached to the Gentiles and the Gentiles welcomed their words and believed. Galilee continues to be important to Matthew, for there people experience the mercy of God (4:23). After the resurrection Jesus appears to his disciples in Galilee (28:7), and from a mountain in Galilee Jesus sends forth his disciples to teach all nations (28:16, 19). Matthew's community, composed of both Jewish Christians and Gentile Christians, moved from darkness to light through their commitment in faith to Jesus and his teaching.

People do not like prophets who tell the truth. John did just that, as did Jesus. They both denounced hypocrisy and called all, especially religious leaders, to lead by example. They received the prophet's reward: opposition and persecution.

Galilee in the time of Jesus was separated from Judea and the area around Jerusalem by Samaria. In this region lived followers

27

of the God of Israel who accepted only the first five books of the Bible and worshiped on Mount Gerizim rather than in Jerusalem. These early Jews had intermarried with other settlers over a period of several hundred years. Many in Judea considered themselves the "true" believers, better than the Samaritans to the immediate north and superior to those who lived among the Gentiles in the Galilee area. This geographical difference will appear throughout the gospel. One group always needs to look down on another.

The people of Galilee supported themselves by farming and fishing. Jesus in his parables used the ordinary aspects of life taken from farming and fishing to teach his listeners. They easily understood his stories and learned their meaning.

Most of this material in this section can also be found in Mark. Here Matthew takes over much of the earlier gospel, but then edits and adds to support his particular audience. Verses 23–25 in particular show Matthew's editorial ability when compared with the parallel verses in Mark.

Unlike the customary method of students seeking out teachers, Jesus seeks out his followers. They respond immediately to the powerful presence of Jesus. With him they begin a ministry of fishing for men who will acknowledge the presence of God. Together with Jesus they will teach and heal and drive out demons. But always the Master leads and they follow.

Too often the followers of Jesus have been portrayed as simpletons; this is evident in the Gospel of Mark. Matthew rehabilitates the earliest followers of Jesus when compared to Mark. Jesus responds humanly by seeming to enjoy the company of some more than others. If Jesus demonstrated such a strong and charismatic personality, naturally certain followers would seem closer to the Lord than others.

Once the ministry of Jesus has begun, Matthew can summarize the teachings of Jesus in the Sermon on the Mount. In Galilee rather than in Jerusalem Matthew presents Jesus as teaching just as Moses taught. On the mountain God taught Moses. Matthew seems to go beyond the similarity of Moses as teacher, for he places Jesus in the role of God. Just as God taught Moses and the early Israelites, so now Jesus teaches all from the mountain.

THE GREAT TEACHER: THE FIRST SERMON, 5:1—7:29

Section Seven: The Sermon on the Mount, 5:1–12

Introduction

Each gospel presents the teachings of Jesus. Matthew, however, seems to gather together and present in an orderly fashion more specific teachings than any other gospel. Jesus in this gospel preaches five great sermons: the Sermon on the Mount in chapters 5—7, the missionary sermon in chapter 10, the sermon on parables in chapter 13, the church sermon in chapter 18, and finally the eschatological sermon in chapters 24—25. After each of these sermons the evangelist remarks, "When Jesus had finished these sayings..." or some similar words (7:28; 11:1; 13:53; 19:1; 26:1). The five sermons beginning with the Sermon on the Mount have encouraged some to see in the Jesus of this gospel the new Moses. Just as Moses taught the people and the first five books of the Old Testament were thought to be written by him, so the new Moses has five great sermons.

Luke also has a collection of teachings of Jesus, sometimes called the Sermon on the Plain (Luke 6:20–49). Like Matthew he begins with the Beatitudes but has only four, to which he adds four woes. Each gospel has its own understanding of Jesus and his teachings. Perhaps Luke is closer to the original source coming from "Q."

The context of the sermon implies that Jesus addresses all of Israel. He makes frequent allusions to the Old Testament, and thus it seems that he is anxious to tell the Jewish audience that he has come "not to abolish the law and the prophets but to fulfill them" (Matt 5:17). After he makes this statement he changes both law and prophets. The sermon may be divided in several different ways whether the evangelist thought of the sermon in sections or not. Clearly, the Beatitudes form the beginning and introduction.

The reference to the crowds at beginning (5:1) and end (7:28–29) sets the audience: people in general or the people of Israel. In the ancient world mountains belonged to the gods. Since the gods live in the heavens, anything close to heaven must be close to them and from the mountains the gods rule and proclaim. In Greek mythology Zeus reigns from Mount Olympus. Moses went up the mountain in Exodus to be near God and from the mountain God taught Moses. Now Jesus teaches the crowds from the mountain. Mountains seem important for Matthew. Besides the Sermon on the Mount, the transfiguration (17:1–9) and the final commission (28:16) take place on a mountain.

Blessed may also be translated as "happy." The form of speech appears frequently in the Old Testament wisdom books. In wisdom tradition beatitudes refer to rewards that are already present. Some see the Beatitudes in the New Testament as eschatological, referring to the future. Perhaps these Beatitudes in Matthew refer to both present and future.

The first Beatitude of the poor, which Luke refers to the needy, Matthew interprets as referring to all those who recognize their poverty before God. He adds, unlike Luke, "in spirit." In some instances those who are financially poor more easily recognize their poverty before God. Some see a reference here to Isaiah 57:15 or Psalm 34:18.

"Those who mourn" finds a background in Isaiah 61:2–3. They mourned for the lost Temple and city of Jerusalem. They needed consolation. The poor in spirit also need consolation. All who suffer can depend on the presence of God for comfort.

Meek in English has the sense of "softness." Perhaps it can better be translated as "gentle." Psalm 37:11 states, "The meek shall inherit the earth." The first three Beatitudes all begin with the same letter in Greek. In fact, they refer to the same type of person: the one who depends on God, suffers in life, and remains gentle throughout it all.

Righteousness refers to God's justice, God's saving activity, and human behavior based on this justice. If people can stand in the presence of God because God tells them to stand, so human behavior should manifest the dignity and value of every human being.

Mercy belongs to God in the Old Testament, but God expects people to forgive each other. Psalm 37:21 speaks of the just showing mercy. Mercy is the correct criterion of the observance of the Law in Matthew. Law in itself never suffices. God wants mercy and not empty rituals (Matt 9:13; 12:7).

"Pure of heart" cannot be limited to one virtue, such as chastity. God demands people to live as pure of heart, with their actions proceeding from a sincere heart: truthful speech, keeping one's word, dealing honestly with others, depending on God. Pure of heart implies people of integrity, whose actions follow their beliefs.

Peace does not mean the cessation of hostilities, but wishing people the best of everything. *Shalom* means to experience the fullness of the gifts of God: long life, faithful family and friends, success in living—all that makes for a good and happy life. *Shalom* means wholeness, a perfect experience of well-being and integration within the individual and in society. Thus, no strife or warfare.

Again, Jesus refers to righteousness, but here he calls for a willingness to accept persecution for adhering to the righteousness of God and living such justice in human relationships.

Finally, the language shifts from the third person to the second person, referring to a more active conflict, perhaps within the Matthean community or between the Matthean community and the Jewish community in general. The words are harsh: revile, persecute, and speak evil. The same happened to the prophets of old and the same happened to Jesus. "Falsely" may be original or not. It is not in all manuscripts.

Questions

42. Can anyone really be expected to live according to all of these Beatitudes?

43. Which do you prefer: "poor" (Luke) or "poor in spirit" (Matthew)? Why?

44. Are those who mourn really comforted?

45. What usually happens to the "meek" or "gentle"?

46. What happens to those who stand up for justice?

47. Forgiveness is one thing; forgetting is another. What do you think?

48. Pure of heart seems easier when it referred only to chastity. What do you think?

49. How can anyone wish everyone else "peace," "the best of everything"?

50. Why not maintain "peace" by avoiding causing trouble?

Conclusion

Unlike Moses, Jesus gives the teachings and does not receive them. Matthew elicits a comparison to Moses and then goes beyond the comparison. It seems he wanted Israel and the Jews to recognize in Jesus the fulfillment of the hope and expectations of the people of the Old Testament. Jesus spoke for God.

Two Beatitudes mention the kingdom of heaven (first and eighth) and twice the Beatitudes call for righteousness (fourth and eighth). Perhaps both Luke and Matthew inherited the Beatitudes from "Q," but Matthew has added to them and has omitted any woes.

The kingdom of heaven or the kingdom of God means a union between God and people and then a unity among peoples. When people live according to the Beatitudes, this union and unity results. The reign of God begins on earth.

Matthew emphasizes righteousness throughout his gospel. His community would have been familiar with the justice or righteousness of God. God had called the people of Israel to stand in the presence of God with dignity and worth. Too often the people of Israel did not afford this dignity and worth to others. Matthew will frequently remind his mixed congregation of their mutual righteousness. Jewish Christians and Gentile Christians both belong and both have value in the sight of God because of their faith.

Although these Beatitudes refer to the future, the anticipation of the reward takes place in the present. The happiness will not be reserved for the future but also takes place *now*.

Each Beatitude describes the type of person who will be part of the kingdom now as well as in the future. Each Beatitude has an Old Testament parallel and each Beatitude goes beyond the general interpretation to apply to the Matthean community. Since this community was in conflict with the Jews, symbolized by the Pharisees and Sadducees, and since the community also had its problems in relationships between Jewish Christians and Gentile Christians, the Beatitudes give the members of the community some guidelines for living.

The individual member of the community need not think he or she must live up to all of these Beatitudes all of the time. If a member once was a peacemaker, or forgiving, or gentle, or dependent on God, or any other of these Beatitudes, he or she can do it again. The Beatitudes remind the followers of Jesus what they have been and what they will continue to be.

Luke had a special affection for the needy, the financially poor. Matthew does not have such interest. He interprets poor in spirit in the sense of the Hebrew *anawim*, those who bow humbly before God, with all trust, willing to accept all from the loving hands of God even if they cannot always understand why. Since they have no money or power, they can rely on God alone.

Life brings sorrow. No one needs to look for it. Sorrow will find you. As Thomas Gray pointed out in one of his poems, "Sorrow never comes too late and happiness too swiftly flies." The teachings and example of Jesus comfort his followers. He promised a hundredfold now and eternal life to come. People who depend upon God, who are gentle and stand for justice, will mourn and God will comfort them.

Christians have stood for justice and they have been persecuted. They follow the example of the Messiah and Teacher. To wish everyone only the best of everything in life demands a large heart and soul. Those who depend on God have such largess.

The Beatitudes describe the true followers of Jesus. They depend on God; they are willing to accept all from the hands of God. They know life brings them pain and sorrow, but their faith supports them. They do not stomp through life but walk gently; they forgive, for they know they need forgiveness. They stand for human dignity and value for all people and do their best to wish all people well. For this they will experience persecution and revilement and slander. But how else can they live if they choose to follow a crucified Messiah?

Section Eight:
Salt and Light, Law and
Prophets, 5:13–20

Introduction

Jesus used images that came from the experience of people. Salt was used to preserve and to give flavor and to purify. Everyone knew that. Leviticus also prescribes salt to be used in sacrifices (Lev 2:13). Usually salt does not lose its flavor, but it can become adulterated.

Without light, no life exists. Frequently the writers of the Old Testament used light as an image related to God. People were to walk in the light of the Lord (Isa 2:5). God intended Israel to be the light for the nations (Isa 42:6). Paul picks up this theme in Romans 2:19. Just as all life needs light, so the lives of the followers of Jesus demand the light of the Lord and his teachings.

The city on the mountain has become a common theme in evangelization. As Jerusalem was built on a mountain for all to see, all nations should come to Jerusalem to learn the Law of the Lord lived by the followers first of Judaism and now of Jesus. Followers of the Lord are to live their lives as examples of light, calling others to bask in the light they have received from the Lord. Good deeds flow from values and the light of the Lord. The teachings of Jesus offer the foundation for the good deeds by which people will glorify God.

"The law and the prophets" sums up the Old Testament. Moses symbolizes the Law and Elijah symbolizes the prophets. Already Matthew had referred to Moses and Elijah indirectly by noting that Jesus had fasted for forty days and forty nights. He will refer to them again in the transfiguration. Jesus fulfills both Moses and Elijah by his teachings, which encompass all of the teachings of the Old Testament when he sums them up with the twofold commandment (Matt 22:37–40).

The passing away of heaven and earth reflects the complete coming of the reign of God. Until then, the law and the prophets remain in place. But Jesus will outlast both since he fulfills both and brings them to completion.

Yodh is the smallest letter of the Hebrew alphabet, much like a comma. Sometimes a decorative stroke was added to a letter. This might be the "dot" or "tittle." The meanings are evident: the law and the prophets remain. "Until all things have taken place" seems odd. Either it refers to eschatological events or to the death and resurrection of Jesus.

Rabbis customarily distinguished between grave and less serious commandments. Matthew recognizes the distinction and then holds to both types for observance. He ends the section with the scribes and Pharisees, who do not practice what they preach. Actions follow beliefs and values. Greatness follows the actions that flow from the beliefs. Jesus gives the interpretation so that those who produce the deeds of righteousness will experience the reign of God.

Questions

51. Which image do you prefer, salt or light?
52. The law and the prophets fulfill all Jewish traditions. How does this affect Christianity?
53. Do Christians observe all of the laws of the Old Testament?
54. Actions follow beliefs and values. How is this true for Christianity?

Conclusion

Somehow the Law remains even if Jesus seems to change part of it. This would please the Jewish Christians. The changes made also would please the Gentile Christians, but all need to respond to new demands. An organic relationship persists between Judaism and Christianity. Something remains even as some things will change.

Salt is no longer used as a preservative in developed countries but less-developed countries continue to use it. Too much salt in a diet can cause problems. Christians need to make a contribution to society without turning non-Christians away from faith. In the past too much "piety" actually hindered the spread of Christianity.

The same can be said for the image of light. Today this symbol retains much of its meaning. Light scatters darkness, and light gives life. Christians are meant to give light to others but like the salt, the light should not be blinding. To illuminate the need for God and Jesus in life does not demand overwhelming the non-believer.

Too often Christians have forgotten their indebtedness to Judaism. All of the teachings in the New Testament by Jesus can be found also in the Old Testament. Some practices may have changed but never their meaning. Even dietary laws were meant to bring discipline into life. That discipline is still needed in Christianity. Jesus made changes in the Law, as will be evident in the rest of the Sermon on the Mount, and in many instances the demands strengthen the responsibilities. Christians must never forget their spiritual kinship to Jews.

What a Christian believes sets the tone for all her or his actions as a follower of Jesus. In the past, Christian beliefs had encouraged missionary activities since Jesus intended his followers to be the salt of the earth and the light to the world. Sometimes Christians went too far in seeing themselves as saviors instead of focusing on the one true Savior but excess never excuses from the actions that should flow from the beliefs.

Section Nine:
Six Antitheses, 5:21–48

Introduction

"What was said of old" appears frequently in rabbinic literature. Usually it refers to Moses and the first generation of Israelites, but it also may be said of later generations prior to the time of Jesus.

Killing of the innocent was always considered a sin. Now Jesus broadens the understanding of human relationships by forbidding anger. Certainly anger curtailed lessens the chance for murder, but Jesus seems to condemn all incidents of anger. Israelites must avoid anger with their brethren, their fellow believers. Perhaps this refers to the Matthean community, but Matthew may intend it to apply to all peoples.

The sanction of judgment in Gehanna will take place not just because of anger but even anyone who calls a sister or brother a fool or *raca* (an obscure form of abuse meaning "empty-headed" or "stupid") can look forward to the fire of Gehenna. Gehenna originally referred to the city dump, "where the worm dies not and the fire is not quenched." The image should frighten and underscore the need for good human relationships.

God wants the offering of the heart, the offering of a life lived well. The offering of a sacrifice presupposes reconciliation. Rather than bring a sister or brother to court, seek reconciliation. Avoid worse consequences by seeking to turn enmity into friendship.

Most societies condemn adultery. Exodus 20:14 and Deuteronomy 5:18 make clear the prohibition, which was seen as an offense against the husband of the adulterous woman and was to be punished by death. Whether always carried out in the time of Jesus, it seems to form the background for the woman taken in adultery in John 7:53—8:11. Jesus goes further by alluding to the ninth commandment. Anger can lead to murder and lust can lead to adultery. Thoughts give rise to actions, just as beliefs give rise to actions. Then Jesus speaks of temptations. Better to lose an eye or a hand than to lose oneself in judgment.

Matthew continues the theme of adultery by referring to divorce. He summarizes the process of divorce as described in Deuteronomy 24:1. Jesus in Matthew makes divorce equivalent to adultery, but with an exception. The same exception clause appears in Matthew 19:9. Unfortunately, no one knows the precise meaning of the Greek word *porneia* (from which we get the word *pornography*). Some translate it as adultery; others fornication, or unlawful union, or sexual irregularity, or unchastity.

Swearing falsely also weakens society and can be seen in the eighth commandment in Exodus 20:16 and Deuteronomy 5:20, as well as in Leviticus 19:12, which prohibits swearing falsely by the name of God. Jesus does not want any swearing. Thus he makes the laws of oaths in the Old Testament useless. Do not use God in any swearing: by heaven or by God's earth or by the holy city of Jerusalem or by your head (the tendency to dye hair while the true color remains?). Rather, say "yes" or "no" and let it be. Anything other than the clear reply of "yes" or "no" comes from the evil one—either the devil or evil in general.

The law of retaliation was meant to limit punishment and avoid any escalation of violence. The punishment should suit the crime and no more. Jesus goes beyond civil law and legal principles to a higher law. "Do not resist an evildoer" does not make much sense. Perhaps it means not to do evil to the evildoer but to respond with graciousness. This would make sense in the context of the following verses. When you are insulted (struck on the cheek), do not retaliate but simply turn away. The verse does not mean pacifism. The taking of the shirt should not create a desire to get even but to give your coat graciously. Forcing into service (a practice of the Roman army) should not cause resentment but is an opportunity to offer greater service. Give graciously to anyone who asks and willingly let anyone borrow what she or he wants.

The Old Testament commands the love of neighbors (fellow Israelites) in Leviticus 19:18, but nowhere does it command

39

hatred of enemies. Here Jesus pushes the limits of brotherly love to include the enemy. Since God lets the sun shine on the good and the bad, so every true follower of the Lord should imitate the graciousness of God and not limit human love. Then, in fact, they are children of God.

Not too much virtue is required to love those who love you and to care for those who care for you. Here Jesus wants a higher order. Tax collectors and Gentiles were not considered to be paragons of virtue but even they love those who love them. True believers do more.

The section concludes with the injunction to "be perfect as your heavenly Father is perfect." Luke in the parallel place has "be merciful" or "compassionate" (Luke 6:36). Nowhere does the Old Testament refer to God as perfect, but it frequently refers to the mercy and compassion of God.

Questions

55. Do you consider calling a person "stupid" or an "idiot" the same as murder?

56. Gehenna, the city dump, is a symbol or image of damnation. How real are images?

57. Empty rituals mean nothing. Rituals should express the reality already there. How do you experience rituals?

58. Is adultery in the heart the same as actual adultery?

59. Temptation should be resisted. Is losing an eye or a hand too much?

60. Does divorce demand an exception precisely because of humanity?

61. How can Christians swear in court?

62. God wants graciousness in human relationships. What does this mean?

63. Which would you prefer: to try to be perfect or to be compassionate?

Conclusion

An antithesis means a contrast. "You have heard it said, but I say…" implies a contrast. Usually the contrast is a contradiction, but when Jesus uses the rhetorical pattern he does not mean a contradiction but an injunction to go further (anger and not just murder, lust and not just adultery, acceptance and not retaliation) or in some cases he makes the first part of the contrast useless (divorce, oaths, love of enemies).

Since these antitheses follow the fundamental statement that Jesus has come to fulfill the Law and not to destroy it, Jesus in the second part of the antithesis implies the fulfillment of the Law. To understand how Jesus fulfills the Law of the ancient Israelites demands an understanding that "Law" or Torah can better be translated as "instruction" rather than the usual understanding of law as a legal instrument. God gives instruction and the followers of God respond. Here action follows instruction.

The biblical foundation for the six antitheses appears evident. But then what do these antitheses mean for the followers of Jesus in the Matthean community? Matthew wanted to show that Jesus and his followers were not in opposition to Torah. In each instance the biblical text forms the starting point and then Jesus goes to the root or meaning of the biblical text and focuses on the internal dispositions of the followers of both Jesus and Torah. Better to go to the source of the sin: anger and lust for murder and adultery and revenge and retaliation as a source for many human problems in relationships. Since oaths can cause problems, why not avoid all of them, Jesus suggests.

The exception clause for divorce makes evident that Matthew and his community participated in the debate on grounds for divorce. In all likelihood the parallel texts in Mark 10:10–12 and Luke 16:18 with no exception reflect the original teaching of Jesus. Here Matthew wants to uphold both the Torah and the teaching of Jesus, but acknowledges that at times exceptions must be made.

The topics covered here—anger, murder, lust, adultery, oaths, responding to evil, loving friends and enemies—have always been controversial for any believer in Judaism or Christianity. Certainly calling a person an idiot should never be considered as bad as murder. Lustful thoughts cannot be the same as adultery. Feeling a need for revenge and at the least avoiding an enemy should not be worthy of Gehenna. And Gehenna is an image not to be taken literally. Gehenna implies pain and when people commit these sins they cause pain for themselves and for others.

Since Jesus came to fulfill the Law, God's instruction, then he and he alone fulfills the Law and not every Christian has reached that same level of fulfillment. Since God allows the rain to fall and the sun to shine on all people, the gracious mercy of God should be the ideal action that flows from the beliefs of Jesus. Since Christians have done this in the past, have risen above the ordinary level of human relationships, then they can do it again. They can resist temptation; they can avoid anger and lust; they can forgive enemies and not seek revenge. Their rituals have expressed their faith and do not attempt to cover up failures in relationships. They have been generous in giving and going the extra mile. And they have failed in all of these. They still live fragmented lives.

Since the Bible does not refer to God as perfect but rather holy and merciful and compassionate and faithful, the idea of perfection probably comes from Matthew. The Greek word used, *teleios,* means goal or completion, and not the usual meaning of perfect, which comes from Greek philosophy. *Teleios* translates the Hebrew word *tamin* or even *shalom* in the Septuagint (LXX). Both connote completeness. So, better to translate the word as "whole" rather than "perfect." Be "whole" and not dissipated or incomplete, just as God is not fragmented. Being whole would then mean the kindness and compassion and fidelity and graciousness found throughout these verses.

Section Ten: Charity, Prayer, and Fasting, 6:1–18

Introduction

Matthew returns to the theme of righteousness: recognizing personal value and dignity before God and then in turn seeing this same dignity in others, especially fellow believers. Three times he uses the word *hypocrites*. The Greek term signifies someone who performs behind a mask. Here the meaning is anyone who pretends to be someone he or she is not. Giving alms, praying, and fasting should signify a reality in the heart and not some false pretense.

In Greek the word for almsgiving, *eleemosyne,* can also mean mercy. The context would demand an expression of mercy such as giving of one's resources to those in need. The trumpet seems like a hyperbole or a metaphor, such as "blowing one's own horn," to make sure people notice the act of giving. People should show mercy in such a way that God alone knows and not even someone as close as your left hand. God will see and repay.

Prayer may be public but should not be a display to manifest piety in front of others. Pray privately, in an inner room, where only God can see. Prayer should mean something and not just empty babble, rattling off formulas. The true God cannot be manipulated by a flood of meaningless words, implying that the gods of the Gentiles can be so fooled. The true God knows people's needs and, like a kind and gentle parent, is anxious to listen and respond.

Then what follows is Matthew's version of the Lord's Prayer. Luke also has his version, which has four less petitions (Luke 11:2–4). Matthew has "our" Father while Luke has only

"Father." Perhaps Matthew's version came from the liturgy. The community of Matthew seems to have had a developed liturgy. In the final commissioning they are commanded to baptize in the name of the Father, Son, and Holy Spirit (Matt 28:19).

The Our Father continues the Jewish tradition of beginning prayer by praising God. The name of God should be revered. Continuing the praise, the disciple wishes that the reign of God be fully realized in the future even as the disciple attempts to live according to the reign of God now. Similarly, the will of God on earth should be accepted and lived just as the heavenly court responds and lives according to the will of God. Harmony will exist between heaven and earth when all accept the will of God.

Then the prayer changes from praising to asking. Matthew prays for bread for the coming day, while Luke prays for bread each day. Perhaps Matthew looks to the future, the eschatological day of the Lord, and maybe this has reference both to the manna in the desert and to the Eucharist.

Matthew in his version of the Lord's Prayer has "debts" and Luke has "sins." Both mean the same and both expect a remission of debts and sins because the petitioner promises to forgive others. "Lead us not into temptation" or "do not put us to the test" probably means "prevent us from being in a situation that we cannot handle." God does not lead people into temptation. Life and people do that. It may also mean a petition to not permit failure in the final test of living as people of faith.

The final petition may mean either the evil one (the devil?) or evil in general or anyone who is evil. The final two verses on prayer underline the need to forgive if people expect forgiveness from God.

The third act of piety, fasting, also should not be on display for all to see. Fasting has always been part of religion, showing discipline and control and sacrifice. People should fast privately but also should fast publicly in time of great need. Private fasting is private. No one should know and people should not change their appearance to make others notice. God responds to those who fast properly just as God responds to those who give alms without ostentation.

Questions

64. Charity, prayer, and fasting characterize all religions. Why are they important?

65. Anonymous donations even today seem to be better than public displays of generosity. Yes or no?

66. The Our Father seems like the prayer of a child who praises the parent and then wants something. Is this a model for all prayer?

67. What does "daily bread" mean to you?

68. Why is forgiveness so important in every aspect of life?

69. Why do people fast? Is it the same as going on a diet?

Conclusion

These sections of Matthew appear only here and nowhere else in the other gospels. Therefore, these teachings of Jesus must have had special significance to the community of Matthew. As a mixed community they had to learn to continue the tradition of almsgiving, prayer, and fasting and also adapt to the understanding of these pious practices according to the teaching of Jesus.

All three acts of piety presented in this section of Matthew—almsgiving, prayer, and fasting—have the same structure: the act, inappropriate behavior (looking for public reward and recognition), and appropriate behavior that God alone will reward.

Jesus does not condemn public acts of giving, praying, and fasting, but taking private actions and using them for personal aggrandizement. Followers of Jesus should avoid public displays of private piety in order to seek honor and recognition.

Giving to charity should characterize everyone who has more than enough of earthly goods. Responding to those in need has long been part of Christian tradition. Some reward flows from acts of charity at least to the extent that the person feels "good." However, the motivation should not be to feel "good" or to receive public adulation. People like to see their names displayed when giving to charity. An anonymous plaque might do just as well.

The Lord's Prayer can be accepted as the center of the section since it presents a model for all prayer. Some think Jesus did not teach such a prayer but that the early church composed the prayer based on the teachings of Jesus and used it as a substitute for the Jewish Eighteen Benedictions to be recited three times a day. In fact, it is a general prayer that can be said by anyone who believes in God and cannot be limited to Christianity.

Matthew's prayer seems particularly Jewish. Some think Luke's version is more geared to a Gentile audience. Since the Matthean community consisted of both Jewish Christians and Gentile Christians perhaps the Lord's Prayer took the place of the traditional Jewish practice of daily prayer. The *Didache* 8:3, an early Christian document, says that "three times a day you are to say the Lord's Prayer." The Matthean community and its gospel, which come from the same time as the *Didache*, probably did use the Lord's Prayer to substitute for the Eighteen Benedictions, thus making the transition to the Christian practice of prayer. This would have pleased the Jewish Christians and not alienated the Gentile Christians.

When a child flatters a parent, the parent knows the child wants something. It seems the Lord's Prayer does just that. After praising God the petitioner asks for daily bread: all that is needed to sustain life for the day—food, clothing, shelter, and people to love and to be loved. Then comes a promise to forgive because everyone needs forgiveness. People do well when the situation is not too much to handle. Here the prayer seems more like the prayer of a parent for a child and the final petition to help in avoiding evil may well mean not just evil in general but evil people and in that sense the devil. Evil people bring out the evil present in everyone's heart. Again, the parent prays to keep the child from bad companions.

Finally, fasting should be part of everyone's life experience. Public fasts used to be called by the church frequently. Now, only rarely does the church ask its members for prayer and fasting. Lent remains a "little fast" when compared to forty days of no more than two meals a day and no meat on Fridays. Fasting brings discipline to a most enjoyable aspect of life: food and drink. Fasting puts pleasure in context and even supports a healthy lifestyle. Dieting is a sad commentary on contemporary life.

Section Eleven:
Further Teachings in the
Sermon, 6:19—7:12

Introduction

Many try to divide the Sermon on the Mount into clear divisions and sections. It seems that Matthew chose to gather many teachings of Jesus into one large sermon and thus it is difficult to neatly divide it. Many verses may be grouped together, but others seem to be a random gathering of disparate ideas. This section seems to be the latter.

Moths destroy clothing. Many dispute the meaning of the word translated as "rust." It may mean "eating by an insect" and thus also refers to clothing or food. If it means "rust," the treasure is metal. Houses made of mud-brick can be easily breached.

Treasure in heaven forms part of a long Old Testament tradition (4 Ezra 7:77; 8:33, 36; Tob 4:8–9). The point seems to be that goals in life dictate actions. The idea that actions follow beliefs forms part of the overall theme of the sermon.

The eye is often called the window of the soul. A healthy eye physiologically enables the person to see the world properly. Otherwise the world becomes a blurred vision of light and darkness. Matthew may also be contrasting children of light (faith) and children of darkness (unbelief). The word translated as "diseased" really means "evil." An evil eye connotes jealousy or envy.

In Israel slaves sometimes were owned by two masters. The sharp contrast between love and hate also fits the general theme of actions follow beliefs. Loving one master brings faithful service. Hating another will cause less service. Mammon means "wealth," "money," or "property." The word may come from the Aramaic *'mn*, meaning "trust," and thus would refer to where one places trust. It may also come from the Aramaic *mwn*, meaning "to supply with nourishment." Whatever its origin the word emphasizes things rather than persons.

The next section (6:25–34) stresses trust in God rather than in things. Life is a good translation of the Greek word *psyche*. Life demands more than food and clothing. Life presupposes these elements but goes far beyond them. Human life means more to God than the birds of the air and worrying cannot add a day to your life or an inch to your height.

The word *lilies* may be understood generically as birds. Matthew includes the animal kingdom and the vegetable kingdom. God's care of humans outshines all other aspects of creation. Even kings (Solomon) in artificial array cannot outshine the beauty of creation. Grass and flowers bloom and fade. God cares for them; thus God will care for people. "Little faith" softens the negative aspect. Matthew also uses this diminutive in 8:26; 14:31; and 16:8. The faith and trust in God needs to be nourished and strengthened but it already exists. Anxiety about eating and drinking and being clothed can lessen the trust in God. Non-Israelites (the Gentiles) are concerned about these, but people of faith are not anxious about these dimensions of life since they are not the most important.

Righteousness has appeared already in the sermon. Being in proper positioning in the sight of God means more than any effort to appear "good" in the sight of others. Worrying about tomorrow never helps. Tomorrow may never come. Each day brings its trouble (evil or wickedness). Take care of today first.

Trusting God should affect how people treat each other. True Israelites should not pass judgment on each other. God alone judges. The Native American proverb demanding walking in another man's moccasins before judgment would fit here. The wood chip and the wooden beam illustrate the context for judgment. How can one judge a chip in another person's eye when a wooden beam exists in the one passing judgment?

Giving holy food (food blessed in the Temple) to dogs or giving pearls to swine will bring unsuspected consequences. Dogs were usually not treated as household pets but considered wild and dangerous. Pigs were unclean and to be avoided. Giving anything to a dog was dangerous. Giving the holy to a dog desecrated the holy. Acting inappropriately will bring unwanted consequences. People must learn to accept the consequences of their actions. Recall the second temptation of Jesus in the desert.

God will respond to people who ask, seek, and knock. The sermon contained the Lord's Prayer. God is like a kind and loving parent, anxious to listen to the prayers of his children. The bread and fish analogies suppose this parent-child relationship. In comparison with God, people are evil. If people do such good things God will do greater. The section closes with the Golden Rule.

Questions

70. Goals are important in life. Do people often think of heaven as a goal?

71. People tend to gather "things." Why so much concern about possessions in American culture?

72. How can one live life without being anxious about food and clothing and things?

73. Judging others comes easily. Why?

74. Fraternal correction should exist. Yes, no?

75. Inappropriate actions bring unwanted consequences. True for all leaders, both civil and religious?

76. Does God really listen to people's prayers like a kind and loving parent?

77. Is the Golden Rule an anthropological principle or a religious principle?

Conclusion

Actions follow beliefs. The goals in life found in the heart should dictate how a person lives. People tend to serve the god of wealth and possessions. American culture sees success dependent on how many "toys" a person owns. Heaven may appear on the distant horizon, but the more proximate horizon offers possessions and then the hope of power. The person of faith serves God alone and puts all else in perspective.

Trusting God in the midst of human failure and need demands much faith. Yet, God does care for animals and flowers. Trusting in God does not mean the lack of concern for daily needs since the person prays for "daily bread," but God remains the overriding presence in all of life's equations.

Judging others comes easily because people need to appear good in their own eyes. Putting someone else down can often bring a momentary sense of superiority. Fraternal correction demands putting one's own life in order first.

Matthew alone has the reference to giving the holy to dogs. It seems to come from a wisdom tradition and thus is a helpful hint for daily life. The most logical meaning can be related to the second temptation of Jesus. Doing something "stupid" or inappropriate can bring results that are at least unpleasant. Religious leaders should not betray the sacred and holy entrusted to them. Unfortunately, in history many have done just that. The same is true for civil leaders. Wearing expensive jewelry in the wrong place at the wrong time may bring unwanted consequences. Actions follow beliefs and values, and actions bring consequences.

God listens to people's prayers even if the answer may not always correspond to the desire of the one praying. Sometimes God says, "No." Just as kind and loving parents must at times deny a child's request, the same is true in the child-parent relationship to God.

The Golden Rule concludes this section. Whether or not a person believes in God or in Jesus, following the Golden Rule makes sense. To be happy in life means contributing to the happiness of others. Matthew says that the Golden Rule summarizes the law and the prophets. This summary may also fit the needs in the Matthean community. The many members coming from different backgrounds and even beliefs should treat each other with respect if they expect to be treated with respect.

Section Twelve:
Judgment and Conclusion,
7:13–29

Introduction

Many ancient cities had narrow gates. People could pass through them but at times, especially if one carried something, the movement was difficult. Following the Torah, the instructions of God, may appear difficult at times but it leads to eternal happiness.

Coming to the end of the Sermon on the Mount Jesus appears to look to the future, the eschatological conclusion of life. The word translated as "hard" usually refers to troubles in the end-times. The image seems harsh: only a few enter the small gate, while many follow the "spacious" way of self-destruction. Matthew offers a warning and an admonition.

Wolves were dangerous; sheep were gentle and comforting. False prophets appeared regularly in the history of Israel. They looked gentle and innocent but within were ravenous, bringing people to destruction.

Many times people find it difficult to discriminate between true and false prophets. Jesus gives the criterion: see their actions. Actions follow beliefs and values. Figs do not come from thorns nor do grapes grow from brambles. Good results come from good values and beliefs. The verse dealing with the cutting down of the tree brings an eschatological tone to the images.

"Lord" to most sounds like a religious title. In fact, it was more a polite title used for teachers. The meaning is evident: actions must follow beliefs. Just as the teacher practiced what he preached so must the disciple. Here also the eschatological theme enters with the hope for the kingdom.

"On that day" also contains eschatological overtones. Here Matthew anticipates the final judgment in chapter 25. "I never knew you" anticipates Peter's denial in 26:72 and the second "depart from me" anticipates the final judgment in 25:41.

The "days of lawlessness" means times when people do not follow the Torah, the instructions of God. *Anomia* (without law) is also used to refer to the Pharisees in 23:38. Hearing and doing follow the general theme of the sermon: actions follow beliefs. The prudent person carefully prepares for the future. Matthew then describes a storm in short phrases in order to image the problems that followers will face (Matt 8:24–27).

Just as Deuteronomy used the formula, "When Moses had finished speaking all these words" (Deut 32:45), Matthew uses the same formula after each of the five speeches by Jesus. The words tie what Jesus teaches to what God taught through Moses. Matthew concludes by contrasting the sermon, the teachings of God's Law by Jesus, with the teachings by the scribes and Pharisees.

Questions

78. Do people think about the final outcome of human life? If so, when?

79. Is following the teachings of Jesus really difficult? All the time? Why?

80. False prophets tend to make things easy. What are some false prophecies today?

81. Prayer without good works is useless. Yes? No?

82. A prudent person anticipates the future with its problems. How does that fit into the teachings of Jesus?

83. Jesus teaches with authority, a right to influence thought, opinion, and especially behavior. Why?

Conclusion

A great deal of the Sermon on the Mount refers to how people live now but also how living now affects the future, especially the final outcome of personal and social history. This final section contrasts those who live correctly, whose actions follow their beliefs, and those who do not. The prudent person lives life based on values and beliefs. The foolish person lives life without principles.

This section develops wisdom themes: two ways of living, two types of trees, two types of rewards. In every instance results follow directly from the decisions made. How a person lives now will dictate the future. Usually young people do not think of the future beyond the coming day or week. The older a person gets the more she or he thinks of the end. Anticipating the future helps a person live in the present. Making difficult decisions when young often makes later decisions easier.

Anyone who offers something too good to be true means it is too good to be true. False prophets live in every century and in every place. Paying attention to how a person lives will give some indication of what a person believes. The person with no principles has no values and offers nothing to anyone else.

Prudence may be an anthropological virtue but in the context of the teaching of Jesus a prudent person views life in the light of the end of all life. How a person lives gives a hint of how a person will die and how a person will live on in eternity.

Some see in this section problems within the Matthean community. Others see the context of Christianity and Judaism. It may be both. False prophets live in the church as well as in society and in other religious traditions. "By their fruits you will know them." The teachings of Jesus provide the rock upon which the person of faith builds his or her life.

Jesus has the right to influence thought, opinion, and especially behavior since he not only takes the place of Moses in this gospel, he takes the place of God by offering instructions to his followers. When people accept the teachings of Jesus, what he taught affects daily actions.

Two themes seem to dominate the sermon: Jesus fulfills the Torah, the instructions of God, and actions follow beliefs. Jesus pays attention to internal dispositions, principles, values, and beliefs and then uses them to interpret the Torah. Thus Torah finds completion in the teachings of Jesus.

These teachings with their eschatological overtones form a fitting conclusion to the Sermon on the Mount. All should look to the future and plan accordingly. The sermon does not mean that a follower actually always fulfills these teachings of Jesus, but reminds the true believer that in the past he or she has actually already made some of these decisions. The person of faith works to see to it that actions follow beliefs. In so doing the person of faith anticipates the future good judgment when life ends. People must live in the present since they can do nothing about the past and cannot anticipate everything in the future. Living in the present, however, affects the future. Followers of Jesus, people of faith, live according to what Jesus taught and thus have no fear of the future.

Section Thirteen:
Jesus Heals, 8:1–17

Introduction

Jesus has taught from the mountain and now he returns to everyday living as a healer. The reference to many crowds seems to contradict the injunction in verse 4 not to tell anyone. This same injunction appears in Mark 1:44, which Matthew has in front of him.

Leprosy in the time of Jesus meant any type of skin disorder and should not be limited to Hansen's disease. Leviticus offers detailed regulations on dealing with lepers (Lev 13—14). They were segregated from the community and touching them would have made a person unclean.

Just as the Magi did Jesus homage (Matt 2:2, 8, 11), the leper does likewise. He uses the honorific title Lord, which as already noted can mean "sir" but to the Christian community took on a christological tone. Jesus heals the man and tells him to fulfill the Law of Moses as prescribed in Leviticus.

Mark frequently mentions the emotions of Jesus. In this parallel passage Mark comments that Jesus was moved with pity (Mark 1:41) and then sternly charges the man (Mark 1:43). Matthew has no interest in the emotions of Jesus. Perhaps because Matthew wants to emphasize the divinity of Jesus he downplays the emotional aspects of Jesus while Mark pays closer attention to the humanity of Jesus.

For Jesus to touch the man shows not only his compassion but his willingness to go beyond the Law, making himself unclean.

The gospel that supports the Law shows Jesus not paying attention to the Law when the Law does not help people. Remember the reaction of Joseph, being a just man, when he decides not to subject Mary to the full demands of the Law (Matt 1:19)?

Leviticus 14 outlines the procedure for declaring a leper welcome back into the community. Jesus touched the man, which was contrary to the Law, and then tells the man to fulfill the Law.

Capernaum seems to have been home base for Jesus in his ministry. Yet, in Capernaum the people did not respond properly to the miraculous activity of Jesus (Matt 11:23).

A centurion commanded a hundred men. Thus the name. Whether Roman or not makes little difference. He was a Gentile who expressed faith and to him Jesus responded. Like the leper, he calls Jesus "Lord."

The Greek word *pais* can mean either "child" or "servant." The other gospels have parallel passages. Matthew offers more details than the others. The response of Jesus can mean "I will come" or "shall I come?" In context it is difficult to determine whether the response means Jesus' positive interest or perhaps a bit of annoyance.

The centurion's reply, "I am not worthy" suggests that the context is the observance of the Law. A Jew would not enter into the home of a Gentile. The polite centurion with faith offers Jesus an alternative method to bring healing without breaking the Law. The question of "authority" seems strange. Does the centurion mean that as Caesar has given him authority over his men, so God has given Jesus authority over illness?

The faith of the centurion, noticeable from the beginning, gives Matthew an opportunity to proclaim the faith of Gentiles, so much a part of his community. Jesus continues with the Old Testament theme of Gentiles joining the people of Israel found in Isaiah and other prophets. The sons of the kingdom are Jews who received the offer but the offering does not mean acceptance. "Weeping and gnashing of teeth" appears frequently in Matthew (13:50; 22:13; 24:51; 25:30). It refers to eschatological and apocalyptic suffering. The episode concludes with Jesus declaring that the hope of the centurion will be fulfilled. The word of Jesus is powerful.

Both Mark and Matthew narrate the healing of the mother-in-law of Peter. In Matthew after rising up (the same word used for the resurrection of Jesus) she serves him and not them. Evidently crowds came to the home of Peter and Jesus healed them by "a word," thus fulfilling the famous suffering servant theme in Isaiah. Jesus heals for he himself will know pain and suffering.

Questions

84. Jesus ignores the Law and touches the leper. What does this tell you about the Jesus in Matthew?

85. Are you interested in the emotions of Jesus?

86. Why Capernaum? I thought Jesus was from Nazareth.

87. Is Jesus treating the centurion with politeness? Who seems more polite?

88. Gentiles have faith greater than Jews?

89. All religions like to be exclusive. How does this apply to Christianity?

90. The mother-in-law serves the men. How is this reflective of the customs of the time?

Conclusion

The Sermon on the Mount demonstrates that Jesus ministers powerfully in words. Now the following chapters will present Jesus equally powerful in deeds. In this section Jesus deals with physical ailments: leprosy, paralysis, and fever, as well as the general healing of crowds. Faith underlies all of the healings, pointing beyond the miracles to the question of the identity of Jesus. Who can perform such deeds?

Whether Jesus came from Nazareth or not cannot be definitively determined from Scripture. Matthew 2:23, "He shall be called a Nazarene," as already noted, can mean that Jesus came from Nazareth or Jesus was a Nazirite, one dedicated to God, or even that he was from the root of Jesse. Perhaps Jesus had two home bases: Capernaum and Nazareth.

The healing of the leper brings up the observance of the Law. Jesus said that he has come to fulfill the Law and then interprets the Law according to his own understanding. The leper needs to feel a human touch and Jesus responds, even if by so doing he breaks the Law.

With the centurion Matthew highlights the almost prayerful attitude of the Gentile. At first Jesus seems to respond as expected of any pious Jew but then the faith of the centurion and his suggestion to help Jesus to avoid breaking the Law give Jesus an opportunity to preach inclusiveness. Jews and Gentiles will be part of the reign of God.

Throughout the gospels women perform the ordinary expected tasks according to the norms of Jewish society. The gospels also present them going beyond the ordinary expectations of society, eventually leading to the quotation in Galatians: "There is neither Jew nor Greek, slave nor free, male nor female, but you are all one in Christ Jesus" (Gal 3:28).

Section Fourteen:
The Stilling of the Storm, 8:18–27

Introduction

The three Synoptics record the stilling of the storm and each gospel offers its own details and meaning. Matthew begins with the context of "following." The scribe wishes to follow Jesus. He refers to Jesus as "teacher." His desire to follow means he wants to be a disciple of Jesus.

Jesus responds by calling himself "Son of Man," which here refers to his lifestyle as an itinerant preacher who has no place to lay his head. Eventually the title will take on a divine aspect, as one coming in glory.

Another individual, who seems to have become a disciple, wants to bury his father much as Elisha wanted to say goodbye to his parents before following Elijah (1 Kgs 19:20). But here it is more than a farewell since the disciple wants to fulfill a religious obligation of burying his father. It may mean a desire to stay with parents until they die rather than an imminent burial.

The response of Jesus seems harsh. Matthew wants to make clear that the heavy responsibility of following Jesus precludes any other obligations, even the sacred obligation of burying parents. Probably Matthew deliberately exaggerates to force meaning upon his listeners. Matthew again repeats "follow."

And then "the disciples followed him" into the boat and the storm arises (Matthew uses a word meaning "earthquake," *seismos*, from which we get *seismograph*), which implies an apocalyptic overtone to the whole episode. Great tribulations surround the boat. Jesus sleeps, trusting in God and in life.

"Lord save us" is a prayer, similar to *Kyrie eleyson*. In Mark 4:40, Jesus says, "You have no faith." As noted Matthew uses a diminutive, "little faith." They have some but not enough. Jesus responds by doing what God does in Psalm 107:29.

Questions

91. Following Jesus demands sacrifice. Why should people bother?

92. Shouldn't people first fulfill family obligations before following Jesus?

93. The boat is often used as a symbol of the church: the "ark of Peter." How does this fit into the context of following?

94. When people are in trouble do they pray?

95. Does Jesus really calm all the storms in life?

Conclusion

Matthew places the stilling of the storm in the context of discipleship. Three times he uses the word *follow*. Discipleship demands a decision that will affect how a person lives. Family obligations must take second place. Everyone can find excuses to avoid discipleship. Augustine prayed to be chaste—but tomorrow, not today. Jesus expects determined decisions, not lukewarm commitments.

They all get into the boat with Jesus. In the Matthean community the boat symbolized the church and the church has its troubles. The first thing that the disciples should do is pray, for they know Jesus is with them. Awakened, Jesus, unlike in Mark, does not immediately calm the storm. First he reminds them of faith and then the storm goes away. The reaction is that all marvel and not just the disciples. They have begun to understand just who Jesus is, for he can command the wind and the waves.

People of faith can deal with any storm, even of earthquake proportions, that life throws at them. They know Jesus is with them and so they pray. Eventually all storms pass, even those that affect the church. Often enough storms arise from within the church caused by members of the church. Whether from within or without, as long as Jesus remains, the storms will pass both for the life of the church and for the life of the individual believers. Matthew assures his community Jesus will be with them "always, to the close of the age" (Matt 28:20).

Section Fifteen:
More Healings, 8:28—9:8

Introduction

No gospel is completely accurate with regard to geography except perhaps the Gospel of John. John was an eyewitness and would know the geography, especially around Jerusalem. The other gospels were written by noneyewitnesses anywhere from forty to sixty years after the stories of the ministry of Jesus took place and were composed in different places than where the events happened. The healing of the sick men in Matthew took place in the land of the Gadarenes some five or six miles southeast of the Sea of Galilee. Mark has the event taking place in the land of the Gerasenes more than thirty miles away from the Sea of Galilee. Wherever it took place, the relationship to the Sea of Galilee is more theological than geographical.

Matthew has taken this section from Mark. In Mark Jesus has power over all evil, even power over the evil forces that live in the sea. Once the demons enter into the pigs they must go to the place where evil forces live, the sea.

Mark has only one possessed man while Matthew has two. Matthew tends to add participants when compared to Mark. The territory was Gentile and thus the herd of pigs would not have been unusual.

Whether the possessed were Jews or Gentiles is not evident, but they were fierce and they seem to recognize Jesus as the one who will battle evil. Has Jesus anticipated the end-times by defeating demonic forces now?

In the Old Testament pigs were considered unclean. Why Jews considered them so remains unknown. Leviticus classifies them as unclean since they have cloven feet and no ruminant stomach

(Lev 11:6–7; Deut 14:8). But why this would make them unclean is still not clear.

Jesus responds to the request of the demons and casts them into the herd of pigs, which Jews would have found amusing, especially since they eventually drown. Once in the pigs the evil forces must get to the sea, to the place where evil forces live. The Gentiles then ask Jesus to leave. Jesus will be rejected by both Jews and Gentiles in his passion. Jesus then returns to his home base to confront another sick person.

In Mark 2:4 the friends of the paralytic go to much trouble to present him to Jesus. Matthew focuses on Jesus and his power to forgive sins. In both gospels, Jesus seems impressed by the faith of the friends. Since people in the time of Jesus associated sin with sickness, Jesus deals with both. In so doing Jesus equates his power with the power of God, thus, in the eyes of bystanders, Jesus blasphemes. Just as Jesus assumes the power of God in forgiving sins, he also reads hearts, just as God reads hearts.

Saying "your sins are forgiven" is easier than healing since the former has no outward manifestations. Since Jesus has power over the paralysis it can be assumed he has power over sins. Nowhere in Scripture does the Son of Man have power to forgive sins. Here the title takes on a divine dimension and the man goes away to his home. The immediate reaction is fear coupled with praise of God. The crowds do not understand precisely who is present among them.

Questions

96. Do people still think evil lurks under the waters?

97. Why does precise geography not matter? I thought the Bible was without errors.

98. Are all evil spirits demonic, associated with the devil?

99. Why do you think the Old Testament limits the kind of food people can eat? Are not all the animals given to humans?

100. Do people still associate sickness with sin?

101. How are sins forgiven?

102. What does "Son of Man" mean to you?

Conclusion

It seems Matthew was aware of the geographical problem associated with the herd of pigs and the Sea of Galilee. He changed the territory from what Mark said but still the pigs ran a long way. Mark throughout his gospel shows the power of Jesus over all evil. Matthew presents Jesus more as the mighty Lord and Master and Teacher. For both Matthew and Mark, geography becomes subservient to theology. The power of Jesus extends to all types of evil.

When people read of demons they immediately think of the devil. In the ancient world any type of illness, even epilepsy, was thought to be associated with the demonic. Even today evil forces, such as greed, can exist in society. Although such forces have nothing to do with the devil, they can be most powerful and destructive.

Christians eat all kinds of pig products, unlike Orthodox Jews. Maybe the prohibition against eating certain food was not to segregate the animals but to bring discipline into the pleasure of eating. This greatly benefits people of all religions.

Very often people think that God punishes through illness. Illness comes as part of human life, often caused by the person individually. Bad things like terrible illness happen to good people. The Book of Job in the Old Testament tries to deal with this classic problem but provides no answer since in the end all is restored to Job and more. Why good people experience such pain in life remains unknown other than accepting that life brings problems to all. God and (for Christians) Jesus remain present with the sick person and help him or her to deal with the tragedy.

Son of Man may come from the Aramaic *bar e nas* or *bar e nasa*, which originally meant "everyman." Eventually it becomes a title associated with Jesus and takes on divine quality. In fact, "everyman" forgives sins for God forgives those who themselves forgive ("forgive us our debts [sins] as we also forgive our debtors [those who sin against us]"). When a person asks pardon for sins, God forgives the sins.

Section Sixteen:
Sinners and Eating, 9:9–17

Introduction

While many want to see each gospel carefully planned out with evident divisions, more accurately the gospels are collections of stories, teachings, and events loosely joined together by similar ideas. Since Matthew had as his sources the Gospel of Mark, a collection of sayings of Jesus ("Q"), and some material proper to his own traditions, at times he would join some sources together without much connection. In these verses Matthew creates a rest before returning to other healing stories.

The name Matthew comes from the Greek word *mathetes*, meaning "disciple." Whether this Matthew, associated with the gospel, was also Levi in Mark 2:14 remains unknown. The Twelve clearly belonged to Jesus in a special way among his many disciples. And like Israel of old, the new Israel, the church, will have twelve stones on which it will be built. The three Synoptics list the Twelve without Levi but include Matthew.

The Gospel of John does not give the list of the Twelve but tells the story of the call of Nathanael in 1:45–51. Is Bartholomew the same person as Nathanael and Levi the same as Matthew? Or were there twelve slots and fourteen names and so two must have had two names?

Jesus called Levi in Mark and Matthew in Matthew and the tax collector gave up his position and followed. Then Jesus eats with tax collectors and other sinners. Whether they ate in the house of Jesus or Jesus ate in their house seems unclear.

Anyone who collaborated with Rome was a sinner to Jews, and often the tax collectors overcharged to fill their own coffers. They were doubly sinners. Jesus eats with this crowd. Pious religious leaders were offended but did not question Jesus directly. On hearing Jesus addressed them openly.

Jesus responds with what seems to be a proverb. As a wisdom teacher Jesus cares about those who need help. To them the master physician will respond. Jesus quotes Hosea 6:6 and Matthew uses the same quotation again in 12:7. Here it implies a concern for outward observance instead of paying attention to internal dispositions, a theme also found in the Sermon on the Mount.

The reference to pious fasting associated with followers of John allows Jesus to present himself as the bridegroom. Just as God was the bridegroom for Israel, now Jesus will be the bridegroom for the new Israel. When he is present all should rejoice in celebration.

The reference to old and new wineskins would have made sense to anyone who made wine. Here the idea seems to be the relationship between old and new. The new wine of the teachings of Jesus will bring new attitudes and new dimensions and new instructions and even new laws.

Questions

103. How much do we know about the twelve apostles?

104. Jesus eats with sinners, rather than with the religious leaders. What does this mean?

105. Do not the pious also need Jesus?

106. When should Christians fast?

107. Does the reference to old and new wineskins make much sense today?

108. Who belongs to religious communities? Only the pious?

109. Which practices are necessary and which are helpful but not necessary?

Conclusion

Whether this section comes from a longer episode in which Jesus enters into debate with his opponents, no one will ever know. It does seem to have many ideas joined together without much thought of how they all fit.

Throughout this gospel Jesus calls and teaches his followers. Matthew means "disciple" and thus a student of the master. Whatever his position, he has always been identified with the Levi of Mark and thus a Jew who collaborated. Caravaggio powerfully depicts the call of Matthew with a light surrounding Jesus as he points to Matthew, holding his money in his hands. The charismatic Jesus looks, calls, and the sinner, the collaborator, responds. History records very little about most of the Twelve. Only legends surround their lives after the resurrection.

The pious need help but sinners need more. Anyone who collected taxes for Rome could easily succumb to overcharge and thus be dishonest. They also must associate with Gentiles. Both would have made them suspect in the eyes of the pious Jew. When Jesus ate with these "probable sinners" and with other "sinners," whoever they might be, he caused scandal.

Pious Jews fasted on Mondays and Thursdays. Evidently Jesus did not expect his followers to have regular ascetic practices and this also would be scandalous. Only after the resurrection did Christians adopt the practice of fasting.

Matthew deals with both by quoting Hosea. Mercy covers a multitude of failures, and God responds more to mercy than to sacrifices. Internal dispositions matter and not just external observance. This may well come from the problems associated with the Matthean community and Judaism as well as Jewish and Gentile Christians within the community.

The "old" and "new" seem to imply that Judaism and the teachings of Jesus cannot fit together. However, this would contradict Matthew's effort to preserve the old. Since Matthew was written after the loss of the Temple in AD 70, which subsequently altered the understandings of sacrifices and priesthood, Matthew teaches that the way to preserve the old is to accept the new teaching of Jesus as fulfilling what preceded. Jesus and his program of mercy not only fulfilled Temple sacrifices but brought God into the ordinary need for forgiveness in daily life. "Forgive us our sins as we forgive those who sin against us."

Section Seventeen:
The Healings Continue,
9:18–38

Introduction

Matthew has taken the episode of the healing of the young girl from Mark. In Mark the girl is near death while Matthew heightens the incident by having the girl already dead. Knowing that his daughter is dead strengthens both the power that Jesus has to heal and the strength of the faith of the official. Like those before him the official (Mark has him an official of the synagogue) offers Jesus homage just as the Magi in chapter 2 and the leper in chapter 8. This strengthens the understanding of the identity of Jesus as divine.

Laying on of hands has much significance in the Old Testament. It can connote a blessing, the passing on of authority, even a sacrificial ritual. Here it implies a transfer of healing power from Jesus to the young girl. Matthew adds the presence of the disciples to relate them to the healing by Jesus.

Matthew also takes the story of the woman with the hemorrhage from Mark. The woman has a magical notion of touching Jesus' cloak but the cure comes from the words of Jesus. Matthew views the faith of the woman approaching from a distance similar to the faith of the centurion. Jesus pays attention to faith and downplays any sense of magic. Since Matthew used the word *sozo*, which can mean "save" as well as "heal," physical healing expressed spiritual healing. The whole person experiences salvation.

The scene shifts to the house of the official. The presence of flute players confirms the death of the girl. Jesus tells them and the professional mourners to leave. He is alone and so Matthew concentrates on the sovereign power of Jesus over death. No mention is made of her parents or his companions. Some think that perhaps Jesus had superior knowledge and that the girl actually was in a coma but since Matthew used the word *egerthe* (the usual term for resurrection) he teaches that Jesus has power over death as he will have power over his own death. Mark notes that Jesus told her parents to give her something to eat. Matthew omits this incident. Jesus touching her is enough to restore her to full health. Mark also adds the injunction not to tell anyone, which is part of his effort to conceal the identity of Jesus. Matthew has no desire to conceal the power and identity of Jesus.

Matthew gathers several traditions to create the story of the healing of the two blind men. Part comes from Mark 1:43–45 and 10:46–52. Matthew presents Jesus as the Son of David, a powerful Jewish christological title. The whole episode centers on faith. The blind men must attest to their belief that Jesus can heal them and Jesus responds by touching and healing. Unlike other instances where Mark calls for concealing and Matthew does not, here Jesus tells the cured not to spread the word but in fact they do just that.

Finally, Jesus heals a mute man. The condition is attributed to demonic possession and thus Jesus will drive out the demon and the man will speak. The reference to Israel calls to mind the crowd to which Jesus preaches, while the presence of Pharisees calls to mind the opponents. They do not deny the power of Jesus to heal but attribute this power to Satan, the prince of demons.

Matthew summarizes the activity of Jesus as teaching, preaching, and healing. Most of the time he avoids references to synagogues since his community experiences opposition from those associated with the synagogues. Here he responds to his own community by commenting that Jesus taught first in synagogues.

The image of the people of Israel as sheep in need of a shepherd figures prominently in the Old Testament (Num 27:17; Ezek 34:5). Jesus will be the shepherd and his disciples will be like harvesters to continue the work of Jesus. The harvest brings again into the picture the eschatological dimension of the teachings of Jesus.

Questions

110. Why would Matthew use Mark and yet make many changes in the inherited text?

111. People like magic. Magic tries to control God. Faith and prayer appeal to the goodness of God. Is magic still around in religion?

112. Is faith healing true?

113. Did Jesus really raise people from the dead?

114. Can faith open eyes? Physically? Spiritually?

115. Why do some people always want to refuse to recognize the goodness in another human being?

116. Why does Matthew continue to bring the final outcome of history into play?

Conclusion

Miracles of healing manifest the power of Jesus over all evil. The more he shows this power, the stronger the opposition grows. People do not like to admit others live filled with the power of goodness and the blessing of God's presence. Putting a good person down somehow makes the opposition feel better. People step on people to get ahead.

Matthew picks and chooses from his sources, preserving only what he thinks is necessary for his community and his purpose. He is not limited slavishly to what he has inherited but is filled with the Spirit of God; he can create his own understanding of what Jesus might mean to his listeners and to his community.

The healing of the two blind men forms a doublet with Matthew 20:29–34. Both have similar words and actions. In this version Matthew centers on a scrutiny of faith: "Do you believe that I can do this?" Faith brings healing. Who can doubt the healings accomplished by a person's faith? Miracles take place every day in hospitals, in nursing homes, and in the lives of ordinary people. Even medical schools now teach the need for the spiritual to be present in efforts to cure and heal physically. The human person has physical, psychological, and spiritual dimensions and they all interact together.

People like magic. Magic fascinates. Ordinary magic shows are nothing more than clever tricks capable of fooling the mind, or at least the eyes. Still, people like to try to control God either by incantations, by repetitions of actions, by the manipulation of things, even by using prayers and objects of devotion, such as statues, rosaries, or candles. Prayers and objects of devotion mean nothing unless they express faith. When they express faith they are no longer magic, and perhaps a kind and loving parent ("Our Father who art in heaven…") will reply.

The Old Testament has stories of raising people from the dead (2 Kgs 4:18–37). The Gospel of John narrates the raising of Lazarus (John 11:28–44). As divine Son of God, Jesus had power over all evil, including death. Whether actual or apparent, physical or spiritual, the true meaning of bringing a person back to life anticipates full eternal life that Jesus offers to anyone of faith.

Finally, as the shepherd, Jesus protects the flock, which at times is harassed and torn apart. He is present with them now and will provide for them in the future through his disciples. They will thus be able to face the final outcome of history with faith and with confidence.

THE MISSIONARY SERMON, 10:1–42

Section Eighteen: The Twelve and Their Mission, 10:1–15

Introduction

Once Jesus has demonstrated his power to teach, preach, and heal, he calls the Twelve to join him in continuing this mission. As Jesus had authority so the Twelve will have authority (*eksousia* means the right to affect thought, opinion, and behavior).

Each of the Synoptics lists the Twelve (Mark 3:16–19; Luke 6:14–16). John does not list the names of the Twelve and in fact rarely uses *twelve* and never uses the word *apostle*. He prefers *disciples*. Matthew lists six pairs.

Simon (Peter) comes first. Peter will figure prominently in this gospel, especially when Jesus gives him the power of the keys in chapter 16. Along with his brother Andrew, Jesus calls Simon first.

Thomas is joined with Matthew, whom the gospel refers to as *telones* (tax collector). The others are listed with little distinction except for Simon the Canaanean, which could also imply a zealot—whether in the religious or political sense is unclear. Finally, Judas is singled out as the betrayer. Iscariot may refer to a geographical place or possibly to what he does: liar, hypocrite, and assassin.

The Twelve are to avoid the Gentiles or the district of the Gentiles and also Samaria (Samaritans were Jews who intermarried and followed only the first five books of the Bible). They are to respond to the needs of all Israel (the lost sheep); they will preach the same as did John the Baptist and Jesus: the coming reign of God.

Like Jesus, they also will heal, raise the dead, cleanse, and cast out. The Twelve will establish continuity between their mission and the mission of Jesus. They do so without cost. They should avoid overpreparing for this mission by acquiring gold, silver, or copper. They should not be overburdened with baggage to make their journey easier and more evident to others that they preach without demanding or needing possessions. Yet, they should expect and accept what they need for life. Their mission will support them. Staying in one house will demonstrate their commitment to the mission without concern for their surroundings.

Peace is the wish for the best of everything. It involves more than a cessation of hostility. The Twelve will wish only the best to all those who listen to their words. When Jews returned from foreign lands, they shook the dust from their feet as a sign of rejection of all that the foreign lands offered. Here the symbol manifests the actual rejection by some Jews of both Jesus and his disciples. Just as Sodom and Gomorrah symbolized wickedness, so the rejection of Jesus, his disciples, and his teachings symbolizes wickedness.

Questions

117. Why are the Twelve important? Does their mission continue?

118. What names of the Twelve mean something to you?

119. How do they continue the mission of Jesus?

120. Why the restriction to Jews, excluding Gentiles and Samaritans?

121. Should missionaries depend only on the support of those to whom they are sent? How practical is this?

122. What does peace mean to you, especially at Mass?

Conclusion

In all probability the mission of the Twelve, the existence of the Twelve, goes back to the ministry of Jesus. Just as Israel had twelve tribes so the new Israel will depend on the Twelve for the fulfillment of their hope for a restored Israel. The lack of knowledge about most of them (some manuscripts have different names) only strengthens the belief that twelve men did function with Jesus as his closest collaborators. Their goal is a restored Israel. Jesus has come not to destroy but to fulfill. The Twelve will aid in this task.

They must first go to Israel. Matthew will use this beginning to create the great missionary sermon of Jesus, which will include all peoples, just as in the ending of the gospel the disciples are sent to "all nations."

What the disciples do, Jesus did. The disciples through the ages continue the mission of Jesus to teach, preach, heal, and cast out evil. Jesus lived a simple lifestyle and dealt with rejection. Their lifestyle should be simple and they have to accept rejection. As Jesus lived as an itinerant preacher, so his followers will do likewise. The same should be true today for Christian missionaries.

In the modern world depending on the free will offerings of others may seem foolish. Yet when the church and its leaders live a simple lifestyle, free will offerings suffice. Only when missionaries and church leaders demand more will free will offerings not suffice.

In the Matthean community the Jewish Christians needed to feel not only accepted but appreciated. In all probability the injunction to preach first to Jews goes back to Jesus. This would suit the Jewish Christians of the Matthean community. In the gospel Matthew will leave an opening to the Gentile mission even in the ministry of Jesus. The centurion was a Gentile and yet had greater faith than that found in Israel. The mission to Judaism showed the fulfillment of the Jewish traditions in Jesus and in his teachings, especially after the destruction of Jerusalem and the Temple in AD 70. Christianity continues this mission with greater sensitivity to the promises of God to Israel.

If peace means wishing the best of everything, then for Christians to do this when celebrating the Eucharist removes any sense of separation and exclusivity. The same wish should be extended to all people, especially those who first heard the word of God in Israel.

Section Nineteen: Missionary Instructions, 10:16–42

Introduction

The second great sermon of Jesus concerns the mission of his followers, especially the Twelve. He has gathered them together and will send them out with specific instructions on how they should act. The image of sheep among wolves highlights the dangers that will surround their mission. Matthew continues the analogy with animals by contrasting the cunningness of the serpent in (Gen 3:1 the serpent is called shrewd) and the innocence of doves. Already the mission of the disciples will prove complicated.

Matthew deals with problems of his own time when he refers to being handed over to the Sanhedrin, the local council of Jewish leaders. Frequently early Jewish Christians appeared before local religious leaders to explain their activities. Matthew has problems with Jews and often has critical remarks about synagogues since Jewish Christians experienced punishments there (Acts 22:19; 2 Cor 11:24–25).

The governors (Roman prefects of Judea) and kings (Herodian princes) also persecuted early Christians. Matthew does not make clear if the Jews dragged the Christians before these tribunals. In both instances, before the Sanhedrin and before governors and kings, the early followers of Jesus bore testimony to Jesus as the Messiah. When they testify they can count on the help of the Holy Spirit. For people unaccustomed to projecting a good defense, this assurance of divine assistance helped the early Christians to stand strong in the midst of opposition. Matthew also anticipated the division among families. This would occur not only among Jewish Christians but also among Gentile Christians.

The section has an apocalyptic overtone, especially with the addition of "enduring to the end." Followers of Jesus will patiently accept the persecution, which may include martyrdom, but ultimately all suffering associated with the final coming of the reign of God will end. The coming of the Son of Man adds to the eschatological and apocalyptic tone. The obvious interpretation seems to imply the coming of the Son of Man in glory before they have completed their tour of Israel. Obviously this was not true. For some this refers to the death and resurrection of Jesus, while others see it as the gift of the Spirit or perhaps the destruction of the Temple in AD 70.

Taken in itself Jesus' reference to his coming would indicate a specific and determinable moment for the coming of the reign of God. Other sayings in Matthew suggest the contrary (24:32, 46; 25:13). Matthew offers a time-conditioned prophecy with a sense of imminent expectation in conformity with the historical situation.

The next verse offers encouragement. Just as the Master experienced persecution so will the disciples. The image involves school (disciple) and home (servant). If Jewish leaders accuse Jesus of being in league with the devil, the same will be true for his followers. No one can follow a crucified master without experiencing pain.

Above all, they are not to fear. Three times Jesus tells his disciple not to fear (10:26, 28, 31). Jesus teaches openly and simply. They must proclaim what they have learned, hiding nothing, not limiting the preaching to what cannot face the light of day, and not whispering. Jesus has nothing to hide and so his disciples must follow his example.

The *psyche* (translated here as "soul") means the real and complete self. The body (*soma*) is the shell. Fear only the possibility of losing oneself in Gehenna (the city dump as a symbol of eternal loss). If God cares for poor sparrows and can number the hairs on a head, how much more will God care for people? Have no fear. Here Matthew makes reference to the cross for the first time.

Matthew returns to the forensic analogy. Testifying on earth for Jesus will assure the support of Jesus for his followers in the presence of God. This will also give encouragement. Such testimony will bring problems: the sword instead of peace. Following Jesus or denying Jesus divides people, even within a family.

Unlike Luke, which uses the word *hate* ("does not hate his own father and mother...," 14:26), Matthew changes the "Q" saying to "loves more than me." Matthew also uses *axios*, "does not deserve to belong to me." A decision for Jesus will affect even those family ties that mean so much in life. Following Jesus may involve much suffering and even a painful death (taking up one's cross). Again, Matthew uses *psyche*, the true self. Following Jesus assures the preservation of the true self, which may entail the giving of one's life.

Accepting Jesus means accepting God and all those who accept the followers of Jesus by that fact accept Jesus and God. The Twelve will go about as prophets, pointing out the presence and absence of God in life. Some will accept them and some will not. The Twelve will offer righteousness, being able to stand in the presence of God, and people should respond properly. The Twelve are the "little ones," just as the community of Matthew are the "little ones." Anyone who responds to the needs of the Twelve or the community of Matthew by offering a cup of water will receive God's reward.

Questions

123. Jesus promises persecution for his followers. Is this still true?

124. How can one be like a sheep and a serpent and a dove?

125. Christianity caused conflict with Jews and even within a person's family. How can "good news" be a cause of conflict?

126. Does the Holy Spirit give guidance to all Christians in their defense?

127. Did early Christians think that Jesus would return soon in triumph?

128. All Christian teachings should be open and transparent. No whispering. Should the church do likewise?

129. Faith drives out all fear. God cares for all people, especially believers. How is this so?

130. Loving Jesus demands a change in living. What does this mean?

131. Prophets are not acceptable, especially in their own families and among their own friends. Is this true?

Conclusion

Persecution from outside and divisions within families will cause pain and sorrow for the Twelve and all followers of Jesus. Deciding to follow Jesus demands a change in lifestyle that might include family relationships. People have to make a decision. No middle way is possible.

Learning from the animal world has long been part of the wisdom tradition. Sheep might look cute but they are not very smart. Snakes are cunning in their ability to hide and lay in wait. Doves look peaceful but often are not. Somehow the Twelve and all disciples are to act as if they are placid sheep, be careful how they move about, and convey an attitude of gentleness. No wonder most fail!

Jesus promised the assistance of the Holy Spirit not just in the case of official conflict but also in the presence of the ordinary conflicts in family and daily life. Following Jesus will give a person the strength to defend a way of living in the presence of opposition and what the world might call foolishness.

The actual persecution of Christians by Jews and Romans probably was minimal but not unreal to those who experienced it. Perhaps the community of Matthew happened to experience more persecution than other early Christian communities.

The problem of family divisions and pain runs throughout the history of early Christianity as well as through the centuries. Very often parents object to the religious aspirations of their children. Brothers and sisters have not agreed on proper religious activity. Divisions persist even among Christians.

Probably in early Christianity many thought or hoped Jesus would return quickly in triumph. Perhaps for Matthew the resurrection of Jesus signaled the beginning of the end. With the passage of time the coming of the Son of Man was pushed into the distant future with no definite time for realization. Some have mistakenly thought that the Son of Man will come only when all the Jews have been evangelized. This prompted the mission to Israel and the persecution of Jews when they refused to accept Jesus as Messiah. Matthew should not be blamed for this mistaken idea.

What Jesus taught should be proclaimed openly. No secret knowledge exists for the "enlightened ones." No distinction should exist in what church leaders know and live above all others. The glory of Christianity should be evident to all as should the failure of Christians.

All prophets, those who tell the presence and absence of God, need to be part of the Christian tradition and need not be limited to Christian leaders. The "little ones" were not just the Twelve but in all probability all the members of the Matthean community. The "little ones" continue in the church today.

Followers of Jesus can expect resistance from outside the community, within the community, and even within one's family. They should not fear since they have been promised the consolation of the presence of the Spirit and know they follow a persecuted Messiah. God has sent Jesus and Jesus has sent the Twelve and with the "little ones," they are all bound together as one.

Section Twenty:
Jesus and John the Baptist, 11:1–19

Introduction

The word *teleo* (to finish) marks the end of the second sermon. It has been used at the end of the Sermon on the Mount (7:28) and will be used after the end of the next three great sermons (13:53; 19:1; 26:1). Matthew, unlike Luke 9:10, says nothing about the return of the disciples.

Matthew has already noted the arrest of John (4:12). Evidently John could communicate with those outside since he sends emissaries; he inquires about Jesus. Since some manuscripts have "Jesus" instead of "Christ" it seems in the early manuscript tradition some confusion existed as to whether John was inquiring about "the Messiah" or about Jesus. Although by the period of Matthew's composition Christ had become a second name for Jesus, such was probably not true for his ministry. The Messiah became Jesus who became Jesus the Messiah or Christ.

John's inquiry if Jesus is the one who is to come seems at odds with the baptism of Jesus by John already recorded. Jesus responds to the question by telling the followers of John to report what they have seen. Either the works of Jesus show that he is in truth the Messiah or the works of Jesus show that the understanding of the Messiah, thought to be a military leader, needs rethinking.

Matthew lists the deeds of Jesus as he had recorded them, from healing the blind to the raising of the dead. Then Jesus praises those who are not scandalized (*skandalidzo*, literally, a stumbling block), those who do not take offense. Throughout the gospel the Jewish leaders take offense at Jesus and his activities. The same will be true for the community of Matthew and the Jews of that period.

John baptized where reeds grew. John was unshaken. Did people pay more attention to shaking reeds, the ritual washing, than to what John preached? When Herod Antipas founded Tiberias in AD 19, he used a reed on coins minted for the occasion. Does Matthew also refer to Herod? This may take on further possibility when added to the "soft garments." John and his teachings contrast with the weak and soft living and teaching of the civil leaders of Judaism and those associated with them.

Jesus proclaims that John was a prophet. He pointed out the absence of God in the lives of the people of Israel. Jesus identifies John with the Old Testament belief that the coming of Elijah would precede the coming of the Messiah. The quotation combines Malachi 3:1; 4:5 and Exodus 23:20. God speaks. The "you" is Jesus and John is the "messenger." In the gospel in 11:14 Matthew explicitly equates John with Elijah. But as great as John was, he belonged to another age in the history of salvation. With John in prison and with the possible veiled references to Herod, the violence may refer to what happened to John. Then the violence against John anticipates the violence against Jesus and the followers of Jesus. Since Jesus and his followers preached the same gospel as John, the opposition maintains continuity. John belonged to the Old Testament as ending and belonged to the New Testament as beginning.

Matthew has Jesus identifying John with Elijah with some hesitation. Perhaps the hesitation comes from the belief that Elijah would be the forerunner of the kingdom and not the Messiah. The lack of political ambition of both John and Jesus also would have caused hesitation in understanding the role of each of these prophets.

"This generation" refers to the opponents of John and Jesus. They accuse both John and Jesus of improper behavior while in fact the true improper behavior belongs to those opposed to John and Jesus. John lived an ascetic lifestyle and "this generation" accused him of being possessed by a demon. Jesus lives an ordinary lifestyle and his opponents accuse him of an inappropriate lifestyle, especially if Jesus was a prophet. John acted as if a funeral was taking place and Jesus acted as if a wedding was taking place and the opponents rejected both.

The final verse seems obscure. Does Matthew use this apparent proverb in the same way as "by their fruits you will know them" (7:20), or do both John and Jesus embody true wisdom, offering guidance for daily life, and the opponents refuse to learn from what both preached?

Questions

132. Was John the cousin of Jesus?

133. What type of Messiah did the people of Israel want?

134. Prophets have problems and cause them. Why should they not expect persecution?

135. Why do people in authority dislike it when those not in authority take on a position of leadership?

136. How does John fit into Christianity?

137. Some prophets are ascetical, some are not. Does it make any difference?

Conclusion

The section on the relationship between John and Jesus involves three elements:

1. John's question about the identity of Jesus
2. Jesus' evaluation of John
3. the opposition that both experienced

Since these same three elements appear in Luke, probably "Q" was the source of all of them.

The Gospel of Luke presents John as the cousin of Jesus but nowhere else in the gospels does this relationship seem to exist. Even in this gospel John seems to have knowledge of Jesus in the story of the baptism but here no evidence of John knowing Jesus appears. Perhaps in the passing on of the traditions different people maintained different understandings of the relationship between John and Jesus and all four gospels have evidence of these disparate traditions. The prominent tradition remains: both John and Jesus were prophets and John somehow prepared for the coming of Jesus. John completed the Old Testament tradition of prophets and ushered in the new traditions of Jesus as fulfilling all of the expectations of Israel. Whether John's role as Elijah preparing for Jesus the Messiah was a Christian adaptation of Malachi 4:5–6 or a Jewish tradition remains elusive. John belongs to Christianity as the one who prepared for Jesus, anticipated the rejection of Jesus, and also formed a pattern that the followers of Jesus would also follow.

The Jews expected a political Messiah who would restore the lost glory of Israel. Jesus was the Messiah but how he lived and what he preached necessitated a change in understanding of the role of the Messiah. Many use this change in messiahship perspective to explain the rejection of Jesus by many Jews. He was not what they wanted and expected. For those Jews who accepted Jesus, he was the Messiah who fulfilled the prophecy of Isaiah 35:5–6: "The eyes of the blind shall be opened, and the ears of the deaf unstopped; then shall the lame man leap like a deer and the tongue of the deaf sing for joy."

John plays the funeral game and Jesus plays the wedding game and both face rejection. The opponents of both prophets want nothing to do with either no matter how they live. Prophets are accepted when they tell people that God is present. People reject prophets when they proclaim that God is absent. Prophets who tell the truth make people uncomfortable and often angry and, when angry, people will tend to destroy those who make them angry. Both John and Jesus did not belong to the religious leaders of Judaism. They unsettled the minds of people and caused problems for the scribes and Pharisees. They had no right to act as they did, so both were rejected and destroyed.

At the time of Matthew many Jews rejected Jesus and his teaching. The community had both Jewish and Gentile Christians. Just as some Jews rejected both John and Jesus, so many Jews rejected the followers of Jesus as they continued his preaching. Just as the Jews of the time of John and Jesus refused "to see" John as Elijah and Jesus as the Messiah, so Jews of the time of Matthew remained blind to what had happened with the coming of Jesus.

Also, long after the death of John many thought him to be the Messiah. By making both John and Elijah prepare for Jesus, Matthew answered the question of the true Messiah. John had a role to play and once it was played, he could leave the stage free for Jesus to complete the mission.

THE CONFLICT BEGINS, 11:20—12:50

Section Twenty-one: Reactions to the Preaching of Jesus, 11:20–30

Introduction

In spite of rejection Jesus maintains his self-understanding and his commitment to his mission. Here Jesus speaks like a prophet, telling the three cities most closely associated with his activities what the future holds for them. Jesus preached but these cities refused to rethink, to repent, to change how they lived. They will suffer the consequences. Actions follow beliefs and values. People must learn to accept the consequences of their actions.

Most Christians are unfamiliar with Chorazin. Located a few miles north of Capernaum, Chorazin was a medium-size town. Today the site is rubble with remains of a synagogue. Bethsaida (house of fish) lies on the Sea of Galilee near the mouth of the Jordan. Tyre and Sidon were Gentile cities on the Mediterranean. Comparing Chorazin and Bethsaida with these pagan cities emphasized their guilt.

Sackcloth came from camel or goat hair. Using it as clothing would have been most uncomfortable. Medieval ascetics and some moderns wore haircloth as a sign of penance. Just as ashes on Ash Wednesday signify rethinking of one's life, repentance, the same would have been true of the ancient world. On judgment day Gentile pagan cities will fare better than the Jewish cities blessed with the presence and preaching of Jesus.

Capernaum served as home base for Jesus' preaching in Galilee. Excavations have discovered a church as well as a synagogue located on the Sea of Galilee. Capernaum had witnessed the cure of the paralytic (9:8). Matthew, however, contrasts the faith of the centurion as superior to that found in Israel. In Capernaum Jesus first encountered the hostility of the Jewish leaders.

Sodom, one of the five cities in the valley in Genesis 19:29, symbolizes both lack of hospitality and sexual wickedness. As bad as Sodom was, Capernaum, by rejecting Jesus and his teachings, will face greater judgment.

But some responded favorably to Jesus and his preaching. Jesus publicly proclaims what God has done. Matthew has already noted the familiar relationship between God and Jesus. Just as in the Lord's Prayer the followers of Jesus acknowledge God as Lord of heaven and earth, so Jesus, the teacher of the model prayer, does likewise.

The "wise and understanding" probably refers to the religious leaders and the inhabitants of the cities mentioned. "Infants," like the "little ones," refers to those who follow Jesus. Although they may not have social position or the knowledge of the scribes and Pharisees, they have perceived the meaning of Jesus and accepted him. God has graciously willed that the lowly ("blessed are the poor in spirit...blessed are the lowly...") acknowledge Jesus as part of the divine plan.

Jesus uniquely reveals God. The authority of Jesus rests on his sonship already declared by Matthew (3:17; 4:3, 6). He teaches and heals as the revelation of God. Father and Son know each other and the disciples know God the Father through Jesus the Son.

The passage ends with the invitation to those weary and heavy burdened. Jesus may address those who are still outside the circle of followers but also those within the group of followers who still experience the heavy burdens imposed by the scribes and Pharisees. Jesus promised rest not just in the future but in the present. "Yoke" in Jewish tradition implied accepting teachings. Referring to Wisdom, Sirach says: "Put your neck under her yoke and let your souls receive instruction" (51:26–27).

Here alone in the gospels Jesus asks for imitation. He wants his followers to be kind and gentle as he is kind and gentle. If so, they will find rest, for his teachings (yoke) are not burdensome.

Questions

138. To whom much is given much is expected. Is this true for the towns associated with Jesus?

139. Repentance, rethinking how one lives, is never limited to once and for all. What place do sackcloth and ashes play?

140. Who are the wise and who are the "little ones" today?

141. Does God seem more concerned with those less gifted than with those greatly gifted?

142. Why does Jesus alone reveal God?

143. How are people burdened?

144. What does it mean to be kind and gentle?

145. When will rest and refreshment come?

Conclusion

Chapter 11 begins and ends with understanding the identity of Jesus. His deeds confirm he is the Messiah. He also lives and teaches as Son of God and as Wisdom. Only because Jesus is God's divine Son can he teach his interpretation of Torah with authority, heal those in need, and cast out demons. The community of Matthew will continue this ministry of Jesus precisely because of their relationship to him, and through him, to God the Father.

Jesus blessed the three cities with his presence. The inhabitants heard his teachings, witnessed his miracles, and refused to believe. Anyone who hears the threats should examine their own sense of repentance, whether in the time of Matthew or today. Those who repented will leave to God the final judgment on those who had opportunities to learn and repent and refused. By using cities from Israel's past, Tyre, Sidon, and Sodom, Matthew reminds all of Israel that they might face the same fate as these ancient cities.

Again, perhaps he is appealing to the Jews of his time to rethink what Jesus might mean to them and to the fulfillment of the Law. Matthew continues to propose Gentiles as more receptive than those to whom so much has been given.

The continual call to repentance demonstrated by one's activity (sackcloth and ashes) remains in force today. Just as the people of the Matthean community had to rethink the meaning of Jesus as their circumstances changed (Jewish and Gentile communities), so the same is true for Christianity today as changes in geography and populations and ethic origins encounter the teachings and meaning of Jesus.

Matthew has Jesus thanking God for revealing to the "little ones," the children, rather than the wise. Jesus can accomplish this because of his special relationship to God as Son. All are invited to accept the teachings of Jesus, which will not prove burdensome.

Nepioi (infants or little children) refer to the disciples of Jesus, the members of the Matthean community, and the followers of Jesus today. They live in faith in contrast to the wise and understanding. Usually the recipients of divine revelation both in Israel and in Christianity are the wise and the understanding, the great religious heroes and leaders. Matthew says, no. God reveals to the children, the "little ones," the *nepioi*.

The reason given in Matthew for the revelation, the close identity between Jesus and God, is sometimes called the Johannine thunderbolt. It sounds more like what one would find in the Fourth Gospel rather than in the Synoptics. Yet, theologically this unique relationship founds the right Jesus has to influence thought, opinion, and behavior in all four gospels.

Christians need to act like Jesus, gently and kindly, and they will find rest. Life becomes burdensome too often. Church regulations seem heavy. Some people go through life stomping rather than living gently. Many quickly pick out what is wrong with others (mean people) instead of what is right with others (kind people). Those who stomp through life and treat others with meanness will never find rest, either in the present or in the future. Those who gently flow with the ups and downs of life and can always find something good in another enjoy refreshment now and in the future.

Section Twenty-two:
The Servant Causes Problems with the Sabbath Law, 12:1–21

Introduction

Sabbath law in Israel always demanded careful observance. For many ordinary people, such meticulous application caused burdens. Jesus and his interpretation of the Law changed that and caused problems between him and the religious leaders.

Deuteronomy offered a humanitarian twist when it allowed the hungry to walk through standing grain, not owned by those who were hungry, and feed themselves, provided they did not harvest the grain (Deut 23:25). This, however, did not apply on the Sabbath, according to the Pharisees. Evidently Jesus thought it did.

Jesus responds to the Pharisees by reminding them that David's men took and ate bread from the sanctuary when they were hungry even though forbidden to all but the priests. Probably the incident with David took place at the shrine of the ark of the covenant at Nob before the Temple was built by Solomon. Leviticus 24:5–9 describes the twelve cakes that should be consumed by the priests alone. David ignored the Law when his men were hungry. Leviticus also allows the priests to violate the Sabbath by performing anything necessary for sacrifice. If others have interpreted the law of Sabbath allowing apparent violations, so Jesus can do likewise, for he is greater than any previous interpreter and greater than any shrine or Temple. And his disciples can do likewise, for as they inaugurate with Jesus the reign of God, they are greater than any Temple, including its priests.

Previously Matthew quoted Hosea 6:6: "I wish mercy and not sacrifice" (9:13). The quotation fits the interpretation that Jesus gives to Torah. Compassion to those in need overrules any demand for ritual sacrifice and for the observance of Sabbath law. As already noted, "Son of Man" may at first have meant "everyman." Thus everyone must make the proper interpretation on how to observe the Law of God. Here it also has the added idea of Jesus and who he is, the divine Son of God. He can offer whatever interpretation he wishes.

"Their" synagogue may be seen in contrast to the synagogue of the Matthean community (church). In this way continuity remains between Jesus and his followers and the opposition that both experienced.

The man with the withered hand was in no immediate danger of death and thus no immediate healing by Jesus was necessary. The Pharisees pose the question about healing on the Sabbath to find fault. Jesus responds by comparing what one would do for an animal on the Sabbath and what one should do for a fellow human being. Jesus takes a liberal interpretation of the Law. Any reason for doing good takes precedent over Sabbath law. Jesus heals the man to manifest his point. The angry Pharisees begin their plot to destroy Jesus. He is allowing ordinary people to decide how the Law must be observed. Such was the responsibility of the religious leaders and not anyone else.

Matthew concludes the section by contributing further to the identity of Jesus. While the Pharisees plot, Jesus goes on to continue his mission of teaching (many followed him) and healing. They are not to publicize what Jesus does. He will not confront the Pharisees directly, for he is the servant of God who will not cry out. Matthew quotes Isaiah 42:1–4. Jesus has already been identified as God's Son. Now Matthew fills out this identity by relating Jesus to the suffering servant of Isaiah. Actually the Hebrew of Isaiah can be translated in Greek either by "servant" or "son." The words, not exactly quoted from Isaiah, recall the heavenly voice at the baptism of Jesus.

The main point of this servant song from Isaiah centers on the gentleness of the servant and not the suffering. Thus "the bruised reed he will not break nor quench the smoldering wick." Justice (righteousness) to victory will belong to the Gentiles as well as to the Jews.

Questions

146. Who is supposed to interpret the Law of God?

147. Jesus says he has come to fulfill the Law and then seems to break it. Why?

148. Do mercy and compassion take precedence over sacrifice?

149. Allowing people to interpret the Law causes problems. Is it not better to limit interpretation to the experts?

150. Why would the Pharisees plot against Jesus? They know the quotation from Hosea.

151. Jesus is the Servant of God who treats all people with gentleness. Do you relate the Spirit to gentleness?

152. When will righteousness come?

Conclusion

When the disciples pick grain on the Sabbath, does this violate the Law? They could do so in someone else's field since they were hungry, but can they do this on the Sabbath? Jesus says, "yes." Human need comes first and not law. Helping one on the Sabbath also takes precedent over observance of the Sabbath. Thus, Jesus can heal the man with the withered hand. If Jesus can do this, so can everyone else. Allowing ordinary people to interpret the Law undermines all law. People can rationalize and become lax. Yet Jesus seems to encourage just that.

The Sabbath observance goes back to Exodus, but especially during and after the Exile its observance formed an essential part of Jewish religious tradition. Even if no Temple existed and thus no sacrifices, people could still observe the Sabbath, honoring their religious heritage. At the time of Jesus Sabbath observance had taken on primary importance along with circumcision and the observance of dietary laws. The same is true today for devout Orthodox Jews. For Jesus to downplay the Sabbath observance, as Christians do today, is tantamount to denial of serious religious traditions.

Fulfilling the Law presupposes mercy as primary. If mercy exists then everyone can interpret freely. Presuming mercy does not exist and thus only religious leaders can interpret the Law relegates people to live without thinking. Jesus took away the sins of people but not their brains and consciences.

Allowing freedom of interpretation of law affects society, both religious and civil. Anyone who teaches this and acts upon it is dangerous and should be destroyed. The good of the religious institutions and civil institutions cannot survive with such freedom. Thus, the Pharisees, as good and pious Jews, need to plot against Jesus. The same problem would have existed in the community of Matthew with their Jewish Christian members. As Jesus took a liberal attitude toward Sabbath observance so probably did at least some Jewish Christians, adding to friction within the community.

Rather than continue to add to the friction with the Pharisees, Jesus withdrew, for he acted gently and kindly. Matthew contrasts the Servant and Son of God with the scribes and Pharisees, who do not act with compassion or with gentleness and kindness. They will plot and Jesus will become the suffering servant of God who will die.

Observance of all law, including church law, depends on how it affects the good of others. Mere observance serves nothing unless people benefit. Righteousness will overcome all law since with righteousness all will stand with dignity before God, both Jew and Gentile, and law will be no more.

Section Twenty-three: This Evil Generation, 12:22–50

Introduction

The conflict begun in the beginning of this chapter continues. The healing of the man, both blind and mute, results in a fierce exchange between Jesus and the religious leaders. The power of healing brings out amazement from the crowds and an accusation from the Pharisees. In the Old Testament, Solomon, the son of David, supposedly had healing powers. Now Matthew uses the title Son of David as messianic and applies it to Jesus. The crowds see in Jesus a continuation of the power of God from David to Solomon to Jesus. The Pharisees see in Jesus one who acts through the power of Beelzebul.

The word *Beelzebul* has a long history. The first part of the word comes from *baal*, the Philistine word meaning "lord." The second part might mean "prince," "dung," or "enmity." At the time of Jesus the title was another word for Satan.

Jesus picks up the accusation and throws it back to the Pharisees. Jesus represents either the kingdom of God or the kingdom of Satan. Since what Jesus does confronts the kingdom of Satan, how can he be part of that kingdom? If Satan acted through Jesus, Satan would be working counterpoint. If some of the Pharisees also enter into conflict with Satan and cast out demons, why is Jesus not doing the same thing?

Matthew has already identified Jesus as functioning through the Spirit of God. Thus, Jesus cannot act for Satan. Jesus makes manifest that the reign of God has begun. Jesus overcomes evil. That should be enough for all.

In the parable Jesus confronts Satan and binds him. As Jesus has power over evil, so Jesus has power over Satan. Everyone must take sides: go with Jesus and the reign of God or go with Satan. The Pharisees and possibly some of the enemies of the community of Matthew follow Satan. They refuse to acknowledge the power of God in Jesus.

The blasphemy (literally, to injure the reputation of another) against the Holy Spirit means to attack the reputation of Jesus by accusing him of working through the power of Satan rather than through the Holy Spirit.

Son of Man sometimes has meant "everyman." Other times when used in the Synoptics it refers to the sufferings of Jesus and still other times it has a connotation of a future divine figure. Jesus as Son of Man represents humankind, "everyman." Speaking against another human being can bring forgiveness but speaking against the Spirit of God, claiming that Jesus' power comes from evil, precludes forgiveness forever.

Actions follow values and beliefs. Matthew returns to this theme from the Sermon on the Mount. Matthew used the same analogy in the sermon in 7:16–20. Vipers (used by the Baptist to refer to the Pharisees: Matt 3:7) cannot produce good effects. If the heart is good the words will be good. Values and beliefs are the treasury. If the treasury is good, the deeds will be good. If evil, the deeds are evil. The words of the Pharisees against Jesus are weak. They accomplish nothing. The words that Jesus uses are powerful. They work. Words form criteria for judgment.

The Pharisees wish to justify their opposition by asking for a sign. Since they have already seen miracles, they apparently want some authentication of the identity of Jesus. When Jesus refers to an adulterous generation he invokes the marriage image of God and the people of Israel from the Old Testament. They have violated their commitment to God by their actions. They have not lived faithfully. To them the sign of Jonah alone will be given. Just as Jonah returned to life after apparent death, so the same will be true for Jesus. But Jesus will truly die and truly be raised.

Jesus continues the reference to Jonah, with the people of Nineveh judging the people opposed to Jesus. They repented and believed Jonah. The evil generation has the opportunity to repent and listen to Jesus and they refuse. The Ninevites join the queen of the south against those opponents of Jesus.

The driving out of the demon has occasioned the speech by Jesus. In the ancient world evil spirits lived in the wilderness as well as in the sea. In the wilderness the devil tempted Jesus. Evil spirits like to find places where they belong. They find that rest in the hearts of the opponents of Jesus. The evil has strengthened as opposition to Jesus grows stronger. The fate of the Pharisees is determined by their opposition to Jesus and his teachings. The evil in their hearts will eventually seek to destroy Jesus.

Suddenly the family of Jesus appears. Historically Catholics interpreted these brothers as possibly children of Joseph from a previous marriage, or cousins or fellow townspeople. Protestants take the words literally to mean children of Joseph and Mary after the birth of Jesus. Matthew probably did not know the tradition of the perpetual virginity of Mary.

Some ancient manuscripts omit verse 47. Probably it is original since verse 48 presupposes a previous remark. Jesus responds by changing relationships. Blood relationship means nothing. Being a member of the family of Jesus demands discipleship, believing in Jesus, and following the will of God.

Questions

153. Jesus heals as the Messiah. Why is he not accepted?

154. The Pharisees seem insincere. Is this true for all who reject Jesus?

155. Why is accusing Jesus of working for Satan so terrible?

156. Can every sin be forgiven? It seems not.

157. How can you apply "actions follow values" to these verses and to today?

158. People must accept the consequences of their actions. Does this apply to the Pharisees?

159. What do you think about the family of Jesus?

160. Can the family of Jesus be enlarged without affecting the perpetual virginity of Mary? Can Protestants be included if they believe Joseph and Mary had children?

Conclusion

Throughout the Gospel of Matthew the identity of Jesus is a theme that recurs. From the beginning Matthew presents Jesus as the Son of God but only gradually does he reveal what this means. Matthew has established Jesus as the one who casts out demons, but the question arises: by what right, with whose power, does Jesus do such things? Jesus attacks the kingdom of evil. Satan cannot be the source of the power of Jesus and therefore it must be God and God alone.

The religious leaders were reluctant to accept Jesus as Messiah because he did not fit what they thought a Messiah should be. By attacking the power of the religious leaders he undermined their authority and so they sought to belittle him by accusing him of working with Satan.

The deeds, the actions, of Jesus show his values and his beliefs and demonstrate that he is a good person, filled with the Spirit of God. This goodness contrasts with the bad character of his opponents. Nothing can be lower than to label a good person evil. The Pharisees are on the wrong side and not Jesus. Often the Pharisees come across as insincere. They are fakes. Perhaps some of them genuinely considered him a threat to traditional Judaism. He was too free with the Law and did not belong to the priestly caste and gave too much freedom to ordinary people who needed guidance from more educated and more enlightened religious leaders. All the Pharisees come across as insincere, but such a judgment may be too harsh. Maybe some sincerely thought they were doing good, but admitting some evil into their hearts by their opposition to a good man only led to greater evil enveloping them.

Jesus forgives all sins but the person has to want to be forgiven and must believe forgiveness is possible. The only unforgivable sin is to refuse to believe in forgiveness. Unfortunately, sometimes individuals have such a sick psyche they actually believe that what they have done can never be forgiven. They refuse to accept the goodness of the Lord Jesus.

Jonah functions in two ways in the episode. First, the story points forward to the death and resurrection of Jesus; second, it focuses on the repentance of the Ninevites. Jonah runs away since he knows God will be merciful to the enemies of Israel as God has been merciful and forgiving to Israel. When Jonah eventually preaches and they repent, the story takes on a character that depicts pagans repenting on the preaching of the Jewish prophet. In Matthew, pagans and sinners follow the example of the Ninevites. The same takes place within the Matthean community. Those who should be expected to repent do not and those not expected to repent, do.

The reference to the queen of the south (Sheba) enhances the actions of the Gentiles. Jesus speaks wisdom, as did Solomon. The wisdom of Jesus outshines that of Solomon. If pagans came to Solomon, how much more should both Jews and pagans and sinners pay attention to the wisdom of Jesus. The Pharisees miss the point. Perhaps they were not evil at the beginning, but their actions against Jesus strengthen the evil within them and eventually they will seek to destroy Jesus. The more Jesus preaches, the greater the reaction against him. He offers wisdom and his opponents refuse to listen.

Jesus experiences alienation from "the evil generation." In Mark 3:21, which Matthew has as a source, Jesus experiences alienation from his family: "He is crazy." Matthew has omitted the remark by the family of Jesus, which he has found in Mark, but hints at the same alienation. The true family of Jesus does not rest on blood but on faith.

In the history of Israel some Jews always judged other Jews and excluded them. Anyone who intermarried (a Samaritan) was not part of God's family. Anyone who did not observe the Sabbath faithfully did not belong. Anyone who acted contrary to the leadership of the scribes, Pharisees, and priests did not belong. Anyone who did not regularly worship at the Temple did not belong—and the list goes on. Something similar must have been happening in the community of Matthew as it has happened in the history of Christianity. The true family of God, of Jesus, consists of people who believe, who follow the will of God. That alone suffices.

Matthew and Luke clearly teach the virginal conception. The New Testament also in certain passages seems to teach that Jesus had brothers and sisters. No gospel explains how Jesus came to have siblings. The perpetual virginity of Mary remains part of Catholic tradition. Protestants, in general, believe Joseph and Mary had other children. The New Testament offers no definitive decision. Such a division, however, should never cause one group to exclude the other from the family of Jesus.

THE THIRD SERMON: PARABLES, 13:1–58

Section Twenty-four: The Parable of the Sower, 13:1–23

Introduction

Jesus has confronted his opponents. Now a clear division exists between the followers of Jesus and many religious leaders. In chapter 13 Matthew presents the third great discourse or sermon by Jesus. In parables Jesus will preach the reign of God, a decisive event in the ministry of Jesus that exposes belief and unbelief. People have to decide. Either people are with Jesus or they are against him.

The parables are not just teachings concerning the reign of God. Parables are word events that demand a response. Jesus does not "teach" in parables but "speaks" in parables. Parables are simple comparisons taken from everyday life. In the classic definition of C. H. Dodd, "at its simplest the parable is a simile drawn from nature or common life, arresting the hearer by its vividness or strangeness and leaving the mind in sufficient doubt to tease it into active thought." Parables arrest attention and often surprise the listener since frequently the parable reverses the expected outcome. Parables are stories or riddles, fables, or allegories or proverbs. Each parable is a form of figurative speech. Jesus freely composes stories with the force coming from a relationship to something else.

The parable of the sower may not be everyone's favorite parable but everyone knows it. The setting is idyllic. The crowds are so great Jesus gets into a boat and teaches the crowd on the shore. Crowds, not the religious leaders, but ordinary people, flock to listen to the words of the itinerant preacher and prophet.

Although everyone refers to the parable as the parable of the "sower," the point is not the one who sows, but the seeds that fall and the yield. The story presents some unpromising places for the seed to fall: the path, rocky ground, thorns. The unusual places add a dimension to the story but in fact present a true reality. When a farmer scatters seeds, some do fall into places that do not offer much for germination and growth. Once the seed is sown the seed is on its own, whether on the path, or on rocky ground, or among thorns, or on good soil. The last place on which the seed falls produces abundantly, up to 100 percent! People should pay attention. Keep your ears open to what Jesus has said!

But it seems the disciples do not have attentive ears. They need an explanation. Whether the explanation comes from Jesus or the early church has been debated for centuries. Much depends on the understanding of the parable as a form of figurative speech. Since the explanation makes the parable into an allegory, some think it was an early church interpretation.

The explanation begins with a reference to the privileged position of the disciples. God has granted them an insight into the kingdom of heaven (a Matthean substitute for kingdom of God). Those fortunate enough to be granted the view into the kingdom will be granted ever greater gifts, while those outside will lose the little they have.

The next verse sounds harsh: "Because seeing they do not see…" In the past some have tried to interpret "because" as "in order that." Unfortunately, the Greek word means "because." Matthew emphasizes the dispositions of the outsiders. They are not open to understand and thus will always remain outside. Matthew concludes by quoting Isaiah 6:9–10. Just as people refused to listen to Isaiah, so people refuse to listen to Jesus. They make the decision and suffer the consequences. Jesus returns to the blessedness of those who are the insiders. They are more fortunate than many prophets and righteous ones.

Jesus then explains the seed is the word of God. Some hear and bear fruit; others hear and, for all sorts of reasons, do not bear fruit or survive. Internal commitment, external temptations, wealth, pleasure, position—anything can rob the seed of fulfillment. But some listen, understand, and respond. They produce and in different degrees.

Questions

161. Are parables easy to understand? Do you like figurative speech?

162. What do you think of the classic definition of a parable?

163. Could not Jesus have spoken more clearly?

164. Did Jesus deliberately intend for people not to understand?

165. If some people are more fortunate than others, is this the same as predestination?

166. How can you apply the parable of the sower to life today?

Conclusion

The third discourse of Jesus (chapter 13) contains seven, possibly eight, parables. A good story or parable gets people to think. It should not be too complicated or too simple. "Teasing the mind" forces people to rethink how they are living and encourages them to make a decision. Figurative speech says more than general prose. The poet can reach deeply into life and pull up an understanding or appreciation that might otherwise be lost. Jesus was a good poet, expressing in his parables insights into the meaning of the reign of God. Figurative speech often manipulates. Jesus and his parables take the listener into areas of life and personal history that often people do not want to face. Making people think brings a greater commitment or at times a greater rejection.

Matthew begins by acknowledging that some, if not many, both at the time of Jesus and at the time of the Matthean community, refused to accept Jesus. In the early church many had problems trying to understand why some Jews accepted Jesus and others did not and why many Gentiles accepted Jesus. Matthew explains the acceptance and rejection by focusing on dispositions. Some people are not receptive for whatever reason; some are receptive. This does not mean that God has predestined some to accept or others to reject. Jesus offers the choice and people have the option of freely accepting or turning away. God does not harden their hearts. People harden their own hearts. Many people are offered myriad opportunities but do not accept what life offers. The same is true for a relationship to God. No one has to accept. Pursuing wealth or power can harden one's heart to the gospel. Being infatuated by pleasure and living only according to human standards of success can close a person's eyes and ears.

The parable of the sower with apparent prodigality in dispensing the seed catches the attention of the listener. When a person grows a lawn from seed, the person does not worry that some seed might fall on the path that leads to the house or on the driveway or in a flower bed. The end result is the lawn; that alone matters and if some seeds never germinate that does not detract from the lawn.

Probably the early church first used this parable to explain why some Jews refused to accept the word of God in Jesus. The parable also could explain some problems within the Matthean community. Some people believed or accepted for a while but then gave up. Some people responded full heartedly; others, to a lesser degree. Some disciples produced more fruit than others. Or, on some days some disciples do better in living a life of faith than other days. Some days are a hundredfold; other days are thirty-fold or sixtyfold. Throughout the centuries the church has always had some who gave up and others who overproduced and others who underproduced. For most Christians, some days are good in living for and in the reign of God and other days are bad and most days are somewhere in the middle.

The disciples in Matthew's community should always acknowledge their blessedness and good fortune. By continuing to listen to the word of God their lives become progressively enriched. Unfortunately, others live outside, either never having accepted the word of God or, once having accepted it, turn their backs on faith.

Section Twenty-five: More Parables and Rejection, 13:24–58

Introduction

The reign of God, or the kingdom of heaven, has always been mystery. Mystery does not imply that people never know anything, but rather that people know something but never know everything. God remains "mystery" just as individuals live and die as "mystery" to others and even to themselves. Understanding something about self and others is part of living, but never understanding everything is also part of living. Each parable will offer some understanding of the reign of God but not everything.

Wheat and weeds grow in every garden and thus in every heart and in every community. Weeds grow in the body of the church as well as in the sanctuary. The kingdom of heaven begun on earth remains imperfect. What should be done to the weeds living in the community? Jesus says, nothing. The judgment between good and bad will come at the end and not now.

The mustard seed is not the smallest of seeds but exaggeration belongs in figurative speech. The parable contrasts the size of the seed with the mature plant. Mustard plants can grow up to eight or ten feet tall but usually would not be thought of as a tree. A good size bush would be more accurate. But the image of the tree fits into the understanding of the people of Israel as God's sturdy tree. Just as the people of God in Israel began as a small group and developed into a large community, so the same is true for the kingdom of heaven. The small community of Jesus would become a large tree, harboring many within its branches.

Leaven acts like a life-giving force. It permeates the dough, making it "alive." A small amount of leaven could create enough bread to feed a hundred people. This parable also emphasizes the contrast between a small amount and a large result.

Matthew includes the reference to the Old Testament (actually to Ps 78:2, with some slight modifications). The quotation suggests that Jesus teaches in accord with the will of God. Here Matthew makes another reference to those who do not understand and accept. Psalm 78 does not have "foundation of the world" and some manuscripts do not have the phrase. It seems to be necessary in context. Matthew places all under the will of God established in the beginning.

To his disciples Jesus now explains the wheat and weeds. Since this is an allegorical interpretation many think it comes from the early church and was not part of the teaching of Jesus. The explanation takes on an eschatological tone. Jesus as Son of Man refers here to a future coming of Jesus. Sons of the kingdom have no fear of the future. The "weeds," those influenced by the evil one, will experience pain and destruction. Weeping and gnashing of teeth has occurred in 8:12 and will appear again in 13:50; 22:13; 24:51; and 25:30. The image—and it is an image—connotes pain and sorrow, not actually weeping, gnashing, and fire. Those who have accepted the seed of the word of God belong to the kingdom of their Father. Jesus will deliver all to God when human history ends.

The parables of the treasure and the pearl may have circulated together since both deal with a treasure, one of which is a surprise and the other is known and sought after. Both emphasize the great value of the treasure, and not what is necessary to obtain it. So the same is true for the reign of God. Anyone should do whatever is necessary to obtain it.

The meaning of the dragnet is a variation on the wheat and weeds. When the net is full the separation begins, just as when the wheat has grown the separation takes place. The conclusion of this parable parallels the conclusion to the wheat and weeds. Angels move like the harvesters saving the wheat and the fishermen saving the good fish. Judgment and punishment add to the eschatological tone of the parables.

Matthew concludes with a question to the disciples: have they understood the meaning of the kingdom? It may begin small, but it will grow and develop silently but surely. The reign of heaven will permeate every aspect of life and will initially include both good and bad until the end is reached, when those who belong will remain and those who do not belong will be cast out.

The verse about the householder and the scribe has often been explained as referring to Matthew himself. He holds on to the old (pleasing the Jewish Christians) and remains open to the new (pleasing the Gentile Christians).

The set phrase "when Jesus had finished these parables" shows the end of the third sermon. Jesus returns to where his family lives and where his neighbors know him and his background. When he teaches in the synagogue, they first act amazed and then the opposition sets in. Jesus taught and healed and the towns-people are confused. Where did he get such wisdom and power? Jesus' father was a craftsman (*tekton*, not a carpenter); they know his mother, Mary, and his brothers and sisters. Here again reference is made to siblings, which can be explained in the ways already mentioned.

Finally, the reaction turns negative. The townspeople are offended. They join the opposition. The same word used previously (*skandalidzo*) means a "stumbling block." His background does not prepare him to be accepted as prophet. Since they know him he will not be accepted and Jesus can do very little among his own townspeople.

Questions

167. Mystery means understanding something but not everything. Does this fit the many uses of the word?

168. Weeds grow everywhere, in families and in the church. How should a family member or a church member react?

169. The mustard seed and the leaven emphasize growth. Right now Christians make up less than one-quarter of the world's population and that number is getting smaller. What does this mean to the reign of God?

170. Do people really value the reign of God?

171. Are people concerned with final judgment? When? How?

172. How difficult is it to hold on to the old and be open to the new?

173. Prophets are not without honor except…Why do people make judgments on another by emphasizing background instead of listening to what they say?

Conclusion

Too often people thought of mystery as not knowing anything. "It's a mystery" when spoken was supposed to stop all thinking. In the Bible the word *mystery* does not mean unknowing or unknowable but never knowing everything. People can grow in understanding of themselves, others, and even God but can never reach the point of total and complete comprehension. People can always be surprised at what they do and what they fail to do.

The parable of the weeds follows an agricultural context familiar to anyone who has farmed. Every field will have some weeds. The audience of Matthew knew that some Jews had accepted Jesus and others did not. They also knew that some who had accepted changed their minds (parable of the sower). The parable teaches patience and tolerance. The same thought underlies the dragnet. If God has patience with people, so people should have patience with each other. The possibility of repentance always exists. No family member and no church member should ever be abandoned or feel abandoned. If God has patience with all people, so individuals have to have patience with others and even with themselves. It took Augustine a long time to repent and Augustine died a saint. Trust in God and in a final judgment.

The reign of God has had a small beginning and has grown and the kingdom of heaven has great worth. Unfortunately, most people live caught up in the daily ups and downs of living and the reign of God becomes an occasional thought. Young people live concerned with the moment. Older people begin to think of their final days and may attempt to allow God some room in a busy life. The reign of God brings peace and contentment now and in the future. If people paid more attention to the teachings of Jesus, life would become more enjoyable. Peace and good will are better than conflict and animosity. Leaving room for God does not mean living in church. Leaving room for God merely involves listening to what God says through Jesus, the Bible, and life.

With the decrease in Christian population and the increase, for example, in an Islamic population in many countries throughout the world, Christians need to rethink the meaning of Christianity as the ordinary means of salvation. Also, many Christians are so in name only. True evangelization based on the word of God needs to take place within Christianity and among Christians. Then by example others may find the teachings of Jesus attractive.

No one finds it easy to hold on to the old and to be open to the new. Change costs and many do not want to pay the price. Cardinal Newman once wrote: "To be human is to change. To change often is to be perfect." People moving from one culture to another, from one country to another, somehow have to hold on to something of the past while adapting to and accepting the new. The problem arises when decisions must be made about discarding some of the old and not fully accepting some of the new. People need continuity but will wither without some discontinuity. The church reluctantly gives up some of the old. For this reason Blessed John XXIII called the Second Vatican Council.

The spiritual family of Jesus, those who accept him and follow him, gradually replaces the natural family of Jesus along with his fellow townspeople. The family of Jesus and the people of the village (Nazareth?) assumed they knew all about Jesus. After all he grew up there. In fact they know little about Jesus and evidently do not wish to know more. Blood lines and even familiarity mean little without faith in Jesus as the divine Son of God. The community of Matthew saw themselves as part of the true family of Jesus even if they were not related to him and did not grow up with him. The people of his hometown dismissed him because they knew him. In so doing they missed much. The prejudice of familiarity caused people to miss the reality in front of them. The same often happens today.

THE MISSION CONTINUES, 14:1—17:27

Section Twenty-six:
The Death of John the Baptist, 14:1–12

Introduction

When Herod the Great died in AD 4, his sons divided up the kingdom. Herod Antipas ruled over Galilee and Perea. Just as his father was curious about the newborn king of the Jews, so Antipas wonders about Jesus. He had John killed and now compares the two. Could John have been raised from the dead?

Josephus, the Jewish historian, records that Herod imprisoned John near the Dead Sea. Herod held court at Tiberius in the north. Herodias, initially married to a paternal half-uncle (not Philip), abandoned her first marriage to marry Antipas. Unlike Mark, Matthew left out the resentment of Herodias against John and his effort to condemn the marriage because of the law in Leviticus 20:21. For Matthew the chief opponent is Herod and thus the actions of Herodias and Salome seem confusing.

On the birthday of Herod, as all know, Salome danced and pleased Herod and he promised to give her whatever she asked. Mark adds "up to half his kingdom." Both Mark and Matthew include Herodias in the decision to ask for the head of John the Baptist. Although Matthew says that Herod was sad, he found himself torn between his oath and the terrible request by Salome. He chose the latter. Passing around the head made the event more gruesome. Just as John preceded Jesus in preaching about the kingdom, so the death of John precedes the death of Jesus and in both cases their followers take care of the bodies.

Questions

174. The civil leaders seem curious about religion but do nothing. Can curiosity help or hinder religion?

175. John told the truth and ended up dead. Why is telling the truth so dangerous?

176. Making foolish oaths helps no one. What should one do if foolish enough to promise something stupid?

177. John parallels Jesus. The disciples will parallel them as well. What can disciples expect?

Conclusion

Herod Antipas, like his father, was curious about religion but did little to either assuage that curiosity or care much for religious practices. Curiosity may engage the mind, just as the parables "tease the mind into active thought," but teasing and engaging the mind remain insufficient. Thinking should lead to conclusions of beliefs and values and then actions follow beliefs.

Earlier Matthew had recorded that John had been arrested (4:12). Now in a type of flashback Matthew records how he died, with the blame going to Herod. Josephus narrates the ministry of John, calling him a good man who exhorted Jews to a more religious life. According to Josephus, Herod becomes suspicious of John, afraid he might lead a coalition against him and so arrests him and kills him. Herod's principal reason for execution was political, according to Josephus.

The story of Herodias and Salome found first in Mark sounds like a parallel to Jezebel (1 Kgs 21). Perhaps some truth lies at the base of the story but with telling over and over exaggeration usually sets in. Besides, the story of Herodias as a scheming and revengeful woman, Salome as a young temptress, and Herod as a weak as water husband, father, and ruler, makes for a better telling.

John told the truth to all who would listen. If he did criticize Herod and Herodias, he merely reminded them of the Law. He told the truth. Some people do not want to hear the truth, and then "kill the messenger" seems to follow. When people hear the truth they cannot pretend to be ignorant and have to make a decision based on the truth. At times, killing the messenger seems easier and less stressful. Actions follow beliefs and values.

The oath of Herod as recorded by Mark and Matthew made no sense. Too often people will make a promise and be unable to fulfill it. When people make foolish oaths, it is better to acknowledge the mistake and get over it. Fulfilling a foolish oath only adds to the foolishness.

John arrived on the scene, preached, was handed over to his enemies, and died. Jesus came, preached, was handed over to his enemies, and died. The early disciples, and disciples ever since, have had the same experience.

Section Twenty-seven:
The Feeding and the Walking on the Water, 14:13–36

Introduction

Matthew sews his narrative together with small phrases even if they do not always make complete sense. "Upon hearing this" seems as if it refers to the death of John, but in fact in the Gospel of Matthew the death is recorded as a type of flashback. Nevertheless, Matthew makes a transition to more miracles.

"Desert" need not refer to true desert. It may mean a less populated area and in the theology of Matthew recalls the wandering in the desert of Israel in Exodus when God fed the people with manna. The reference to towns where food could be purchased supports the idea of a less populated place rather than a true desert.

The crowds follow Jesus and he heals them. Perhaps the motivation for following was witnessing the miracles. Jesus fulfills their hopes by healing and feeding. When the disciples suggest Jesus dismiss the crowds, Jesus tells them to feed the people themselves.

Over the centuries people have sought some symbolism in the numbers 5 and 2 and questioned the presence of the fish. Exodus makes mention only of manna. Some concluded that perhaps early Christians ate fish with the Eucharist symbolized by the bread. Jesus gives orders for the crowds to prepare for eating and the disciples obey.

Blessing the bread forms part of the ordinary role of the father of the family at a Jewish meal. Blessing and breaking also hints forward to the Last Supper (Matt 26:26). The disciples give out the bread but no mention is made of the fish. All ate and were satisfied and the remains filled twelve (tribes of Israel? apostles at the Eucharist?) baskets. The number of people seems spectacular, not counting women and children! Matthew frequently exaggerates, as do stories told over decades.

Jesus leaves the disciples to pray alone, and forces them to get into the boat. Jesus remains in control and the disciples obey. Unlike the other gospels, especially Luke, Matthew makes few references to Jesus praying. Setting Jesus apart from the disciples sets up the context for the second miracle.

The Sea of Galilee is about four-and-a-half miles wide. The disciples in the boat are far from land and under pressure from the wind and waves. Between 3:00 and 6:00 a.m. (the fourth watch) Jesus appears walking on the water. The reference to a ghost strengthens the fear in the disciples. "It is I" translates *ani hu* from Isaiah and serves as a substitute for the divine name. Since only God can walk on water, and Jesus now walks on water, so Jesus must be identified with God.

Peter, the spokesperson for the Twelve and who figures prominently in this gospel, speaks out and wants to do what Jesus does. Just as the disciples prayed, "Lord, save us" in 8:25 during the stilling of the storm, so the fearful Peter does likewise. Jesus again refers to their "little faith." They have faith but that faith needs help. The storm passed and both Jesus and Peter are in the boat. Like many times before in this gospel the disciples do homage to Jesus. They recognize he is the presence of God among them. They arrive at their destination and the people gathered all those who were in need to come to Jesus and he healed them. In chapter 9 when recording the miracle of the woman with a hemorrhage, Matthew had omitted the reference to the fringe of his garment, found in Mark. He includes it here. It may refer to the fringe or tassels worn by pious Jews to remind them of the presence of God and the commandments.

Questions

178. What was the miracle?
179. Bread and circuses pleased the people of Rome. Miracles

and food pleased some of the followers of Jesus. Do bread and circuses still exist, fooling people into false security?

180. The miracle of the feeding occurs six times in the gospels. Why so much attention given to it?

181. If Jesus is *ani hu*, why do more people not recognize him?

182. Did Jesus really walk on the water?

183. Why make a fool of Peter?

184. "Little faith"—does it still exist in the church?

185. Why do some people seem anxious to accept Jesus and others become ever more reluctant?

Conclusion

Twice Mark records a feeding miracle (6:35–44; 8:1–10). Luke has one feeding story (9:12–27) and John has one feeding story (6:1–15). Matthew has an additional feeding miracle in 15:32–39. Unlike the disciples in Mark, the disciples in Matthew have more understanding of Jesus and his message.

Elisha in 2 Kings 4:42–44 also feeds a large crowd with few provisions, and food remains afterward. Matthew points backward to a miracle in the Old Testament and points forward to the Last Supper. Several themes occur: the Old Testament relationship both in the sense of desert and feeding and also Elisha; better understanding on the part of the disciples; the reference to the Eucharist and, probably for the Matthean community, a reminder that Jesus continues to feed them in the Eucharist.

Over the centuries many have wondered just what happened. Nowhere do any of the accounts refer to multiplication of loaves and fish. Some have thought that no ordinary citizen of Palestine would go into a wilderness without some provisions. By the example of Jesus and his disciples with their provisions, others imitated them and all ate and were satisfied. No one knows with certainty what happened. The multiple attestation (six times in the gospels) shows that something happened with Jesus and his disciples and meals. If Jesus is the presence of God surely Jesus could multiply food at will, but usually God and Jesus do not act in such a way. It seems better to pay attention to the meaning and not get concerned about historicity. Jesus enjoyed the company of disciples and followers at meals. He wanted them to be fed and satisfied. The same is true in the celebration of the Eucharist today and the banquet fits well the full realization of the kingdom. Jesus feeds spiritually now and fed physically in his ministry.

Food and entertainment please everyone. Unfortunately, people can miss the meaning. Too much attention can be paid to entertainment without seeing the meaning of enjoyment coming from a life of faith. Church leaders can fool people into thinking all is well as long as the show looks good. Sometimes behind the scene the show is shoddy. Better to clean up the whole scene than settle for a good-looking show.

Ani hu means the presence of God. The Gospel of John more than any other gospel stresses the divinity of Jesus and uses the Greek equivalent of *ani hu* frequently. Matthew also wants to present Jesus as taking the place of God. He did this on the Sermon on the Mount. Now he feeds and walks on water. Matthew will use many images to help people to believe that Jesus lived and lives as the presence of God in human history. Walking on the water and proclaiming *ani hu* demonstrates for the readers of Matthew that truly Jesus is God among them.

Peter may be the rock in 16:16, but he fails by denying Jesus three times. Here he seems impetuous. How ironic that Jesus chooses a weak and even boisterous leader. Peter even has trouble with faith. He has "little faith" that needs support and encouragement. He flounders when he loses trust in Jesus. The same is true for anyone who follows the Lord.

Internal dispositions, a common theme in Matthew, help to explain acceptance of Jesus. Some people live disposed to faith and following Jesus while others lack the basic internal sense of acceptance. Cynicism and sarcasm make it hard to accept any miracles and any belief in a divine presence. Acceptance and appreciation of life make it easier to see the divine in the commonplace.

Section Twenty-eight:
Jewish Traditions, 15:1–20

Introduction

Traditions are values, beliefs, practices, rituals, events, and symbols passed on from one generation to another. People pass on traditions intact and at other times changed with a shift in circumstances. Pharisees and scribes, committed to Jewish traditions, come from Jerusalem, implying that the discussion about certain customs and traditions with Jesus and his disciples takes place in Galilee.

The washing of hands does not refer to personal hygiene but ritual purification. According to the scribes and Pharisees, the disciples of Jesus violate Jewish tradition. They pose the question to Jesus, who ignores them and turns the question back to the Jewish leaders. Jesus accuses them of violating the Law by their tradition! They should look to themselves before criticizing others.

Jesus combines words from Exodus 20:12; 21:17, Deuteronomy 5:16, and Leviticus 20:9 regarding parental obligations of caring for and supporting elderly parents. The Jewish custom of declaring a gift to God and thus avoiding the parental obligations violated the Law of God. Jesus accuses the religious leaders of hypocrisy (literally, living behind a mask as in a theater). They pretend to be religious but in reality live the opposite. They pretend to worship God but fulfill the prophecy of Isaiah. They offer lip service, which God rejects.

Jesus continues the discussion by calling to mind the difference between ritual defilement and moral defilement. The moral issues eclipse any ritual issues. Once again, the Pharisees take offense and Jesus appears frustrated. He implies that God did not plant the Pharisees and they will be rooted out. Like the previous parables involving seeds and plants, Jesus calls for tolerance: "Let them alone." They are blind and if people are foolish enough to follow them, they all fall into the pit.

Peter again acts like a spokesperson and again seems dense. In Jewish traditions feelings and understanding come from the heart. What enters through the mouth involves the stomach and bowels and leaves in an uncomely manner. What comes out of the mouth (words, evil thoughts, violations of the Ten Commandments) arises from the heart and that alone can cause defilement. Eating with unclean hands pales when compared with the defilement from the heart.

Questions

186. Should all traditions be maintained?

187. People often rationalize to avoid obligations. Why?

188. Hypocrites live both in the sanctuary and in the body of the church. What should be done?

189. Do people pay lip service to the commandments of God?

190. Moral defilement is more significant than ritual defilement. Are they ever related?

191. Jesus seems frustrated. Does this seem strange for a divine Son of God?

192. Foolish people still follow the blind. How can such a situation be avoided?

Conclusion

Mark, when dealing with this controversy, declares that all food is clean. Probably for Matthew his community still debated these issues and so he avoids the more general declaration of food and concentrates on ritual purity. The tradition of categories of food so strong in Jewish tradition becomes abrogated in Christianity. Some traditions need to change. The problem always involves what to hold on to and what to discard. Pharisees wanted to observe all of the traditions of the fathers, even if they went far beyond the Torah. Jesus has already made interpretations that affect Torah, as seen in the Sermon on the Mount. Jesus has already changed things.

Eating with unclean hands may have been a Pharisees' tradition but does not come from Torah and probably was not a universal custom. Perhaps only the most pious observers would have followed the practice. When the Pharisees accuse Jesus and his disciples of not following the tradition, they presume he should do more than the general population with regard to ritual observance. Jesus ignores them and becomes frustrated. Why do people not understand! The human Jesus reacts very humanly when faced with human density in thinking! Here Matthew shows Jesus with some emotion but in a limited fashion.

Pharisees followed the tradition of *korban*. They could declare something sacred and belonging to God and thus no one could demand any obligation coming from the declaration of *korban*. People avoided parental obligations by declaring *korban*, which violated the Law of God. As the attitude of the Pharisees against Jesus hardened, so the attitude of Jesus toward the Pharisees becomes one of frustration. They pretend to be following the Law of God and do the opposite.

Living behind masks (a good explanation of hypocrites) unfortunately happens in the church and in society. Too often leaders, both civic and religious, hide behind masks. Eventually the masks come off and all suffer, both leaders and subjects.

Throughout history people have thought God will pay attention to ritual observance even if the rituals fail to come from the heart. The warning of Jesus has as much meaning today as it did two thousand years ago. Ritual lies take place daily in churches, temples, and mosques. And God is not pleased. Rituals are supposed to express the reality of faith present in individuals and in the church. Otherwise they mean nothing.

People who do not think and who pay no attention to "by their fruits you will know them" will find themselves following leaders who do not know what they are doing. Jesus came to take away sins but not brains. Individual believers have an obligation to follow their own conscience, paying attention to church leaders but weighing carefully both what the religious leaders say and how they live.

Section Twenty-nine:
More Healings, 15:21–31

Introduction

Jesus in Matthew is less divine than in the Gospel of John but more divine than in the Gospel of Mark. In this episode he seems not only human but petty. It is not nice to refer to anyone as a "dog."

Tyre and Sidon lie on the Mediterranean coast. Gentiles lived there and Jews avoided the area. Did Jesus go in the general direction, or did he actually go as far as these coastal cities? The problems between Jewish Christians and Gentile Christians in the community of Matthew existed and at times they fiercely debated each other. The context of the Matthean community may have set the scene for the story of the Canaanite woman.

Did the Canaanite woman hear of Jesus and travel to see him? Did Jesus leave the general Jewish region to teach among Gentiles? Did Matthew create the scene to help deal with the problems within his community? Did Matthew modify an event in the ministry of Jesus to deal with this same problem?

The pagan woman used a Jewish title of Jesus: Lord, Son of David. The disciples suggest to Jesus either that he dismiss her, send her away, or exorcise the demon tormenting the daughter. Either way, the disciples did not want to deal with the woman.

Jesus responds harshly by first referring to his mission to the lost of Israel and then using a diminutive "little dogs" or "house dogs." The remark sounds insulting. Jesus acts out of character.

The pagan woman continues the tradition of Gentiles doing homage to Jesus and makes a clever response to the harsh words of Jesus. House dogs are fed within the house, and the implication is that God feeds both Gentiles and Jews. The community of

Matthew would have listened carefully to the dialogue. Jesus rewards the woman's faith and heals the daughter. Matthew continues with a summary of Jesus' healing activities. People respond by glorifying God.

Questions

193. Jesus says he was sent to the lost of Israel yet he goes at least near the Gentile community. Why the contradiction?
194. How could the woman have learned of the title for Jesus?
195. What do you think of the response by Jesus?
196. The woman did homage and had faith. Is that sufficient?
197. How do you feel about the reference to "dogs"?

Conclusion

Jesus and the Canaanite woman have an extended conversation, with the woman trumping the teacher. The woman addresses Jesus as Lord and Son of David. If Matthew records accurately then the woman did her homework to use the proper title and assumed the attitude of prayer in the presence of Jesus. If Matthew created or modified the episode, then Matthew presents the Gentiles in a favorable light. If Jesus remained in the general territory of the Jews, to conform to Matthew 10:5, then the woman had to travel to encounter Jesus. She studied how to approach Jesus and traveled into Jewish territory. Both present Gentiles in a positive light.

Although Jesus honors the call to ministry among the Jews, he now leaves an opening to the Gentiles. In fact, this happened in the time of Matthew. Gentiles belonged. They prayed with Jewish Christians and honored and gave homage to Jesus as Lord and Son of David.

Jews often called Gentiles dogs, just as today many cultures refer to those considered inferior as "dogs." "Little dogs" or "house dogs" may lessen the insult but does not take it away. If

Jesus followed the custom of referring to the Gentiles as dogs, here he also acknowledges the Gentiles have faith, just as he admired the faith of the centurion.

Perhaps the disciples referred to the woman as a dog and wanted Jesus to get rid of her. The reference to "dog" precisely because it is insulting, however, would support the belief that Jesus said it. If the disciples said it, by moving it to the lips of Jesus Matthew or Mark strengthened the place of Gentiles within Christianity. Faith and prayer change a status of a person and that happened in early Christianity, especially within the Matthean community.

Section Thirty:
The Second Feeding
Miracle, 15:32–39

Introduction

Matthew tends to exaggerate and in this second feeding story the crowds have been with Jesus for three days. No wonder they were hungry and Jesus had pity on them! The reference to the wilderness and the bread recalls Exodus: God's feeding of the people of Israel with manna. The disciples in spite of the previous miracle seem surprised. They reply that they have bread, seven (not five) loaves, and a few fish. The number 7 in the Old Testament refers to Gentiles.

Jesus gives thanks (*eucharistesas*). The use of the word for *give thanks* more explicitly anticipates the celebration of the Eucharist. With the leftovers Matthew again makes reference to "seven," a further possible reference to the Gentiles. Matthew adds to the spectacular number of people fed by adding, "not including women and children." The region of Magadan is unknown in archeology.

Questions

198. What differences can you see when comparing this feeding with the previous miracle?
199. Why would Matthew make references to the Eucharist?
200. Why the references to the Gentiles?
201. Why two miracles of feeding?

Conclusion

Since Matthew used Mark as a source and Mark has two miracles of feeding, Matthew decided to include both in his gospel. Luke had the same source but omitted the second miracle of feeding. Both miracles follow the same pattern with some minor differences: the three days, less emphasis on fish, and the references to the Gentiles. Did Jesus first feed a Jewish crowd and now a Gentile crowd? If so, how does this fit into the general command to minister to the lost of Israel?

No indication exists that the feeding took place in Gentile territory, but then no one knows where Jesus was and where Jesus went after the miracle. Whether or not the miracle took place in Gentile territory, the veiled references to the Gentiles distinguish this miracle from the earlier feeding miracle.

The lack of interest in the fish and the further references to the Eucharist probably arose from the greater interest in the celebration of the Eucharist, which people saw prefigured in the miracles of feeding. The second feeding expands the role of disciples just as the celebration of the Eucharist did. Each may refer to some aspect of the Matthean community: the place of Gentiles, the functions of leaders, the importance of the celebration of the Eucharist. Matthew must deal with both Jewish Christians and Gentile Christians. The gradual increase in references to Gentiles would support the general trend in the Matthean community (probably in Antioch) to have a continued increase in Gentile converts and a lessening in the numbers of Jewish converts to Christianity.

Section Thirty-one:
Further Controversies,
16:1–12

Introduction

With the increase in controversies with the Pharisees and now the Sadducees, Jesus' level of frustration rises. Even the disciples offer little comfort to a distraught Jesus. The Sadducees have joined the Pharisees as adversaries. In itself, this strengthens the opposition to Jesus since these groups had enough differences among themselves. They "test" Jesus, which would throw the readers of the gospel back to the "testing" of Jesus by Satan. Matthew continues to darken the portrait of the Jewish leaders.

The Jewish leaders may know how to read the signs of the weather, but they fail to read what is actually happening in their personal lives and in their religious traditions. The evil and adulterous generation has returned (Matt 12:39). Just as the people of Israel failed in their relationship to God in the past, so the same is true for the present generation in the time of Jesus. Again, Matthew refers to the sign of Jonah as he explained in 12:38–42.

Somehow they have crossed the sea and complain about bread. Jesus takes the occasion to use a different interpretation of leaven. As Jesus used the image in a parable now he uses the image to avoid the influence of the Pharisees. Of course, the disciples ignore Jesus, which adds to his frustration. Jesus has to remind them again that their faith needs help and support. They have already forgotten about how Jesus fed large crowds on two occasions.

Matthew frequently uses plays on words. In Aramaic leaven is *hamira* and teaching is *'amira*. Finally the disciples understand that Jesus warns them to avoid the teaching of the

Pharisees and Sadducees. They should listen to him and not the religious leaders of their times.

Questions

202. What are the differences between Pharisees and Sadducees?
203. The opposition grows. Why does Matthew highlight this?
204. Jesus seems frustrated by both the Jewish leaders and disciples. Why?
205. Religious leaders can influence people for good or ill. What can a follower do?

Conclusion

The controversies involve the two principal religious groups of leaders. The Sadducees come from the priestly segment of society and the Pharisees come from a group of pious Jews committed to strict observance of Torah. They usually did not get along because of their differing interpretations of Torah. By the time of Matthew the Sadducees had lost their influence with the destruction of the Temple and the end of sacrifice and then priesthood. Together they add to the opposition to Jesus.

Matthew writes his gospel culminating in a full rejection of Jesus by his crucifixion and death. He continues to increase the opposition so that the ultimate decision to destroy Jesus reaches a culmination that began with the effort on the part of Herod to destroy Jesus as a child. Just as an evil king (Pharaoh) tried to destroy Moses, so an evil king (Pilate and the religious leaders) attempts to destroy Jesus. Throughout the ministry the evil begun in the opening chapters continues to grow stronger until it leads to crucifixion.

The failure to understand on the part of both religious leaders and the disciples adds to the frustration of Jesus. He does not want to destroy the Torah but to help people to see it fulfilled. He wants people to rethink how they are living and pay more

131

attention to their relationship to God rather than worry about bread and earthly things. He fails with regard to both religious leaders and, too often, in dealing with his dense disciples.

All religious leaders are supposed to act like leaven, influencing people for good. Unfortunately, in the history of all religions some religious leaders fail in their responsibility and pay more attention to their own needs and to the needs of the institution than the needs of ordinary believers. In Christianity the Holy Spirit has been given to all followers of Jesus. When they distrust the leadership in the church they can fall back on the presence of the Spirit. If the decisions they make give them peace and contentment, believers can be sure they are following the inspiration of the Holy Spirit.

Section Thirty-two: Peter and the Passion Prediction, 16:13–28

Introduction

Peter has already appeared in this gospel as the spokesperson for the disciples. In this chapter Jesus gives him authority in the church after Peter has professed his faith. Matthew alone among the gospels uses the word *church* (*ekklesia*) and twice within these few verses. Peter and the church belong together in this gospel.

Caesar Augustus gave the city originally called Panion to Herod the Great. When Philip the son of Herod rebuilt the city, he changed the name of the city to Caesarea Philippi in his honor as well as that of Caesar. The name itself connotes both Jewish and Gentile dimensions. When Matthew uses the title Son of Man here it is as a specific title of Jesus and not as the generic "everyman" that he used before.

Jewish tradition expected a return of one of the great prophets in anticipation of the coming of the Messiah, or perhaps a figure like Moses (Deut 18:15). The disciples answer with the classical list of names. Matthew adds Jeremiah probably because of his interest in Jeremiah as a figure of Jesus. Matthew alludes to Jeremiah in several instances and actually refers to him in three texts (Matt 2:17; 16:14; 27:9).

Peter responds with a profession of faith: "the Christ the Son of the living God." For the first time a disciple professes faith in Jesus as both the Messiah and the Son of God. This same Peter will deny Jesus when forced to choose between his own safety and his faith.

Jesus responds to this profession with a declaration. Peter alone receives a blessing from Jesus. Jesus gives Peter his full title:

Simon son of Yohanna (probably John and not Jonah). In contrast to a human revelation (flesh and blood) Jesus attests that God has revealed this to Peter. Peter has a special blessing from Jesus and has a special relationship to God.

Again Matthew uses a play on words: in Greek *Petros* (Peter) and *Petra* (rock), in Aramaic *kepha* (Peter/Cephas). Perhaps Peter had a nickname: Rocky. *Petra* could mean a solid rock but also a small pebble. This might fit Matthean irony when one considers just how solid Peter was with regard to faith in Jesus.

"Gates of hell" refers to the domain of the dead. It does not mean the domain of the devil. Jesus declares that anything opposed to God will not triumph over the church. Keys refer to authority. Peter is the gatekeeper, an image that continues into popular images of heaven.

Binding and loosing covers several ideas: including and excluding, laying down rules and easing rules, forgiving and refusing to forgive sins. Here Peter alone receives this power while in 18:18 Jesus gives the same power to the community.

When Matthew tells the disciples not to tell anyone, perhaps Jesus wanted the disciples to rethink just what the Messiah might mean. Peter evidently misunderstands and Jesus must rebuke him. Jesus predicts for the first time his suffering and death and resurrection. Peter wants no part of it. He probably wanted the glory but not the pain. Once again Matthew uses the word *skandalon* (stumbling block). Peter the rock does not want Jesus to suffer. He joins the list of tempters going back to the temptations in the desert that preceded the public ministry of Jesus.

Jesus finishes his remarks to Peter and turns to address his disciples alone. The sufferings of the disciples will link them to Jesus. The whole world would include all that the devil offered to Jesus in the temptations. They mean nothing when compared to true life. Depending on how a person lives (actions follow beliefs) Jesus as the Son of Man will reward. Judgment depends on deeds. The presence of the eschatological and apocalyptic tone will reach a climax in chapter 25.

Questions

206. Jesus was the Messiah. He was one of the prophets but not the prophet that preceded the Messiah for he was the Messiah. Why does Matthew insist on Old Testament continuity?

207. Peter again assumes a leadership role. Just how much of a rock was Peter?

208. Both Peter and the community receive authority. How does this apply to the church today?

209. Peter was also Satan and a stumbling block. Has this been true for the successors of Peter?

210. How does carrying one's cross fit into spirituality today?

Conclusion

Matthew continues to trace all of the teachings of Jesus and all of Christian traditions and beliefs to the Old Testament. In this way he maintains continuity and pleased the Jewish Christians. At the same time he continued to make changes in Old Testament traditions, pleasing Gentile Christians. He does his best to preserve the old and to be open to the new, however difficult.

Matthew alone among the gospels has the personal proclamation to Peter giving him authority and power in the church. Peter professes his faith and receives a blessing from Jesus. The use of word plays and Aramaic suggests a pre-Matthean source for the saying. Some think the saying came from Jesus himself. But then why no clear reference in any of the other gospels? Others think it came from Antioch, the probable place of origin of the Gospel of Matthew and where Peter was held in high regard as a centrist, bridging both Jewish and Gentile Christians. Still others think it is a remembrance of a postresurrection appearance of Jesus to Peter. No one can make a definitive decision. It is part of the canon of Scripture and should be accepted as such.

If Peter had the nickname Rocky, then his nickname prefigured his role as the foundation of the church. The use of rocks as foundations occurred in the Old Testament in Isaiah 51:1–2 and

135

Psalm 118:22. In the New Testament Jesus is the rock and not Peter (1 Cor 3:11). But in Ephesians the household of God rests on the foundation of apostles and prophets (2:20). But was Peter a rock? He denied Jesus three times and often seems like a weak leader. Pebbles are annoying. If *petra* means pebble, was Peter also annoying to Jesus? How ironic that the one chosen to be the leader also comes across as weak and even a tempter for the Lord! This has been true for the two thousand years of Christianity. Chosen leaders often have feet of clay.

The gift of authority both to Peter and to the church in Matthew sets up a balance. The church needs Peter and Peter needs the church. Together they work to bring about the reign of God. Often enough conflict may arise as to which has the most authority. The gospels give no clue. Each gospel has some reference to Peter as a Christian leader but none presented as strongly as Matthew. Matthew alone gives Peter the keys and he alone gives the same authority to the church. The relationship between Peter and the church will continue throughout history and, like other dimensions in this gospel, something of the old will remain as both Peter and the church remain open to the new.

Jesus carried a cross; Peter carried a cross and eventually died like his Master. No one should be hung on some mystical cross but no one can avoid problems in life. How a person integrates pain, problems, and sorrow into life determines the worth of a person. Believing in an ultimate positive future, God, helps people to live. Jesus predicted his passion but also the resurrection. The same exists for all followers of Jesus.

Section Thirty-three:
The Transfiguration and the Disciples' "Little Faith," 17:1–20

Introduction

People long for theophanies. "If only God would give me a sign I would be able to…" People want to have a vision of God, a manifestation of God's power and goodness. In the Old Testament, Moses and the people of Israel enjoyed a vision of the glory of God at Sinai. They saw the power and goodness of God and everything changed.

The transfiguration of Jesus, found first in Mark and then included with some minor changes by Matthew, gave to the chosen inner circle within the Twelve (Peter, James, and John) a vision of the glory of God in Jesus. They saw and were overwhelmed and were changed.

Some find in this episode allusions to Sinai and Moses. There are similar details: the high mountain, the reference to six days, the companions of Moses, and the three companions of Jesus. If Matthew wants to present Jesus as both the new Moses and the manifestation of God, the transfiguration suits his purpose.

Transfigured means a change in form. Here the disciples see the spirituality, the divinity of Jesus, made manifest in his body. His face shone, just as the face of Moses shone when he came down from the mountain (Exod 34:29).

The appearance of Moses and Elijah with Jesus shows Jesus' superiority over the law and the prophets. They become his companions. Their appearance may also anticipate the resurrection of

Jesus since both were taken up into heaven (Deut 18:15, 18; Mal 3:23–24).

The never understanding Peter speaks up, acknowledges that Jesus is Lord (not Teacher, as in Mark), and volunteers to build tents for Jesus and the two visitors. The coming of the cloud, a symbol of God's presence, and the voice like that at the baptism of Jesus preclude any attempt by Peter to prolong the experience by building tents. The experience frightens them. Jesus approaches them and it is over.

William James speaks of four characteristics of mystical or religious experiences. They are ineffable. They cannot be named. They contain a noetic content; the individual learns something. The person is passive and the experience is transient; it passes and usually quickly. The transfiguration fulfills James' criteria of a mystical experience.

Matthew calls the event a vision. Jesus tells his disciples to tell no one until the Son of Man has risen from the dead. For the second time Jesus makes a reference to his resurrection.

The reference to Elijah reflects the Jewish tradition of the return of the prophet to herald the coming of the Messiah. Jesus makes clear that John filled the role of Elijah. As he made reference to his resurrection, Jesus concludes the episode by referring to his suffering.

Coming down from the mountain Jesus encounters a distraught father. The other disciples had remained below and evidently had tried and failed to cure the man's son. With characteristic reverence the father makes his request and prays "Lord, have mercy"—not unlike the prayer of the disciples in the boat and the prayer of Peter when he attempted to walk on the water. The Greek refers to "moonstruck" and probably means the boy suffered from epilepsy as translated into English.

Once again Jesus seems frustrated. Whether the "faithless generation" refers to the disciples or the people in general seems unclear. Jesus heals the boy and turns to his disciples and accuses them again of "little faith." How often must he remind them that their faith needs strength and support! Jesus then recalls the parable of the mustard seed and assures them of their remarkable ability if they have faith.

Some manuscripts add: "This kind never comes out except by prayer and fasting." Mark includes it in his version and Matthew omits it. Perhaps a later scribe added it to copies of Matthew. People usually remember the phrase. However, the meaning remains obscure in the context of the healing.

Questions

211. Can the physical manifest the spiritual?
212. Have you ever had mystical experiences?
213. Peter continues to misunderstand. What does this tell you about Peter and the disciples in the early church?
214. Moses represents the Law and Elijah the prophets. How do they fit into the needs of the Matthean community?
215. Jesus seems frustrated by a lack of faith. Can faith really cure people and move mountains?
216. Do prayer and fasting help in healing?

Conclusion

Over the centuries many have attempted to delineate the precise genre of the transfiguration story. Since Mark has no resurrection appearances some see it as a transferred resurrection story. Matthew calls it a vision. What kind of a vision? No doubt Jesus had a mystical experience and the disciples have had a mystical experience of Jesus. The episode easily fulfills the criteria of William James. Many people over the centuries have had similar experiences. The other most famous one in the New Testament takes place on the road to Damascus with Paul the apostle.

The material without the spiritual does not exist. The human being in biblical anthropology has physical, psychological, and spiritual dimensions. They all interact and sometimes the spiritual shines through. The artist can see the spiritual in the physical. Such perception creates the artist. Michelangelo could look at a piece of marble and see David or Moses or a sorrowful mother holding her only son. The transfiguration is the feast of artists. The spirituality of Jesus shines through the body and the disciples see the glory of God in Jesus. They witness the power and goodness of God in Jesus.

Moses and Elijah, representing the law and the prophets, bring an apocalyptic element since their passing and their future role remained unsure in the history of Israel. They appropriately converse with Jesus as the disciples foresee the full manifestation of Jesus in glory in the future.

In the Gospel of Matthew the transfiguration story links Christianity and Jesus to the Old Testament Law and prophets, a common theme and need in the Matthean community. The Jewish members of the community continually must face Matthew's attempt to assure them of the continuity between Israel and Torah and Jesus.

Peter, held in esteem in the Antiochean/Matthean community, recognizes the relationship between Jesus and the law and the prophets. He could serve as a model for other Jewish Christians. Peter the centrist might lack full understanding and his faith needed help, but he still belonged to Jesus.

Historically Christians have interpreted the transfiguration as an attempt by Jesus to prepare his disciples for the passion and crucifixion. In the final days of Jesus the spirituality, the divinity, gets lost in the cruel and painful death. Whether this was true for the disciples of Jesus, it has been true for anyone who reads the Synoptic Gospels.

After the religious and mystical experience of the inner circle of the Twelve, Jesus again becomes frustrated by the "little faith" of his followers. From chapter 16 on Matthew will focus on the disciples. They appear in a more favorable light than in Mark but still manifest the ordinary failures of fallible human beings. They have faith but not sufficient faith. Their faith will be further tested in what will happen in the final days of the ministry of Jesus. The weakness of those closest to Jesus offers encouragement to the community of Matthew. If some have trouble understanding and believing, they need not be surprised. Those closest to Jesus had the same problem. Such is true today.

Faith healed people in the time of Jesus because Jesus said so. Faith heals people today. But sometimes God says, "No," and faith does not heal. When faith no longer heals, perhaps God calls the person home and the person of faith accepts. As for moving mountains, sometimes faith has moved the mountains that people create within themselves and in others.

Section Thirty-four:
The Temple Tax and the Second Passion Prediction, 17:22–27

Introduction

Each gospel has three predictions of the passion of Jesus and each gospel deals with them differently. The greatest differences exist between the Gospel of John and the Synoptics. Since Matthew and Luke follow Mark, the differences in these gospels are slight.

In the first prediction by Matthew the author specifies the elders, chief priests, and scribes will put Jesus to death. In this second prediction Jesus refers only to "men." The reference to the resurrection, like that in Mark, seems more like a refrain. Like Mark the final prediction in Matthew (Matt 20:18–19) has more details than the previous two. Also, unlike the disciples in Mark, who do not understand, here the disciples become sad.

Peter lived in Capernaum and Jesus probably used this town as one of his two home bases. Capernaum also had a tax office. Peter has a conversation with the tax collector and then with Jesus. Peter tells them that Jesus honors the Temple tax.

The conversation of Peter and Jesus concerns who should be obliged to pay the tax. The word used includes both indirect taxes (or custom duties) and poll or head taxes. More likely the words just mean any general tax. When Jesus asks who should be obliged Peter answers that rulers collect taxes from others. Then Jesus informs him that the sons are free from such obligations. The implication is that since Jesus is God's Son he is excused from Temple taxes. To avoid scandal, Jesus instructs Peter to go fishing and he finds a coin in the mouth of the fish that will pay for both Peter and Jesus.

Questions

217. Here men in general are guilty of the death of Jesus. Is this true?
218. Why would Jesus bother to pay the tax?
219. How is Peter depicted here?
220. Do you believe that Peter caught a fish and it contained a coin in its mouth?

Conclusion

The first and third predictions of the passion in Matthew make specific references to Jewish religious leaders. In this prediction "men in general" are guilty. Anyone who seeks to destroy what is good, especially a good person, has participated in the death of Jesus. When Paul says Jesus died for our sins (1 Cor 15:3), he does not imply that God demanded the death of Jesus for appeasement. Jesus dies for our sins because individuals seek to destroy what is good. Jesus was good. To lessen his influence, people who did not want to deal with goodness decided to kill him.

The tax probably referred to the annual tax every Jew paid for the upkeep of the Temple. The episode comes from the material proper to Matthew since it appears only in this gospel. The story supports the belief that Jesus is the divine Son of God and therefore he has no obligation to pay the tax. But who would be scandalized?

If the followers of Jesus did not pay the tax, then they would not be considered Jews. Gentile Christians would feel no such obligation since they had no personal relationship to the Temple. The Temple tax would have made sense to all Jewish Christians before the destruction of the Temple, but after AD 70, when the Romans continued to collect the tax and used it to support the

Temple of Jupiter in Rome, all Christians needed a proper response to paying such taxes. Since Jesus paid the tax with no obligation, so all Christians could continue to pay the Roman tax to avoid problems with the Roman authorities. Early Christians practiced a general observance of civil taxes.

Rabbinic literature has a similar story in which a pearl is found in the mouth of a fish. In folklore rings and coins are found almost regularly in the mouths of fish. Whatever happened, it is a good story and it has a good purpose.

THE FOURTH SERMON: THE CHURCH, 18:1–35

Section Thirty-five: The Church Sermon, 18:1–35

Introduction

Chapter 18 presents the fourth great sermon or discourse by Jesus and concerns the church. Jesus had gathered a group of followers during his ministry. While he was with them they continued to learn and always had his presence. By the time Matthew was written (around AD 80–85) that community had become a "church" with clear lines of authority (especially Peter and eventually the Twelve), a mission (28:18–20), rules and regulations (the Sermon on the Mount), and specific guidelines for the church community (chapter 18).

The disciples wanted to know their status in the reign of God. Jesus used a child to teach them. The child has no social status or political significance and lives completely dependent on adults. Since people paid little attention to children, so the disciples, who acknowledge dependence, do not assume any superiority over others. Then they will be recognized as great in the reign of God. Humility involves truth. The true disciple follows the truth by imitating the example of Jesus.

The "little ones," the disciples, should live and act as children with no pretense and no sense of superiority over other "little ones." Accepting "little ones" means accepting Jesus. Social status means nothing in the church of Jesus.

Matthew returns again to the word *skandalidzo*. Six times Matthew uses the verb or noun. In a religious context the stumbling block refers to apostasy or a temptation to sin. The "little ones" refers to members of the Matthean community. Anyone who causes one of the members of the church to sin should drown in the deepest part of the sea with a large stone around his neck to make sure of the drowning. Even if scandals must come the one who causes the scandal must accept the consequences of his actions (second temptation of Jesus).

People must make decisions regarding priority. Matthew likes exaggeration and here he uses hyperbole of the various body parts to teach his point. Perhaps also the reference to the body parts refers metaphorically to the members of the family, the body of the church. When individuals cause scandals they should be cut off, excommunicated. They do not belong.

They may be "little ones" but their guardian angels assure the awareness of God to their plight. They must not be despised, neglected, overlooked, or hurt. In the church they belong and must receive their rightful acceptance.

Ezekiel 34 criticizes the bad shepherds of Israel. Jesus himself is the good shepherd in John 10, and in Luke 15 the parable of the lost sheep supports the image and function of Jesus as taking care of the least of the brethren in the community. If Jesus acts in this way, so the same must be true in the church. Since this sermon deals with church issues, Matthew calls to the attention of the church leaders how they are to act.

The church will have problems and Matthew tells the community how to deal with them. Fraternal correction demands a reproof, which should first be done privately. If that does not work, follow the dictates of Deuteronomy 19:15 and seek two assistants. If that fails, turn to the church community. If that does not work, never give up but treat them like tax collectors or Gentiles who always have the possibility of repentance. Excommunication does not mean eternal exclusion.

As Peter received the power to bind and loose in chapter 16, so the same power belongs to the church. The church community can excommunicate or lift the excommunication, can forgive sins or refrain from forgiving. Here the use of this power does not rest upon any special position in the church. The community has the authority and the responsibility.

If members of the church agree on earth the Father will accept in heaven. Since the chapter concerns the church then such matters as prayer, government, and requirements of membership belong to the whole church. While the context of the reference to the presence of Jesus in the midst of his disciples has a juridical tone, common in the whole chapter, the reference to prayer takes on a liturgical context as well. When Christians pray together Jesus assures them of his continued presence.

Forgiveness has always caused problems in the church. To Peter's generous offer, Jesus tells his followers that no limits should ever exist with forgiveness. If God places no limits on forgiveness, humans can do no less. Jesus concludes with the parable of the unjust servant. Ten thousand talents would be equivalent to a billion dollars. (Remember, Matthew likes to exaggerate.) The selling of family members was not part of the Jewish tradition at the time of Jesus but did exist in Gentile communities. When the servant pleads, the master dismisses the debt as a forgiven "loan."

When the same servant deals cruelly with his fellow servant who owed him a hundred days' wage, his fellow servants take action. "Forgive us our debts as we also have forgiven our debtors." Mercy experienced is mercy given. Otherwise God does not forgive.

Questions

221. What constitutes status in the church?

222. Scandals occur. What should be done to those who cause the scandal?

223. "The "little ones," the unimportant members, often suffer. They are ignored, despised, often humiliated. What would Jesus say?

224. What are the responsibilities of church leaders concerning the "little ones"?

225. How should the church deal with dissenters?

226. If Jesus is present where Christians gather, does this apply to the Eucharist of non-Catholic churches?

227. Why is forgiveness so important in the church? Does it apply to church leaders as well as the "little ones"?

Conclusion

Status in the church depends upon faith. Holiness develops in the body of the church as well as in the sanctuary. Weeds can grow in both areas. Position in the church rests on dependence on God and on Jesus and not on office. Some who hold office belong to the "little ones" and some do not. The child had no social status and would have been ignored. Jesus wants his church members, especially the leaders, to be social "nobodies." They have a ministry and should fulfill it without demanding social status. They fulfill their service with no regard to prestige or personal importance.

The references to priorities in body parts can refer to the actual community. Some people belong and others do not. Those who seek social status, cause scandal, and pay no attention to those members in need do not belong. Cut them off! Matthew offers strong words, especially concerning church leaders. The worst seems to be those who fail in their ministry to the forgotten, the marginalized, the misunderstood, and the abandoned.

Differences will always exist in the church. People will disagree and cause pain for themselves and for others. Different interpretations of the Jesus tradition existed, as evidenced in the various books of the New Testament. What should one do in the church? Begin privately. Then seek help and turn to the whole church. If nothing works, exclude but never abandon. The whole church binds and looses. As already mentioned, this authority functions alongside the authority of Peter. Neither exists exclusively.

If Jesus is present when Christians gather, how can anyone say Jesus is not present when non-Catholic Christians celebrate the Eucharist? Some will admit a presence but claim the presence differs from the Eucharist in the Catholic Church. No one seems able to explain the differences in a theological sense and then turn to a juridical understanding of validity.

Forgiveness has no limits. This teaching causes problems. People like to hold grudges. "Christian Alzheimer's disease" means one forgets everything except the grudges and resentments. Some will forgive but not forget. Jesus challenges his followers to live with limitless forgiveness. No one said it would be easy. Even the most hardened sinner can rethink and live differently. Redemption means every person has a value, a worth, and a dignity that no one can destroy, not even the person himself or herself. People need to acknowledge their redemption and forgive themselves. People need to acknowledge the redemption of others and forgive. Both leaders and members of the church have experienced redemption and everyone needs to receive forgiveness and offer forgiveness. Jesus says, "No limits!"

THE JOURNEY TO JERUSALEM CONTINUES, 19:1—20:34

Section Thirty-six: Marriage, Divorce, Celibacy, Children, and Wealth, 19:1–30

Introduction

Jesus has finished his fourth sermon or discourse with the usual wording in Matthew: "When Jesus had finished saying…" He has given the instructions to the church community and now travels from Galilee to Judea. Like many pious Jews he moves from north to south by crossing the Jordan to avoid Samaritan territory. Jesus moves toward Jerusalem and along the way he continues to heal; in Jerusalem, he no longer performs miracles. The opposition follows him and attempts to trip him up with the question on divorce.

For the second time in Matthew Jesus deals with the issue and once again quotes Genesis. "Let no man separate" refers not to men in general but to the husband. In traditional Judaism marriage was a contract that could be abrogated by the husband. The Pharisees interpreted Moses' command as a law. Jesus interpreted it as a concession. As in 5:32 Matthew again offers an exception: apart from *porneia*.

151

The remark from the disciples seems odd. They act as if marriage is not desirable unless the man can divorce his wife! "This teaching" probably refers to the question of the eunuch saying. Jesus calls for celibacy for the sake of the kingdom.

Just as Jesus presented a child as an image for how one should enter the kingdom of God, so here Jesus uses a child to teach that they must accept the kingdom as a gift. A child can lay no claim on anything. A child receives from a loving parent. God acts the same way.

Wealth brings its own temptations. The wealthy young man shows an interest in Jesus and his teachings and tells Jesus he has kept the commandments and wants to know what else he lacks. Matthew again refers to perfection (cf. 5:48). Jesus challenges the young man to give up his possessions and follow him. The challenge is too much and the young man leaves with sadness. His possessions prove an obstacle to following Jesus.

Things can hinder a person from entering the kingdom but need not. Wealth seems to make it harder. A camel passing through the eye of a needle implies the impossibility of a rich man entering the kingdom. The tradition that Jerusalem had a small gate called the needle that a camel could pass through only with much difficulty has no basis in fact.

If wealthy people cannot experience the kingdom of God, who can? Jesus responds that no one can unless God so wishes. All things are possible for God. God freely gives to anyone, including the rich. No one can buy their way into the kingdom.

Peter speaks up, but what has he given up? The boasting Peter wants something and Jesus promised to give them all a share in power and glory by judging the tribes of Israel. Jesus also promised rewards now but mainly in the future. Then the great reversal will take place: the last first and the first last.

Questions

228. Why does Matthew return again to the question of divorce?

229. Does celibacy makes sense in the contemporary world?

230. What does it mean to be like children to enter the kingdom in this century?

231. Why does wealth hinder discipleship?

Conclusion

Within first-century Judaism the religious leaders debated the grounds necessary for divorce. Matthew has Jesus enter into the debate. God's will for man and woman comes first and then the concession from Moses. At the time of Jesus and Matthew some liberal rabbis, such as Hillel, allowed divorce for any cause, including spoiling a dish or being displeased with one's wife. For others only moral transgressions could form the basis for divorce. In Mark and Luke the teaching of Jesus seems most strict: no divorce at all. Matthew modifies the teaching from Jesus with his exception. As already noted, no one can be sure of what constitutes the exception. He deals with the issue twice to make sure his listeners understand the importance of marriage. Jesus rooted his prohibition against divorce in the primordial will of God. God created a partnership that should last. In all probability the apodictic prohibition against divorce found in Mark and Luke goes back to the historical Jesus. Matthew, the one who favors the Law, allows an exception.

Celibacy was unusual in ancient Judaism. At the time of Jesus some Jews, such as the Essene community at Qumran, lived a celibate life. John the Baptist and also Paul appear to have been celibate. The use of the image of a eunuch seems strange. It can mean a natural and congenital or accidental incapacity for marriage. It also can mean creating eunuchs to have castrated attendants for a harem in Eastern courts. Certainly Jesus does not advocate self-mutilation as Origen believed. Jesus used eunuchs as a metaphor. The eunuch saying offers motivation for celibacy: the sake of the kingdom. Celibacy is a gift and not for everyone. In a world obsessed with sex, the voluntary refraining from sexual activity along with a lifestyle given up to serving others can stand as a means of forcing people to think of values other than personal pleasure. Church law demands priestly celibacy for the

Roman Catholic Church but not the Eastern Catholic Church. The law presupposes the charism of celibacy. It makes sense only when practiced with the motivation given by Jesus in this text: for the sake of the kingdom.

Blessing of children always formed part of Jewish traditions. Jesus, however, not only blessed the children but took them seriously and used them as an example for adults to imitate. "Let the children come to me..." counsels the community to afford to children their rightful place now and in the future. Weak, helpless, the vulnerable belong to the kingdom of God and they should never be excluded. If people learned from children they would more easily understand and become part of the kingdom of God.

With the rich young man Matthew seems to present two levels of religious observance: the commandments and the additional following of Jesus. The second is not necessary and not everyone receives the call. The young man does not accept discipleship and goes away.

Wealth brings two temptations: those who have money want more. They are never satisfied and they will do anything to protect what they have. Giving in to these temptations might prevent participation in the kingdom of God. But with God hope for redemption and salvation always persists. Wealth can be an obstacle, but it all depends on how wealth is used. Matthew exaggerates wealth as an obstacle: a large object going through a small opening (the camel and the needle). That implies that for the Matthean community wealth was a problem, just as wealth often creates problems for Christians today. Just as the weeds grow in the sanctuary as well as in the congregation, so the problem of wealth exists for the leaders of the church as well as the flock. Still, redemption has taken place. God has offered salvation through Jesus. No one should ever feel excluded, even the wealthy.

Do the Twelve receive a special reward in the re-creation of the world at the end of time? Certainly Jesus' choice of twelve reflects the twelve tribes of Israel. Might it mean that now the true tribes are followers of Jesus and that Christianity sits in judgment on Judaism? Since the gospel comes from a highly Jewish Christian community, the saying may have been included to encourage the Jewish Christians to see the fulfillment of Judaism in Christianity, rather than the complete abrogation of Judaism.

This chapter of Matthew deals with issues of debate within Judaism and within Christianity: divorce or no divorce; celibacy or marriage; children in the kingdom and adults in the kingdom; and the problems associated with wealth. Giving in to the temptations focuses all attention on wealth so little time and energy are left for such things as God and religion or even other people. Wealth can become a false god, just as multiple wives, or the arrogance of adults, or even celibacy can become false gods. Actions follow values and beliefs. It all depends on why!

Section Thirty-seven:
The Parable No One Likes,
20:1–16

Introduction

Most Christians have their favorite parable from Jesus. Many like the prodigal son and others the good Samaritan or the good shepherd. No one ever likes the parable of the workers in the vineyard. It seems so unfair!

The vineyard often symbolizes Israel and may also symbolize the church. The householder goes out, not the steward, and invites workers into the vineyard. No one has to come and the workers in the vineyard are promised the going rate for day laborers.

The third hour was 9:00 a.m., the sixth, 12:00 p.m., the ninth, 3:00 p.m., and the eleventh hour, 5:00 p.m. After the first hiring, the master promises "to pay what is just." Why did the master continue to go out to hire? Did the workers hired earlier not work efficiently? Was there more work than he had anticipated? Was a storm coming? All such questions, although interesting, miss the point of the parable.

At the end of the day each worker receives his pay, beginning with the last, and eventually all receive the same amount. The last paid were the first hired and so they watched the whole process. They had agreed to the normal day's pay but since they worked twelve hours and the last worked only one hour, they expected more. And most would agree. Did the last do as much in one hour than those hired earlier did in more hours? This also misses the point of the parable.

The master does not appear angry since he calls one of them "friend" and reminds them to what they had agreed. Can he not do what he wants with his money? Does he have to be fair to everyone?

"Is your eye evil" refers to jealousy and envy. The final saying also appeared in 19:30. The great reversal will take place: the first last and the last first. But here it refers only to the order of payment. All receive the same amount. The parable seems strange and obtuse. No wonder people do not like it.

Questions

232. Do you think the master is fair?
233. Why do people dislike this parable?
234. What do you think of the various explanations in verses 13–16?
235. Is there any relationship between this parable and the parable of the prodigal son?

Conclusion

The parable has two distinct divisions: the hiring and the payment. The hiring causes no problems. The payment does. Why should the person who worked one hour receive the same pay as the one who bore the heat of the day and worked twelve hours? That goes against any sense of American fairness.

The various endings from verses 13 to 16 seem to imply that Matthew has trouble with this parable as well and continues to try to find an answer. The material is unique to Matthew and so no comparison can be made to the other gospels. Some ancient manuscripts also add after verse 16, "many are called but few are chosen," which appears at the end of another parable in Matthew 22:14. That implies that even some copyists struggled to understand the meaning of the parable.

The image of the vineyard appears in Isaiah 5:1–7. Israel is the vineyard of the Lord and the Lord cares for the vineyard. Jeremiah 12:10 also refers to Israel as a vineyard. The image can then be transferred to the church. The notion of harvest connotes the idea of the final judgment with the giving out of rewards, but here there are no punishments, only what some think are unfair rewards.

Householders, or vineyard owners or wealthy people, are not free to do what they want with their money, at least not in the Christian context. Charity is one thing but justice is another. This does not seem like a good explanation. It may satisfy some but not all. The great reversal seems out of place, especially since it was also found in the previous chapter. The explanation that makes the most sense involves envy and jealousy.

The envious person wants something that someone else has. The jealous person thinks that someone has something that rightfully belongs to him or her. Can members of the Christian community rejoice in the good fortune of another? Or do grudges and claims of "unfair" cloud the ability to celebrate when something good happens to somebody else?

The older brother in the parable of the prodigal son could not rejoice in the good fortune that his brother had returned and was rewarded. After all, the prodigal brother had squandered all of his inheritance while the older brother stayed home and worked. It all seems so unfair!

Jesus and Paul, in particular, make it clear that no one can lay claim to salvation and redemption. God freely gives and all the person has to do is be open to receive. Jewish Christians had observed the Law from birth and over centuries. Now Gentile Christians lived on the same level. They both received the gift of God, which they did not deserve. The Jewish Christians found it hard to rejoice in the good fortune afforded to the Gentiles. The same problems persist today.

A parable: "a woman had a distant relative whom she did not like. This relative, however, always bought Christmas gifts for the children and so she felt an obligation to buy the relative some small gift. One year she decided on Lottery tickets and bought ten. The relative won a million dollars and graciously gave the giver of the ticket fifty thousand dollars." End of parable. If you were the buyer of the ticket, would you rejoice in the good fortune of the winner and be grateful for the fifty thousand?

Section Thirty-eight:
The Passion, Discipleship, and the Blind Man, 20:17–34

Introduction

For the third time Jesus predicts his passion. In this final prediction Matthew offers more details. The religious leaders will hand him over to the Gentiles and they will mock, scourge, and crucify him. The resurrection refrain follows. The Romans used crucifixion as punishment for major crimes. The Jews used stoning but also, as in some Middle East countries today, beheading. Jesus talks of pain and the disciples look for glory.

In Mark, James and John approach Jesus. Matthew has their mother making the request, perhaps to soften the lack of understanding on the part of the disciples. Sitting on the right and left as designated seats of honor had greater meaning in the past as compared to today.

The conversation takes place between Jesus and the two disciples. When Jesus refers to the cup perhaps they understand this as the cup of suffering but also, perhaps, they miss the point and just are anxious to get the reward they desire. Quickly they say, "We can." Jesus seems less frustrated here by his disciples but perhaps he smiled as he told them they would indeed drink the same cup of suffering as he would drink. Matthew knew. They did not but would learn.

Jesus will not assign such places of honor. That belongs to God alone. The ten other disciples (apostles) became indignant, but why? Because James and John beat them out in asking or at them for asking? In general the Twelve seemed most interested in sharing in the

159

honor and glory of Jesus. Only eventually would they learn of the pain involved in following him. If Jesus would be handed over after preaching, as was John, the disciples should anticipate the same.

Jesus takes the opportunity to teach about true discipleship. They are not to lord it over each other. The Gentiles used and abused power. The disciples will be servants and slaves. Jesus lived as a servant and slave for others, and he will give his life for his followers. "As a ransom for many" alludes to the deliverance of one held captive. The "many" may refer to Isaiah 53:11–12. Jesus redeems. Jesus assures his followers that the goodness, dignity, and value God has given them will never be destroyed. He has delivered them from the power of evil, which they also possess, but the evil will never destroy the goodness. People are redeemed.

Jericho lies fifteen miles northeast of Jerusalem. It is one of the oldest human settlements and appears frequently in the history of Israel and Christianity. Again, Matthew has two blind men, unlike Mark, who has one called Bartimaeus (Mark 10:46). Matthew prefaces the prayer of the blind men with the title "Lord," which by the time of Matthew meant more than just "sir." Jesus took pity; he touched their eyes and they saw and followed him. Matthew does not make clear if they became the followers of Jesus or followed him to Jerusalem from Jericho.

Questions

236. Why did Jesus have to suffer and die?
237. Sharing in power and glory is better than pain. Correct?
238. Who "lords it over" whom in Christianity?
239. Who are the servants and slaves in Christianity?
240. Why the multiple healings of blind people?

Conclusion

Jesus journeys closer to Jerusalem and has taught the disciples on the way by word and example. This chapter deals with the suffering of Jesus and the disciples and the type of leadership that Jesus expects. The disciples seem confused by the third prediction of the passion, just as people today wonder why Jesus had to die such a cruel death.

People tend to destroy what is good. People do not like good people since good people remind them of what they might be. Better to destroy the good person by cutting remarks or insinuations, or even lies. The ultimate method is death. Some Jews and some Romans tried to destroy Jesus. He was too good. He caused problems for the religious leaders by giving people too much freedom. He disturbed the social and civil order and should be done away with. But God would not allow the goodness of Jesus to be destroyed. God raised Jesus up in the resurrection.

Honor and glory appeal to everyone. Pain and suffering do not. The cup of suffering appears frequently in the Old Testament (Jer 25:15; 49:12; 51:7; Isa 51:17). The disciples could have understood it as suffering but probably did not. People need not hang on a mystical cross, but life brings pain and sorrow. Integrating the troubles of life into one's person only adds to one's glory: the manifestation of God's power and goodness. Seek the power and glory in the right place and never allow any pain and sorrow to destroy the gift of hope.

In most religious communities leaders claim titles. They exercise their authority by telling people what to do and not to do under pain of excommunication, exclusion from the kingdom, and even eternal punishment. Whether Judaism, Christianity, or Islam, the same temptation not only exists but many religious leaders seem to fail in living as servants and even slaves of the flock. Too frequently the servants and slaves are the flock who serve the leaders. Neither Jesus nor Matthew would approve.

Blindness can refer to physical "not seeing" but often in the gospels it refers to a spiritual "not seeing." John 11 makes it clear. Those who pretend to see, do not, and those who are thought not to see, actually see. The beginning of seeing properly lies in prayer. Seeing and not seeing, like the parable of the weeds, may be found in the sanctuary and in the body of the church.

THE HOLY CITY: THE CONFLICT STRENGTHENS, 21:1—23:39

Section Thirty-nine: Jerusalem, 21:1–17

Introduction

And so Jesus arrived in Jerusalem. The three Synoptics, Mark, Matthew, and Luke, provide a simple geographical outline for the ministry of Jesus. He began in the north, in Galilee, the land of the Gentiles, and traveled to Jerusalem for his death and crucifixion. The Gospel of John has several journeys to Jerusalem and thus has a greater leeway in presenting Jerusalem events.

The holy city lies on the crest of the central range of mountains in Palestine, between 2200 and 2400 feet above sea level. Thus, in the Bible, people go up to Jerusalem. The city has two hills, on the east and west, with the higher western hill given the name of Zion. Herod the Great added considerably to the structures of the city, including the Temple and the Fortress Antonia and his own palace in the western part of the city. David conquered the city after his accession to the throne of Israel and made it his capital. Since the city was not identified with any tribe, David, great politician that he was, chose a neutral capital. He probably also made the priests of the pagan city his own and thus unified his kingdom by controlling religion with priests not identified with any particular tribe. It is to this city Jesus would travel and where he would die.

Bethphage (house of figs) lies east of Jerusalem. The Mount of Olives runs north and south, parallel to the city. "Ass" and "colt" may refer to Zechariah 9:9. "The master" may mean teacher but to early Christians the word has become "Lord." The quotation combines Isaiah 62:11 and Zechariah 9:9. Zechariah included in his prophecy "righteous and victorious." Matthew used only "meek." Throughout the episode Jesus seems to know everything. Sitting on the cloaks and the animal, Jesus receives the homage of the inhabitants by accepting the branches thrown before him. Hosanna originally meant "save we pray," and here expresses homage.

To describe Jesus' entrance into the city, Matthew used a strange word (*eseisthe*), shook, which more properly was used referring to an earthquake. It may mean that the arrival of Jesus was like an earthquake that stirred up everyone. In fact, that happened. The reputation of Jesus had preceded him but the inhabitants had not yet witnessed his teachings or his miracles. They acknowledged that Jesus was a prophet.

Jesus enters the Temple for the first time in this gospel and immediately confronts the buyers and sellers. Only Jewish coins could be used in the Temple and so money changers were necessary to change Greek or Roman coins into the correct coinage. People also needed animals for sacrifice and thus sellers of animals were also necessary for the sacrifice. The priests of the Temple would have controlled the franchises for buying and selling.

Jesus throws out the money changers and sellers of animals, restoring the Temple as a holy place of prayer. The "den of thieves" refers to Jeremiah 7:11. When thieves steal they run to a safe place to hide. Here the safe house has become the Temple of God. The thieves have made the Temple their hiding place!

Jesus performs no specific miracles in Jerusalem. Almost as an aside, Matthew mentions that he healed the blind and the lame to set the stage for the opposition to reappear: the chief priests and scribes. The leaders accuse Jesus while the "little ones," the forgotten and abandoned, offer him homage and praise. Jesus leaves the city and uses Bethany as home base while in Jerusalem.

Questions

241. What do you know about the city of Jerusalem?

242. Why was Jerusalem so important for Jesus?

243. People change from homage to crying for crucifixion in a short period of time. Why is this so?

244. Jesus drove out the money changers and the sellers. What does this action mean for the future of the Temple and its worship?

245. The opposition starts immediately. Why would the chief priests and scribes be so opposed to Jesus?

Conclusion

The present city of Jerusalem was built north and west of what was the original city. The Temple mount, or the holy mount in the tradition of Islam, is a large platform on which Herod had built his Temple and on which now rests the Dome of the Rock. The Holy of Holies, which originally contained the ark of the covenant in Jewish tradition, had become the sacred space in which once a year the high priest uttered the holy name of God.

The outer court contained the altar of sacrifice and the altar of incense, and an additional court contained the stalls where pilgrims could exchange money and buy animals for sacrifice. The economy of Jerusalem depended on the buying and selling. Any change in the system would have deleterious effects on the economy.

For every pious Jew, Jerusalem since the time of David was *the* holy place. If possible, pilgrims should go up to Jerusalem yearly, especially at Passover, to experience the sense of Jewish tradition and to pray and offer homage to the God of Abraham, Isaac, and Jacob. In the Gospel of Luke, Jesus goes first to Jerusalem around the age of twelve. Now in Matthew he goes for the first time during Passover.

Matthew has many fulfillment citations in this section to assure his readers, especially the Jewish Christians, that Jesus has fulfilled all the ancient prophecies. Jesus will die in

Jerusalem since it is not fitting that a prophet die outside of Jerusalem.

The entrance into the city begins Holy Week, which concludes with the death of Jesus. On Sunday people proclaim the coming of the Son of David. On Friday they call for his death. People are fickle. The religious leaders call for his death because he undermines their authority even though they acknowledge that he performs some good deeds. But he violates the Sabbath and tells people they can make their own interpretations of the Law. His actions in the Temple undermine the Jewish liturgical system and affect the economy. Only religious leaders can interpret the Law and they alone can establish how to worship. They benefit from the Jerusalem economy. The civil leaders go along with the destruction of Jesus to curry favor and to avoid unrest.

The chief priests controlled the franchises for money changing and selling animals. Their livelihood and support rested on this source of income along with free will offerings. With no means of support the priesthood would not last. With no animals the priests could not offer sacrifices. The symbolic action of Jesus demonstrates the end of traditional Judaism with its system of priests and sacrifices. Actually, the system survived until AD 70, when Titus destroyed the city. Since then Judaism has become the religion of the synagogue with no priesthood and no sacrifices. Today some Jews would like to see a restoration of both priesthood and sacrifice and this would begin with the rebuilding of the Temple. Unfortunately for them, the Temple area is under the control of Islam and on it Muslims have built two mosques, the one most famous over the rock from which Muhammad ascended to heaven. It seems the Jews will not again have a Temple in Jerusalem.

The opposition to Jesus by religious leaders has existed from the beginning of the Gospel of Matthew. The evangelist offers many suggestions for the rejection of Jesus by the religious leaders. No doubt he undermined their authority and position. Usually that is enough reason for opposition to any person. The drama of Holy Week has begun!

Section Forty:
The Fig Tree and the Authority of Jesus, 21:18–28

Introduction

Most people do not like the parable of the workers in the vineyard and most people do not like what Jesus did to the poor fig tree. His action seems out of character and contributes little to understanding his ministry. Matthew has taken the story of the fig tree from Mark, who has sandwiched it by the cleansing of the Temple. In Mark Jesus first curses the tree, then he goes to the Temple, and then the disciples see the withered tree. Actually what Mark does helps to make sense of the whole episode.

Mark also notes that it was not the time for figs, which makes the cursing have less rationality. Matthew makes mention only of the leaves. In Matthew the tree withers as if by magic. Matthew ends the story by using the episode to stress the power of prayer.

The ministry of John returns to the scene when the chief priests and elders question the authority of Jesus. Authority is a right to influence thought, opinion, or behavior. Power is the ability to do so. The Greek has two different words. Here Matthew uses in both instances *eksousia*, which means "authority." Many translations use "authority" the first time and translate the word as "power" the second time. Clearly, the opponents want to know who gave Jesus the right to do what he does.

Jesus avoids answering the question by posing one of his own. Jesus puts the opponents on the defensive. If they say, "from God," Jesus can ask, why then did they not believe him? If "from men," then the religious leaders face opposition from those who acknowledge John as a prophet and some even as the Messiah. Since they refuse to answer, so Jesus refuses to answer.

Questions

246. Why do you not like the story of the fig tree?

247. Can Jesus allow frustration to become irrational anger?

248. If the right to do as he does comes from God, then why do people not believe him?

249. The way Jesus deals with opposition must have made them angry. Could he not have done things differently, just as he could have done things differently regarding the fig tree?

Conclusion

Mark makes the story of the fig tree worse with his comment, "it was not time for figs." Matthew has lessened the impact by referring only to the leaves, but both show an unusual Jesus. If this is a miracle it is the only one that occurs in or near Jerusalem. Most interpret the story as a parable that has become a metaphor. Both Mark and Matthew used it as an event to demonstrate the power of prayer. It still seems out of character.

The fig tree in Israel offers both shade and food. Together with the grapevine, they convey a sense of contentment, peace, and prosperity. In a desert area fig trees and grapevines also connote water. What more could a person want! Jeremiah in 8:13 mentions both the fig tree and the vine: "When I would gather them there are neither grapes on the vine nor figs on the fig tree." Clearly here the fig tree and the vine represent the people of Israel. They have no fruit and the leaders are responsible (Jer 8:4–12).

The cleansing of the Temple and the cursing of the fig tree both symbolically refer to the leadership of Israel, which has led the people into infidelity to God. Evidently Mark found the story and used it to stress the power of prayer. Both he and Matthew

168

see no problem with Jesus becoming frustrated and cursing the fig tree. Such actions do not contradict the divinity of Jesus, although Mark seems to make the action more irrational by commenting it was not the time of figs! Originally it probably referred to the failure of leadership and eventually the end of traditional Judaism with its priesthood and sacrifices, which was replaced with the synagogue. In the tradition it becomes an episode in which Jesus acts irrationally. The inclusion of the irrationality of Jesus in the gospels for some proves it happened!

Matthew presents five controversies with the opponents of Jesus in Jerusalem. If Jesus says he has his right from God, he blasphemes, which Jesus avoids by his own question. The Jewish leaders worked closely with the Romans to provide peace and security. Their activity revolved around the Temple which, following the lead of David, they could use to control the people by controlling religion. John's ministry did not include the Temple and posed a threat to their authority. John also posed a political threat since some saw his ministry as a means to overthrow the occupation. In either case, the chief priests and elders would not want to acknowledge that John's ministry came from heaven. They could hardly dismiss it, at least publicly, since the people considered John a prophet. Just as they were not open to receive the ministry of John from God, so their personal agendas prevented them from accepting the ministry of Jesus.

No doubt Jesus could have done things differently to avoid criticism. When faced with a lack of integrity on the part of religious leaders, he had no choice but to act. Actions follow beliefs. The actions of the religious leaders flowed from their values and beliefs. Jesus opposed those same values and beliefs and offered his own. He had no choice. What he did had to come from his beliefs and the opposition's came from their beliefs. A final confrontation would lie ahead.

Section Forty-one:
The Parables Return,
21:28—22:1–14

Introduction

Jesus taught in parables. Storytelling has long characterized good teachers since people find it easier to remember the stories than some abstract theory. Some of the parables of Jesus seem easy to understand while others involve more activity: "teasing the mind into active thought."

The parable of the two sons joins the section to the previous discussion on Jesus and John since both are God's sons. The reference to the vineyard joins this parable to the next parable. Certain manuscripts have a reversal on who does what but the meaning remains the same. One said, "Yes," and did nothing and the other said, "No," but repented. Sinning does not condemn a person. A refusal to repent, to rethink, condemns a person.

Again, the parable refers to the religious leaders. Jesus contrasts them with the tax collectors and prostitutes. The former are collaborators and usually cheaters; the latter are guilty of sexual promiscuity. Yet, these groups repented; they rethought how they were living and followed John and then Jesus.

Matthew continues with another parable involving a vineyard. Clearly this parable goes back to Isaiah 5:2, with the reference to the hedge to keep animals out, the wine press to make the wine, and the tower for both watching and providing a place for the workers to rest.

The master sends two groups of servants and the workers mistreat them. Thinking they will respect his son, the owner sends him and the workers kill him, reasoning that they will inherit the property if the master has no heirs. However irrational this

170

appears, the parable is not meant to make sense in every point. The comparison remains clear: Jesus is the Son. The master will avenge the death of his son by putting the workers to a miserable death and then give the vineyard to others.

Matthew quotes Psalm 118:22–23. Jesus, the rejected stone, has become the stone that keeps everything together. Since the chief priests and Pharisees know the parable applies to them, Matthew insinuates that they will lose their authority and the meaning of Israel will pass to another group. By the time this gospel was written the Temple was destroyed and the authority of the priests and scribes was lost.

Finally, Jesus tells the story of the wedding feast. This parable also refers to the chief priests and Pharisees. Matthew makes the parable a wedding feast instead of a great supper as found in Luke 14:15–24. Since the parable appears in Matthew and Luke and not in Mark, it comes from "Q."

The sending of the servants and the bad treatment they receive parallels the previous parable. The burning of the city may refer to the burning of Jerusalem in AD 70. Finally, the servants make every effort to invite guests by going beyond the city. They invite both the evil and good, much like the weeds and the wheat.

The king inspects the guests and finds a man without a wedding garment. This action might appear irrational since an uninvited guest could obviously not prepare for a wedding feast unless he had been given enough time. Some think that in such an occasion wedding garments are supplied. No doubt the garment had some symbolic significance. Since the person did not belong, he was cast out with the appropriate Matthean punishment. Many were invited but not all passed the scrutiny of the king.

Questions

250. Do you get tired of trying to figure out the meaning of the parables?

251. Have you ever been in the position of saying, "No," and then rethinking and saying, "Yes"?

252. The second parable has allegorical elements. Does this help or confuse the meaning?

253. Why the question of the wedding garment? What do you think it means?

254. Jesus in Matthew almost taunts the religious leaders. Why does Matthew do this with such vigor?

Conclusion

Parables are meant to be simple explanations. The context in which they are spoken, however, adds to their meaning. The controversies with the religious leaders grow stronger as Jesus approaches his death. The three parables are meant to pinpoint the problems that Jesus sees in how the Jewish religious leaders are functioning. They profess one thing and do another. They situate themselves above the sinners and tax collectors and in the meantime ignore the teachings of both John and Jesus. The sinners pay attention to what John and Jesus have said and change their way of living. They are all children of God, but the "black sheep" of the family respond with fidelity while those who are supposed to be models of fidelity refuse to listen.

Repentance does not mean a once-and-for-all decision. The word *repentance* both in English and in Greek means to change one's mind or rethink. Repentance means turning a page over in the book of life and starting to write again. Repentance is a frequent if not daily occurrence. Very often the most faithful followers of the Lord need to rethink and act differently. Sometimes saying "yes" is wrong and other times saying "no" is wrong. Just as belief needs to be reaffirmed often, so repentance needs to become part of the ordinary life of the followers of Jesus.

The parable of the vineyard expresses the harsh treatment the prophets received in history and the manner in which the religious leaders of Judaism reacted to Jesus. The allegorical elements seem evident: Israel is the vineyard, the owner is God, the workers are the religious leaders, the servants are the prophets, and Jesus is the son. Since Matthew composed the gospel after the destruction of the Temple and with all of the allegorical elements, in all probability the early church reworked what might have been a simpler parable from Jesus.

The parable deals with the leadership of Israel and not with Israel as a whole. In Isaiah the vineyard is destroyed, but in this parable the vineyard is not destroyed but instead given to others, which means to better leaders. In the past the better leaders have been interpreted as Christian leaders. Historically Christian leaders have often been as bad as the religious leaders of Judaism. The vineyard remains God's holy people, which surely maintains the covenantal relationship between God and the people of Israel as well as those faithful followers of Jesus. When the church added the allegorical elements the parable became more obscure. Some have also tried to apply the hedge and the wine press and the tower to an allegorical interpretation. This adds more confusion. The parable concerns the failure on the part of the religious leaders of Judaism in the time of Jesus. It applies to all religious leaders of all times.

The final of the three parables has two parts: the invitations and the casting out. The final verse sums up the parable: many are called but calling does not mean acceptance. Some have considered the parable composed of two parables but Matthew has joined them together for his own purpose. The end of the second part has characteristic Matthean components: the weeping and gnashing of teeth.

Extending invitations to all, both wise and foolish, formed part of the Old Testament wisdom tradition, especially in Proverbs 9. Wisdom calls out and encourages all people to learn from life. See what works and what does not work and act accordingly. God has planted an order in the universe and the wise person discovers the order and follows it. Wisdom offers helpful hints to live a good and happy and prosperous life. Unfortunately, some do not listen and instead follow the counsels of foolishness. They do not belong.

Matthew used the parable to explain the different reactions to Jesus and his teachings in Israel. All were invited but some, mainly the Jewish leaders, refused the invitation and even mistreated the messengers. Then others were invited—those who were considered the dregs of society, the sinners and the tax collectors. This might have included Gentiles as well in the understanding of the early church. But not all passed the scrutiny of the king.

The theory that the king would provide fitting garments does not explain the situation since then all would have suitable clothing. The problem seems to mirror the situation in the early church. Some in the church are unworthy for whatever reason. The expulsion of the unworthy guest would remind the church members of their calling and how they are to live up to that vocation. Repentance would help explain the expulsion. If a person does not frequently repent, then that person does not belong. God offers freely and the individual has responsibility to respond. If failure occurs, then repentance always remains an option. Refusal to repent brings exclusion.

In these three parables Matthew continually criticizes the Jewish religious leaders. He must explain to the Jewish Christians that Judaism did not fail but was fulfilled in Jesus and his teaching. The religious leaders failed. By rejecting Jesus they opened the door not only for all Jews, even sinners, but also for Gentiles to become followers. But even within the church, some people really do not belong. This could apply to leaders as well as to the members of the community. The warnings of Matthew apply today to the Christian church as they once applied to Judaism.

Section Forty-two: Four Questions: Taxes, the Resurrection, the Greatest Commandment, David's Son, 22:15–46

Introduction

Matthew has taken the following controversies from Mark with little or no change. He situates each question with a group or with Jesus himself: taxes (Pharisees); resurrection (Sadducees); greatest commandment (a scribe); and David's son (Jesus himself). Some think Matthew, following Mark, presents a rabbinic schema of questions: law, a mocking question, conduct, and finally an apparent contradiction in Scripture.

Matthew begins the first controversy by presenting the Pharisees in a bad light since they plot to entrap Jesus in speech. The presence of the Herodians, supporters of the dynasty begun by Herod the Great, adds weight to the controversy. They would have supported the tax since they depended on Rome for their position in Israel.

With guile they acknowledge that Jesus teaches the way of God in truth. They want to know if God would allow them to pay taxes to Rome. Jesus knows their malice, that their hearts are evil, and asks to see a coin.

Since the coin had the image of Caesar, the coin belonged to him. Jesus tells them to give it back. By adding "give to God what is God's," Jesus challenges his opponents to pay as much attention to what belongs to God as they do to what belongs to

Caesar. The amazement may have come from the ability of Jesus to avoid the trap and transfer the question to obligations to God.

The second controversy involves the Sadducees. Matthew begins by stating the belief of the Sadducees against resurrection. They quote Deuteronomy 25:5–10. The seven husbands add in their opinion to the absurdity of resurrection. The seven may also allude to Sarah, the daughter of Raguel, who outlived seven husbands (Tob 3:8; 6:14).

Jesus tells the Sadducees they understand neither the meaning of the Pentateuch (Torah) nor the meaning of the resurrection. Resurrected life differs from earthly life and so no easy comparison exists. In the Torah Moses taught that God maintains a relationship with the ancestors of Judaism and thus they must be alive; they have been resurrected. The Sadducees should know this if they know the Scriptures. Contrary to the religious leaders, the crowds, the ordinary people, were amazed.

Two groups down. Now a scribe or lawyer in Luke posed another question to test Jesus. Rabbis counted 613 commandments in the Torah. With so many, the question should quickly arise of which is the greatest. Does a hierarchy of commandments exist?

Jesus quoted Deuteronomy 6:5, which forms part of the *Shema Israel* (Hear, O Israel…) prayer recited by pious Jews several times a day, especially when entering or leaving the house. But then Jesus adds the second commandment to stand on an equal plane with the first: the love of neighbor. Here Jesus quotes from Leviticus 19:18 with "neighbor" meaning fellow Israelite. The reference to "hang" (better translation than "depend") connotes an image of a large mass depending on or hanging onto two ropes.

Finally, Jesus posed a question to the Pharisees. In Jewish tradition, the Messiah would be David's son. And thus the Pharisees respond. This gives Jesus an opportunity to force them to do some thinking based on Scripture. How then could David under divine inspiration call him "Lord"? Jesus quotes Psalm 110:1. "Lord" in Greek *(Kyrie)* was used for God. If David speaks in Psalm 110, then the Messiah is superior to David. The Messiah must be more than David's son but God's Son. With that remark they all fall silent.

Questions

255. Does the coin have anything to do with the separation of church and state?

256. What does the resurrection mean to you?

257. John has only one commandment. How many are there?

258. Jesus used the Scripture to confuse his opponents. Can this still be true today?

Conclusion

Roman taxes, like taxes today, gave an individual a right to enjoy the peace and prosperity of Rome. Members of the empire had to pay in Roman coinage and it amounted to a full day's pay for a laborer. At the time of Jesus the coin bore the image of Tiberius. Pharisees and Herodians who had to coexist with the Romans paid the tax. They all hated the tax and some nationalists opposed the tax and used it as a cause for rebellion.

The Pharisees want Jesus to make a public statement on the matter. If he opposes, he causes trouble for himself with the political leaders. If he accepts, he might lose face with many Jews. By pointing to the image on the coin, Jesus avoided the issue. If it has Caesar's image it belongs to him. Give it back.

Over the years many have used this text to as a basis for separation of church and state. It offers no such foundation. Church and state have two different forums to operate and at times they overlap. They should not be absolutely separated. Take care of what the state obliges and also do not forget what God obliges is about all that can be drawn from this controversy.

Josephus explains the background for the second controversy: "The Sadducees hold that the soul perishes with the body." They held that since the texts in the Jewish Scriptures that support the resurrection of the body are not from the Torah, they need not be accepted.

Pharisees accepted a belief in the resurrection that Jesus shared. By quoting from the Torah Jesus attacks the fundamental premise of the Sadducees' argument. Jesus can debate using Scripture with the best of his opponents and win.

Whatever the "resurrection of the dead" means, it implies some physical dimension. To be human means to have a physical body and so resurrection does not mean just that the soul lives on in eternity. A glorified body includes a body even if no one knows exactly what that entails. Some think a resurrected body includes a relationship to the whole physical universe. Whatever it means, it will be beyond our imagination, so says Paul in 1 Corinthians 15:42–58.

The next Scripture debate involves the greatest commandment. The Pharisees would have been pleased by the answer Jesus gave to the Sadducees, but now they must deal with how he answers them. By quoting both Deuteronomy and Leviticus Jesus sums up the Torah. How could anyone ever attempt to observe 613 commandments! There must be an easier understanding. In traditional Judaism teachers summed up the commandments much as Jesus did in this episode. And they believed in a hierarchy of commandments. Some were heavy and some were lighter. Jesus' love commandments not only summed up the Law but go to the root of the Law. He provides a coherent principle on which people could evaluate all the other commandments and know that they had fulfilled them.

All three Synoptics have this episode. The Gospel of John does not. The Fourth Gospel has only one commandment: "to love one another as I have loved you" (John 13:34). Loving the neighbor includes loving God. Refusing to love the neighbor means a refusal to love God (1 John 4:20).

Finally, the fourth controversy involves the proper interpretation of Psalm 110. "Son of David" does not limit the meaning of Messiah. The original context of this psalm involves the crowning and enthronement of the new king. In the ritual use of this psalm, God promises honor and protection to the new king of Israel. In this psalm God speaks to the new king, the Messiah, and thus the new king must be more than David's son. Matthew has already hinted that the lordship of God and the lordship of Jesus are the same. This claim would have offended pious Jews at the time of Jesus and also would have caused problems between the Matthean community, especially its Jewish Christian members, and other Jews. Even today, many Jews accept Jesus as a great teacher but not as the Messiah or as the divine Son of God.

Over the centuries people have always abused Scripture, making claims that the Bible never made. Taking verses out of context causes only problems. The Bible should be used to interpret the Bible. The New Testament will never be understood without knowing the Old Testament. The individual books of the Bible, especially the New Testament books for Christians, need each other for proper interpretation. The Bible appears to be filled with contradictions that can be resolved only by understanding the context of each book and the hierarchy of beliefs.

Section Forty-three:
The Pharisees, 23:1–39

Introduction

Matthew wants to settle the final score with the Pharisees. The controversy between Christians and Pharisees has reached a high point in the time of Matthew. He knows he must conclude the argument against them. Jesus hurls his final accusations against the Pharisees and then will not speak to them until he stands before the Sanhedrin (26:64). Matthew developed this final discourse to the Pharisees from his own experience and his community's dealings with them, together with material he has taken from Mark and "Q."

The speech has three divisions: verses 1–12 condemn the Pharisees for their hypocrisy and status seeking; verses 13–33 contain seven prophetic woes; and finally verses 34–39 recount the persecution of Christian messengers and a lament over the city of Jerusalem.

Jesus seems to be talking to his disciples, the Pharisees, and the Matthean community. Since Matthew begins with mention of the scribes and Pharisees and does not include the chief priests and elders, the actual time period may come more from that of Matthew than of Jesus. Matthew combines the time of the ministry of Jesus with his own historical situation.

The scribes and Pharisees ran the day-to-day operations of Judaism. The "seat of Moses" signifies the teaching and authority that the scribes and Pharisees claim. Jesus acknowledges this authority and then criticizes it. They do not practice what they preach. Their actions do not flow from the values of the Torah. They lay burdens too heavy to carry in their interpretation of the

180

Torah, especially with regard to the Sabbath. They allow no interpretation other than their own.

The Pharisees do all for show, including emphasizing the outward signs of piety. Certain passages from the Torah were written down, enclosed in little leather boxes, and strapped on the forehead and on the arms during prayer. Many Orthodox Jews continue the practice today. They also wore fringes or tassels on the corners of their outer garments that were originally meant to remind them of the Torah and God's presence. They liked to be seen in prominent places, seeking status, enjoying their position and how they looked. Titles, such as rabbi and teacher, added to the status.

Suddenly the audience seems to shift to the disciples alone. Jesus tells them to avoid such honors and titles. Matthew reserves "Father" for God alone and the disciples have one Master, Jesus. Self-exaltation means nothing.

Next follow the seven woes. Seven times Matthew accused the Pharisees of hypocrisy, living behind a mask, pretending to be something they were not. By refusing to accept Jesus and his teachings they excluded themselves and others from the kingdom. Some manuscripts have the woe concerning widows, which is usually seen as an interpolation from Mark 12:40 or Luke 20:47. Major manuscripts do not have this verse.

Jesus accused the Pharisees of missionary activity to make one convert and then the new proselyte becomes worse than they are with their hypocrisy. They are blind since they use the name of God as they think will fit their needs. Any true oath demands an appeal to God, and no effort to use casuistry to fit a personal desire can excuse the oath taker.

Tithing meant the giving of one-tenth to God through contributions to the Temple. The religious leaders increased the goods that needed to be tithed and thus received more income with the supposition that they used the tithing for their own benefit while they ignored the important aspects of the Torah—mercy, justice, and forgiveness.

A camel was an unclean animal. Jesus exaggerates to drive home a point. Those who claim to be most observant live just the opposite way. Interior purity means more than external observance of purity laws. Whitewashed tombs helped people to avoid impurity by contact with the dead. Jesus used the image to accuse the Pharisees of internal defilement while outwardly they had the appearance of piety.

The children of those who killed the prophets now wanted to express their piety by building monuments to the dead prophets. The Pharisees continue a line of those who rejected the teaching of God by rejecting the prophets sent by God.

Jesus used the image of serpents and vipers as John did in Matthew 3:7. What comes out of them is poison. The reference here to prophets may refer to Christian missionaries after the death of Jesus, which would also explain the reference to the crucifixion. Historically, Jews persecuted Christians following the claim by Christians that Jesus had been raised from the dead. The prime example is Paul, who traveled from city to city to persecute the church.

The reference to Zechariah may refer to Zechariah the prophet, Zechariah the son of Jehoiada in 2 Chronicles 24:20–22, or Zachariah son of Bareis mentioned in Josephus. Probably all three have been mixed together.

"This generation" refers not only to the generation at the time of Jesus but also to the generation at the time of Matthew. By then they had already experienced the destruction of the city of Jerusalem with the loss of the Temple.

Finally, Jesus laments over Jerusalem, the city he loved. Jerusalem symbolized the presence of God in Israel and now, as Matthew wrote, Jerusalem lay in ruins. The final verse looks forward to the second coming of Jesus in triumph, which will become a major topic in the following two chapters.

Questions

259. What was wrong with the Pharisees as religious leaders?
260. Was Jesus too harsh with the Pharisees?
261. What images that Jesus used did you find most harsh?
262. Could what Jesus said about the Pharisees apply to all religious leaders?

263. What problems do you see in today's religious leaders that mirror those present in this chapter?

264. What is your general impression of the Pharisees?

265. Do you think this chapter comes mainly from Jesus or from Matthew?

Conclusion

Moses wrote, according to tradition, five books. If Jesus is to be the new Moses in Matthew he also should have five sermons. Chapter 23 is clearly a sermon or a discourse, but since it does not end with the usual formula "when Jesus had finished..." commentators will ignore this as a sermon and see it as a polemic against the religious leaders of the time. It seems Matthew has enlarged the warning in Mark 12:38–40 against the Pharisees into a long diatribe. Probably the speech mirrors more what the Matthean community thought about the Pharisees and their dealing with them than what Jesus experienced.

The scribes in the time of Jesus involved themselves in governing affairs and the people considered them the intellectuals of Jerusalem and Judaism. They aligned themselves with the Pharisees, together with the other religious leaders, against Jesus and his followers. They relied on their knowledge of Scripture and their ability to use Scripture in arguments.

Pharisees believed in free will, the resurrection of the body, and rewards and punishments after death. They knew the Torah and relied on oral traditions and teachings of the rabbis. The word *Pharisees* implies the "separated ones." As a religious movement they centered on ritual purity, the observance of the Sabbath, and tithing. They also had political influence.

Matthew, unlike Josephus, presents the Pharisees in a negative light, probably more negative than the experience of Jesus himself. Matthew contrasted them with what he thought should be Christian leadership. They become the foil, the straw man, to be taken down by their failed efforts to lead properly.

They failed in leadership by desiring titles, honor, and privilege while imposing impossible burdens. For Christians all are equal with one Father in heaven and one Master, Jesus. Christians serve each other. Christians had begun a new, nontraditional community based on equality of disciples. Matthew attacked the Jewish leaders to add legitimacy to his own community, especially among the Jewish Christians.

While Matthew criticized Jewish leaders, his own community, with its emphasis on rules and authority and especially on Peter and the Twelve, contributed to a lack of egalitarian sense of community that followed in later centuries. Titles multiplied from an anthropological need for distinction and clear lines of authority, to ensure the community lasted. Matthew preached an equality and actually contributed to a developed hierarchy.

Matthew has seven woes while Luke has four woes against the Pharisees and three against lawyers. Matthew joins them all together and applies them to all Jewish religious leaders. The woes rest on hypocrisy—the failure to live with actions following values and beliefs. Appearance should reflect reality; leaders should walk the walk and talk the talk and no separation should exist between what they believe, who they are, and how they live.

The woes also reflect the conflict between early Christianity and the rabbinic movement after the destruction of the Temple. The Pharisees hinder the spread of the gospel; they raise up enemies against it by their proselytizing; they engage in useless casuistry; they have misplaced priorities, pay attention only to the externals, and join the long list of those who opposed those who speak in the name of God. Throughout the gospel Matthew has built up his opposition to religious leaders and it now reaches a climax in this chapter.

The chapter should serve as a critique of all religious leaders. The excesses denounced here remain in every religious tradition. The critique against the Pharisees historically could also be made against Christian leaders or against any religious leaders. The temptation to pay attention only to externals, to live behind masks, to fail to act according to proper values and beliefs, has plagued religion for all recorded history.

In the past some have used this chapter to characterize Judaism instead of seeing it in context. Matthew deals with his period primarily. He also wants to warn Christian leaders not to fall into the same trap. He does not denounce Judaism, just as he would not denounce all of Christianity because of failures in Christian leaders.

The Pharisees insisted on rewards and punishments after death. Matthew concludes with a threat they will be punished for what they do and what they fail to do. He accused them of persecuting Christian missionaries. The members of the Matthean community would have understood the reference to Zechariah as the one murdered in the Temple area by two Zealots and the destruction of the city to the fall of Jerusalem in AD 70.

This generation will be punished for what they do both to Jesus and to his followers. Their fathers did the same to the prophets. Matthew here functions as a Jewish prophet speaking in the words of Jesus to the people of Israel and especially its leaders. They have failed and they will be punished as they have already seen their house destroyed in the burring of the Temple and the destruction of the city of Jerusalem.

The Pharisees failed because they lived a life centered on themselves and their privileged position. They forgot that leadership, especially in religion, means service. They settled for externals and forgot that the externals are supposed to mirror the internal. Like all religious leaders they experienced the temptation to pleasure, honor, and glory and the failure to accept the consequences of their actions. And they succumbed. Matthew had started the ministry of Jesus with these same temptations. Jesus conquered them, while in the eyes of Matthew the religious leaders of Judaism failed. This chapter stands as a warning to all Christian leaders today as well as in the time of Matthew.

Section Forty-four:
The Final Sermon: The
Temple and the Signs,
24:1–14

Introduction

Jesus directs the final sermon to his disciples and to future faith
communities. Because it speaks of the future coming, the end of
the world, and the time approaching the end, many refer to this
final discourse as the "eschatological sermon" or the "apocalyptic sermon." Each of the Synoptic Gospels has a similar discourse
by Jesus, and each has its own variations. Matthew has joined
together some material from Mark and from "Q" as well as his
own traditions to create an extensive sermon covering two chapters. He writes chronologically, from the birth pangs of the end
to the final judgment. Eventually he exhorts the community to be
watchful and vigilant.

Jesus left the Temple area. He had arrived there in 21:23 and
it seems all of the verbal controversies took place within the
Temple area. In verse 3 Matthew has Jesus sitting on the Mount
of Olives. As Jesus left the Temple area and approached the
Mount of Olives he and his disciples could have looked back
across the valley to see the Temple with all of its buildings glow-
ing in the sunlight. Even today the view of the city of Jerusalem

is magnificent from the Mount of Olives, especially when the sun bounces off the buildings, making them glow with a pinkish light. And in the middle of the Temple mount, the gold of the Dome of the Rock adds to the wonder today. In the days of the Temple of Herod Jesus and his followers would have sat in amazement at the beauty of the buildings across from them. Jesus then tells them of the coming destruction of the Temple of Herod. Since Matthew wrote after the destruction of the Temple the words of Jesus could have been a prophetic warning or comments by Matthew after the event.

The comments by Jesus prompt the disciples to ask when and what would be the sign of the coming of Jesus, the messianic age, and the end of the world. Jesus then gives some general signs that precede the coming of the messianic age. The terrors and wars and famines and earthquakes will announce the beginning of the birth pangs. Matthew added the persecution by the nations. Certainly the Matthean community experienced such suffering from both Jews and Gentiles. People within the community will betray each other. Families will find themselves separated and divided. And many deceivers will arise both from within and from without the community. People will lose love. Some will endure to the end and some will not. The good news, the victory of God over evil, sin, and death, will be proclaimed in all the world and then it will be over. This final sermon of Jesus does not sound very happy or like it is about good news of victory over sin and evil and death!

Questions

266. What does eschatological mean to you?

267. Does Jesus respond to the disciples' questions?

268. The signs that Jesus spoke of have been present in every age. Is this age more eschatological and apocalyptic than previous times?

269. False prophets exist in the church and outside the church. How is this true today?

270. Does persecution exist today for Christianity?

Conclusion

The word *eschatology* comes from the Greek word *eschaton*, meaning "last thing." Eschatology concerns the future and since the ultimate future for the human race is "God" the future must be good. The present is filled with evil because people regularly destroy the good. Jesus preached and brought the good of the future into the present. The conquest of evil and sin began with him and the victory over death occurred in his resurrection. In Christian theology eschatology studied the four last things: death, judgment, heaven, and hell. These ideas are all found in this sermon by Jesus.

Apocalyptic means that things will get worse before they get better. It connotes a catastrophic in-breaking of the divine into human history with pain and sorrow abounding. Apocalyptic literature arose at a time when people needed hope in facing problems. Eschatological is more positive and apocalyptic is more negative. Often the two ideas go together but they should be distinguished.

Jesus gives some general answers that can apply to every age. For two thousand years false prophets have arisen to tell Christians exactly when Jesus is returning, only to realize that Jesus has not returned. No one knows. Some previous ages were clearly apocalyptic (e.g., the Black Death), but Jesus did not return. Many think today is an apocalyptic age, especially with the rise of religious fundamentalism and terrorism. Join this to natural disasters, the spread of war, the exploitation of the weak, and the general decline in religious observance, and many are convinced this century will be an apocalyptic century.

False prophets have existed within and without the church in every age. "By their fruits you will know them." Pay attention to what they say and how they live. The messianic age may begin tomorrow or in a thousand years. In the meantime be careful of false prophets who pretend to be what they are not.

Matthew includes in this beginning of the sermon references to internal community problems. Enough evidence exists in non-biblical Christian literature to testify to dissension within the communities that involved betrayal of church members, including church leaders. Things in early Christianity were as bad as or worse than today and yet Jesus did not return.

Matthew joined the apocalyptic to the eschatological. The coming of the Messiah will bring the triumph of goodness but it also will witness much pain and sorrow. Believers should have patience and endure to the end and have hope in the good news and in final victory.

Section Forty-five:
The Coming of the Son of Man, 24:15–31

Introduction

Few people understand this passage and fewer yet find it helpful. From the desolating abomination, to the flight to the mountains, to the suffering greater than anything previous or anything to come, to the shortening of the days for the elect, most people are left without a clue as to its meaning. And then Matthew says, "Let the reader understand"!

This section of Matthew comes from a writing circulated among Christians in Israel during the Jewish War. The time of Matthew, however, is at least a decade after the destruction of Jerusalem with its Temple and Jesus did not return. Matthew may be recalling past events but also may be including some material so that it can apply to future events, especially with the approach of the end of human history whenever that occurs. Matthew recognizes a darkening of world history, with Christians bearing heavy burdens through persecution. Hope can give them the ability to bear with the temptations and the failures as they await the coming of the Lord.

In 167 BC Antiochus IV Epiphanes erected something in the Temple of Jerusalem, perhaps a statue or an altar to a pagan god. Matthew takes this image from Daniel and then seems to imply an anti-Christ type or perhaps it was something that happened during the Jewish War. Since the writer urges people to flee, it must have been a specific event but as yet no one can be sure precisely to what he refers.

The way the flight is portrayed presupposes a Palestinian situation. "Not on the Sabbath" may refer to a Sabbath's day journey since the strict observance of the Sabbath when in danger no longer applied since the time of the Maccabees. The suffering seems to transcend any historical scale and thus may refer to the final turmoil and suffering preceding the end of human history. No doubt this is apocalyptic. The shortening for the elect offers some consolation.

False messiahs pepper Jewish history just as false prophets have arisen in every Christian age. The same previous warning continues with the thought in the background that the criterion needed to identify the true prophets should be remembered: "by their fruits you will know them." Since Jewish Christians accepted Jesus as the true Messiah they are helped in their ability to avoid false messiahs.

The coming of the Son of Man will be a public event. No hidden appearance will characterize the second coming. People will be surprised but will not mistake the event. In Greek culture vultures were considered part of the eagle family and so perhaps a better translation of the Hebrew word *neser* would be vulture. It makes more sense.

The cosmic signs of the coming of the Son of Man add to the apocalyptic tone of the passage, but should not be interpreted as the destruction of the world. The images come from Isaiah 13:10 and 34:4. Together they orchestrate a final and divine judgment over all creation. Since the ancient cosmology has God living above the sky, then the judgment will begin from the heavens and all will be shaken.

The sign of the Son of Man may be interpreted as a banner or a flag around which all the elect will gather. The image of the Son of Man coming in glory comes from Daniel 7:13 but here in Matthew it refers to the coming of Jesus. Angels take care of the gathering of the chosen.

Questions

271. Does the apocalyptic mean anything to you?
272. Do you think we live in an apocalyptic age?
273. When you read that Matthew combined events from his

own period with events of the time of Jesus does this cause you concern?

274. Should anyone take the events so described literally?

275. What does this passage mean to you personally?

276. Do you prefer the eschatological to the apocalyptic?

Conclusion

Most of the images in this passage come from the Old Testament, especially the Book of Daniel, and are gathered together to form a piece of apocalyptic literature. The Book of Daniel was written during a period when Judaism was under attack both culturally and politically. Apocalyptic literature was written to encourage hope in the midst of what seemed like a hopeless situation. Telling people that everything will be back to normal soon does not help when normalcy does not come. Telling people that the problems will be around for a long time and they should trust in God's providence can offer hope in the midst of human despair.

The eschatological does not carry the same sense of gloom. Some writers will use eschatological almost synonymous with apocalyptic but this muddles the meaning. Eschatological helps Christians to believe in the "already presence of God's grace" while the fullness awaits the future. People tend to destroy what is good but God does not. The apocalyptic comes from a particular period of great suffering and pain and problems from within as well as from without. Whether the time of international terrorism and moral decay within society and even religions constitutes an apocalyptic age remains to be seen. Certainly in such an age hope supports efforts of Christians to remain faithful to who they are and what they are called to be.

The abomination may have been a sacred stone placed on top of the altar in the Temple in Jerusalem. It happened during the time of the Book of Daniel. In the time of Matthew the abomination may also have brought to mind the attempt of Caligula to have a statue of himself erected in the Temple around AD 40. For Matthew the event is still in the future but also may have referred to the actual destruction of the Temple in AD 70. The suffering calls to mind the same ideas in Daniel 12:1–3.

Many books in the Bible combine historical periods. Looking back from a perspective of a generation can help individuals to recognize the meaning of events in a previous generation. Each of the gospels combined events from the ministry of Jesus with the life of the early church. The gospels are not biographies but books of faith that combine theology with history to bring out meaning. Matthew brought some episodes from the life of Jesus into his own period to help his listeners and members of his community to understand how they were to live as people of faith.

Over the centuries readers of the Bible have not paid sufficient attention to the meaning of apocalyptic texts and have interpreted them literally. Understanding symbols and images of the past, especially from more than two thousand years ago, can cause confusion to people today. This section of Matthew looks forward with hope to the coming of the Son of Man. For the elect of God such a coming will bring not tribulation but celebration. In the meantime life itself brings its pain and sorrow. The actual situation of persecution taking place during the time of Matthew contributes to the apocalyptic. Christians should focus on the eschatological, the future of the human race, which is God alone. That will sustain them in the midst of any pain. Forgetting the images used, the apocalyptic offers hope in a final victory of God and God's goodness in the midst of all evil.

Section Forty-six:
More Parables:
Watchfulness, Maidens,
and Talents, 24:32—25:30

Introduction

No doubt Matthew likes to use parables. Early Christians wanted to know exactly when Jesus would return. Many Christians today would like to know the same. Instead of giving clear answers, Matthew resorts to stories about watchfulness and readiness, for no one really knows. The fig tree tells of the passing of seasons. People can learn if they look. The events previously described offer some hint as to when Jesus will come, but Matthew offers no exact time. Probably in the early church people believed that Jesus would return quickly and thus Matthew adds to the tradition by his telling of the meaning of Jesus and his return. That Matthew personally does not subscribe to an exact return becomes evident in verse 36.

Before the second coming all must first be fulfilled. Everything ordained by God must be accomplished. Then the Son of Man can come. By the time of Matthew and with the death of many of the early followers, people probably began to project the coming into the distant future while holding on to the tradition that soon Jesus would return. They recognized the delay and hoped for the imminent coming of the Lord.

The reference to Noah points to the suddenness. The flood happened when no one expected it. The same will be true for the coming of the Son of Man. The reference to two men and two women connotes the idea that people may look like they are the same but one of the two belongs to the elect and the other does

195

not. The true Christian watches with vigilance. The reference to the thief adds to the sense of vigilance and watchfulness and preparation.

The brief parable of the servants offers two types of servant: one acts reliably with prudence; the evil one acts in the opposite manner. With the delay of the second coming the evil servant abuses his fellow servants. Does this refer to internal church problems in Matthew? Does it refer to the persecution from the Jewish community? The parable ends with a warning, against hypocrites, a favorite word used by Matthew to refer to religious leaders, similar to the warning in chapter 23. The usual Matthean punishment of weeping and gnashing of teeth will follow.

The setting of the parable of the maidens (Matthew used the Greek word *parthenos*, which means virgin, the same word used for Mary in Matt 1:23) imagines the return of the groom from the house of the bride's father to take her into his own house. The maidens would welcome the bride and groom and the celebration would begin.

It seems they carried some kind of oil lamps, with some thinking ahead in case of delay and bringing extra oil. Many times negotiations took longer than expected, which would account for the delay in the return of the groom with his wife and party members. The maidens also would have welcomed the couple a distance from the house, which would necessitate the full supply of oil to make a lighted procession to the new house. The dilemma comes from not enough oil for both groups to form the lighted procession. Refusing to share the oil does not denigrate efforts to be charitable. Being charitable would make the matter worse for all, since no one would be able to greet the groom and his party with the lighted lamps.

Then the parable changes, with the foolish maidens left outside and refused entry. Such would not be the usual result but for the meaning of the parable, exclusion is necessary because of a failure to be prepared and vigilant. Both the wise maidens and the groom reject the foolish maidens. They failed to think ahead and provide for the unexpected and thus met with exclusion.

A talent meant a lot of money—something similar to the expression "a gazillion dollars" today. Each was given according to his ability. (Today the word *talent* has come into English from this parable meaning the ability to accomplish something.) The first two invested and the third buried his talent. Burying money in those times was equivalent to using the mattress as a bank. The delay in the coming of the master continues the theme of the earlier parables.

When the master arrives he rewards those who used their talents, accepting their responsibility. The servant who buried the money remarks that his master is a hard man and because of fear he buried the money. The master expected interest and got nothing. Responsible activity brings its reward. Or here, it seems the rich get richer and the poor get poorer but the poor deserve to be poor because of their actions. Matthew returns to his theme of accepting responsibility for one's actions as seen in the second temptation of Jesus by Satan. The parable ends with the usual Matthean weeping and gnashing of teeth.

Questions

277. Do these parables make too much of a simple truth?

278. How can the parable of the two servants be applied to the contemporary church?

279. Should the wise virgins have shared their oil?

280. Is the punishment of the foolish virgins too much? Does it fit the crime?

281. Does the punishment of the servant who buried his talent fit the crime?

282. Why is accepting responsibility for one's actions so difficult?

Conclusion

Matthew offers five little vignettes: the fig tree, Noah, the two men, the two women, and the thief. All have to do with preparedness and vigilance. Since no one knows when time will end, all should be watchful. Actually, it seems as if Matthew has just expanded Mark 13:33–37, with the ever-occurring theme of watchfulness. In ancient Judaism calculating the exact time of the messianic kingdom began in the time of the Book of Daniel. When the kingdom did not come and two hundred years passed, skepticism set in within Judaism. The same would have happened within Christianity for those who expected Jesus to return within their lifetime.

This passage, especially the parable of the servant who mistreated his fellow servants, may also refer to problems within early Christianity. This could have been true for Jewish Christians mistreating Gentile Christians, or vice versa, or it could be applied to the leadership. The context may also be the problems between Christianity and Judaism. The Jews would have ridiculed the Christians, who claimed that Jesus would return, and he had not. This would have fit in well with the mocking of Christians by Jews. Matthew responded by saying that no one knows when but Jesus will come! This same attitude has influenced Christian theology since the time of Matthew. Christians should act as if Jesus were coming tomorrow. Actions follow beliefs.

The parable of the maidens contrasts two groups just as the previous parable contrasted the good servant and the evil servant. But here not so much evil but foolishness divides. Over the centuries many have offered an allegorical interpretation of this parable. Jesus is the bridegroom; the delay refers to the second coming; the maidens refer to the church filled with wheat and weeds or the maidens refer to Christians and Jews and the exclusion is the final judgment. Some allegorical elements may be present, but the comparison between Christians and Jews finds no foundation in the text. It better fits the church. The moral of the story may be twofold: watch and be ready, and know that some who are in the party do not really belong.

The bridegroom in the Old Testament was God and the people of Israel was the bride. Here Jesus seems to take the position of God. Matthew adds another brick in his building up the theology of Jesus as divine. The situation within the community of Matthew first may apply to the Jewish opponents who have no interest in Jesus or in his return. In spite of the efforts of Matthew to root Jesus and his teaching in Judaism, the opponents will reject everything Matthew has tried to accomplish in his writing. They are the foolish ones and will learn that they do not belong when Jesus does return.

Also, within the Matthean community petty partisanship divided the group. Some because of their treatment of others do not belong and the time will come when they will be excluded. They are the evil servants who will get their just reward in the future.

Finally, the parable of the talents deals with living responsibly. How a person acts will affect the final outcome of the judgment of God. This parable leads into the final judgment scene. The master wanted evidence from the servants with regard to their living responsibly and if they were capable of more responsibility. Reward would come if the person lived properly and proved that he or she could assume more responsibility.

Perhaps Matthew again referred to the Jewish community after AD 70, which tried to preserve the old traditions and failed to see the fulfillment in Jesus. Christians were supposed to take the traditions of Judaism and bring them to fulfillment in Jesus. The first two servants would have been Jewish Christian missionaries and the third servant was Judaism after AD 70. At least some Christians thought of Judaism after the destruction of the Temple in this manner. Like the householder of Matthew 13:52 the Christians took from the storeroom the old as well as the new.

But perhaps this reads too much into the parable. It may refer to a constant theme in Matthew of accepting the consequences of one's actions, including a final judgment when history has passed. Sometimes simple parables can become too complicated.

The punishment of the foolish maidens and the servant who buried his talent seems too much. Why should a little foolishness and fear exclude someone from the kingdom of God? Where is God's mercy and forgiveness? In both instances living for the present only never suffices. Eschatology brings the future into the present and this should affect how a person lives. Then how a person lives now will influence the final outcome, which completes and fulfills the value judgments and actions that have been present in life. God does not decree the judgment but individuals create their own judgment by how they live. Living with no sight of the end, failing to allow the end to influence present activity, will bring its own punishment. The foolish maidens blamed the wise ones because they would not give them some share in the oil. The servant who buried his talent blamed the master because he was a hard man and created fear. None would accept the consequences of their own actions.

Section Forty-seven: The Judgment, 25:31–46

Introduction

Matthew writes dramatically. His eschatological sermon reaches one climax with the coming of the Son of Man and then comes the final climax: the judgment. The Son of Man comes in glory with the angels and now the judgment of the nations takes place. The first two verses set the scene and then the king proclaims judgment. The reward of the righteous is described in verses 34–40 and the punishment of the guilty takes place in verses 41–46. The king deals first with the righteous and then with the condemned.

The whole section seems carefully constructed: the sentence, the grounds for the sentence, and the clarification with the overruling of the objection. Matthew writes rhetorically, pulling in the reader and surprising all with the single criterion: the treatment of the "least." Then the judgment is over.

God or the angels or the Son of Man gather the nations. Some think the nations include Israel but in other instances in Matthew *panta ta ethne* (all the nations) means the Gentiles. The primary scene involves Gentiles. In the history of Israel separate judgments for Jews and Gentiles were part of the tradition.

Mixed flocks existed in Israel. The goats needed more warmth than the sheep and so were separated at night and brought inside. The sheep preferred the outdoors, but they were more valuable and needed more protection. The image fits the story. Goats also have horns, which add to the bad image.

Jesus assumes his role as king, a function hinted at from the infancy narrative of Matthew by the Magi. During his passion, ironically Jesus will also be called king. As Son of Man Jesus judges and then those found worthy enter into the joy of the kingdom of God.

The righteous have shown hospitality to those in need. Jesus identifies with his brethren and the least of them. This seems to mean the Christians and so nations will be judged on how they treat Christians. Although earlier in the gospel nations did not include Israel, nothing forces the interpretation to exclude Israel in the final judgment. How people treat Christians forms the criteria for judgment for reward or punishment for both Jews and Gentiles. Of course, the same is true for how Christians treat each other or how people treat each other. The everlasting fire creates an image of punishment and belongs to the age to come.

Each receives according to his or her deeds. Actions follow values and beliefs, and rewards or punishments follow the deeds. The deeds are deeds of love either done or omitted. It seems the judgment involved individuals as well as nations. The enumeration of deeds of love is illustrative and not exhaustive. Similar deeds are mentioned in the Egyptian Book of the Dead and also in Judaism and in nonbiblical literature.

In the mind of the evangelist all nations, including Israel and members of the church, stand in judgment. Christians and non-Christians face the same judge with the same criterion for evaluation of admittance into the kingdom of God. The judgment stands as a warning for those who believe in Jesus and a hope for those who do not even know Jesus. It all comes down to how people treat each other.

Questions

283. Matthew likes law and yet he says the only criterion for salvation is how people treat each other. What do you think of this?

284. Does this criterion apply to all people, even of different faiths?

285. Why is this a warning to Christians?

286. Is Matthew a conservative or a liberal?

287. What are your thoughts on judgment (individual and general)?

288. Does everlasting punishment make sense for a merciful God?

Conclusion

Over the centuries scholars have debated the literary form of this section of Matthew and from whence it came. It has some elements of a story or a parable but also elements of a prophecy. Matthew alone contains this section, so no comparisons with other gospels can be made. The scene involves a final judgment event for all the nations. Some receive reward and some receive punishment.

Three parables about being prepared for the coming of the Son of Man precede this judgment scene and set the context. If the parables come from Jesus, the audience would have been Jews; if from Matthew, the audience would have been Christians, both Jewish and Gentile, as well as other Jews. Somehow all are involved.

If "nations" refer only to Gentiles, then Matthew offers a criterion by which non-Christians will be judged: how they treat Christians. The criterion involves works of mercy and kindness and compassion. Many may want to see the judgment apply first to Christians, but Matthew makes a case first for the judgment of Gentiles as well as Jews: how did they treat the brethren of Jesus? "Whoever receives you receives me and whoever receives me receives him who sent me" (Matt 10:40) and "as you did it to one of the least of these my brethren, you did it to me" (Matt 25:40). Certainly, if this is valid for Gentiles it must also be valid for Christians. How do Christians treat each other?

Throughout this gospel Matthew has dwelled on the Law, on the Torah. Jesus preaches that observance of the Law always remains primary. Yet, in this final judgment scene Matthew offers only the criterion of taking care of the least. He seems to reject all that preceded in favor of this. He wants continuity with the past but also sums up the Law by how people treat each other.

This Jesus had already done in the twofold commandment of love of God and love of neighbor.

Augustine once observed: "Love and do what you want." It seems Matthew says the same thing. Conservatives seem to like law and order. Liberals often are more spontaneous and ignore law when it conflicts with what they think are higher values. Matthew has already ignored the Law in the story of Joseph and Mary when Joseph discovers Mary is pregnant. Evidently in the final judgment the highest value is not law but how people treat each other.

In an age when people debate just who can be saved and what other religions offer to their adherents and how Jesus as the one Savior fits into this picture, Matthew has something to say. At this present period in history perhaps one-quarter of the world's population is Christian, 17 percent of them Catholics. How do people enter the kingdom? Evidently for Matthew it depends first on how others treat Christians and then how they treat each other.

In Catholic theology the final judgment has been depicted in literature by Dante and in art by Michelangelo and countless others. Most use Matthew as a model. Devils and hell, fire and torture are all depicted in a frightening manner. Actually, the Bible speaks of damnation as eternal darkness as well as fire. Clearly, damnation cannot be both. Pope John Paul II once remarked that the images of hell fire are just that: images. They represent an attempt to portray the meaning and effects of damnation. Never having loved and never having been loved is a good description of damnation. Surely that is damnation on earth. No one will deny. Will the same be true for eternity?

Do people judge themselves and then God ratifies human decisions? That seems to be the opinion of the Gospel of John. Matthew would agree since he teaches that actions follow values. If people believe and value only themselves, then they will die only with themselves. Judgment has begun by how people live.

Many of the early fathers of the church debated whether any sin a human being could commit could possibly be greater than the love and mercy of God and thus believed in universal salvation. Even in Catholic theology traditionally the church has taught the possibility of eternal damnation but no one has to believe that anyone is damned. Much speculation has centered on eternal damnation and eternal salvation. If God is the future of the human race, then eternal salvation is the future of the human race. How an individual experiences this salvation will depend on the individual and on the merciful judgment of God.

The text probably comes from Matthew, perhaps originally from Hellenistic Jewish circles with which Matthew had some relationship. The basic teachings go back to Jesus but they have been adapted after the Easter experience and the experience of some two or three generations of Christians living the gospel. The early church has taken the demands of Jesus as already seen in the Sermon on the Mount and presented them in a final and dramatic manner. The actual judgment scene should not be interpreted as a real event to come. After death, no one wants to wait around for a final judgment scene before experiencing the fullness of God's saving presence. But the words of Jesus that proclaim the criterion for eternal salvation remain forever. Both individuals and the human race must wait for the final outcome.

THE PASSION AND DEATH, 26:1—27:66

Section Forty-eight: The Plot, 26:1–16

Introduction

For the last time Matthew concludes a sermon with the words "And when Jesus finished..." Now he turns to the passion and death of Jesus. The evangelist follows the general outline and content of Mark and adds some material unique to his own sources, including the death of Judas, the wife of Pilate, and the guards at the tomb. Continuing his interest in the Old Testament Matthew attempts to show the fulfillment of Old Testament writings in the actual events of the passion of Jesus. He also will add to his Christology by stressing Jesus as the Messiah and the Son of God. The time of Passover has arrived and Jesus informs his disciples of his impending passion. Jesus knows what will happen and accepts it as coming from the will of God. The end has begun.

Unlike during the ministry of Jesus, when the adversaries were the scribes and Pharisees, during the passion the chief priests and elders become the main antagonists. They direct the events that will lead to his death. After the death of Jesus, the Pharisees join the chief priests in setting the guard at the tomb. The chief priests and elders assemble in the courtyard, which may not necessarily mean an external courtyard. Wherever it was, it afforded a meeting place to plot.

Caiphas was the high priest from AD 18 to 36. He succeeded his father-in-law Annas. Both seem to have had a role in the passion and death of Jesus. They did not want to arrest Jesus during the feast but since they did (Matthew follows Mark's account) either they wanted to arrest Jesus before the feast began or wait until after and do it privately outside public scrutiny. Judas made it possible to arrest Jesus quietly before the feast.

Jesus was in Bethany, his home base while in Jerusalem. There the woman anoints his head, which some see as a reference to a regal anointing. Whatever the possible interpretations and motivation, the woman evidently wants to show love and respect to Jesus. Matthew, unlike Mark, does not describe the oil or write of its cost.

In Matthew the disciples become indignant. In other gospels it was Judas (John) or the Pharisees (Luke). Matthew may have made it disciples to teach a lesson to his own community about wealth. Jesus supports the woman. He does not oppose almsgiving but this anointing Jesus accepts as burial preparation. The timing makes it right. As a result, when the good news is preached about Jesus she will be remembered. Matthew does not name the woman; the Gospel of John calls her Mary of Bethany. Some have identified her as Mary Magdalene. In Matthew she remains anonymous, which seems better.

Judas, one of Jesus' disciples, betrayed him. Since this appears in all of the gospels and the early church hardly would have made it up, the great sadness is that one of those closest to Jesus betrayed him. Judas goes to the religious leaders and asks for money. Matthew alone gives the exact amount: thirty pieces of silver, the price of a slave in Exodus 21:32. With a promise from the chief priests to satiate his greed, Judas seeks an opportune time.

Questions

289. The religious leaders decide to kill Jesus. Are they alone responsible?

290. Jesus is anointed. Does it matter that no one knows the woman's name?

291. There is a time for everything, a time to give alms and a time to anoint. Does this make sense?

292. Betrayal happens in every family and in every group. Was Judas completely evil?

293. Why is greed so pernicious?

Conclusion

Matthew sets the scene for the passion and death at the time of Passover. Jesus controls the events even as characters enter the scene. The Jewish leaders plot, the woman anoints for death, and Judas betrays. The Passover celebrates the liberation of Israel from Egypt. Passover celebrates joyously freedom and God's goodness and glory. Anointing on the head can mean an acknowledgment of luxury in life, a consecration, divine approval, or a preparation for death. The woman contrasts with the Jewish leaders who plot to kill during a feast and Judas who plots to betray. The woman honors Jesus. The woman seems to waste money according to the disciples and Judas wants money. The leaders want to get rid of Jesus but do not want to disturb Roman authorities, who often expect problems during the feast of Passover. Jesus faces opposition from the Jewish leaders, from his own disciples who object to the anointing, and from Judas who seeks to betray him for money. The only positive character in the episode other than Jesus is the unknown woman!

The religious authorities seek to destroy Jesus because he gives people too much freedom in interpreting the Law. He has assumed some divine prerogatives and might cause political problems, but above all Jesus undermines religious authorities. Jesus dies because people destroy what is good. Some Jews, especially some religious leaders, were responsible for the death of Jesus, as were some Romans, but ultimately all are responsible for the death of Jesus since all destroy what is good.

So often in life good people do good things and remain anonymous. The deed outshines the doer. Whoever the woman was, she performed a good deed. And in the judgment of God, she will be rewarded. In the meantime, all who read the Gospel of

Matthew remember that when men plotted against and betrayed Jesus, a woman loved him and honored him.

Jesus makes clear extravagances are good at the right time. People need celebrations and opportunities to go beyond the ordinary, mundane aspects of life. People can both enjoy the good things of life and help the poor. Timing is everything.

Judas was one of the Twelve. He followed Jesus and no doubt Jesus loved him and Judas loved Jesus. What happened? If Judas was a Zealot, maybe he wanted Jesus to start a revolution to overthrow the Roman occupation. The arrest would force Jesus and his followers to act. But such was not the plan of Jesus and it did not work. Judas could not have been totally evil. He was a follower of Jesus. Someone had to betray Jesus and, unfortunately for Judas, he filled the need. His plan went too far and he along with Jesus suffered.

Whatever the true motivation of Judas, Matthew says it was greed. Who knows? Perhaps it was power. Greed often causes the greater challenge in life and in following Jesus. People want more and more money and want to protect what they have. They have little energy for anything else. Greed, once entering the human psyche and spirit, controls time and energy and envelops and consumes everything else. Generosity alone cures greed.

Section Forty-nine:
The Passover and Last
Supper, 26:17–35

Introduction

The Feast of Unleavened Bread, a spring feast, at the time of
Jesus was joined to the Passover commemorating the Exodus
from Egypt. In the evening the family celebration began. His disciples had become his family and so Jesus celebrated with them.
Jesus as the one who presided asked his disciples to do the prepa-
rations. Jesus will be in charge during the whole passion and
death. Judas and the Jewish authorities seek an opportune time
and Jesus acknowledges his time is near. The disciples do as
instructed and they gather to keep the Passover as a family. They
recline at dinner following the Greek custom adopted by the Jews
for special feasts.

Jesus begins by informing the Twelve that one of them will betray
him. They address him as "Lord," now clearly a christological title.
Jesus does not give the name of the betrayer but instead remarks
that one who shared a meal and shared the Passover will rise up
against him. Betrayal by one so close is the worst kind. But all falls
under the divine plan.

Unlike the other disciples, Judas calls Jesus "rabbi," teacher.
Jesus responds with the same expression that he will use with the
high priest (Matt 26:64). Judas may have expected a negative
answer but he received a positive answer. Jesus knows. The
Gospel of John adds that Judas departed (John 13:30). In
Matthew, Judas disappears. Judas will return with the Jewish leaders in the garden.

Jesus performed the ordinary Passover ritual but adds to it a
new meaning for the bread and wine. Now when they celebrate

the Passover they will share in his death. The joining of the offering of the bread with the wine instead of the separation customary during a Passover meal may come from the liturgical practice of the community of Matthew.

The "blood of the covenant" refers to the practice in Exodus 24:8, when Moses sprinkled the blood of the sacrificed animal on the people, sealing the covenant with God. Matthew adds "for the forgiveness of sins." When they share in the death of the Lord in this sacred meal they will experience the forgiveness of sins. The promise of Jesus, "I will not drink…," may suggest that the Last Supper anticipates the final coming of the kingdom of God with its eschatological banquet. The Passover meal concludes with the singing of Psalms 113—118 and from the room they go to the Mount of Olives, across the valley from the city and the Temple.

Once there, Jesus informs his disciples that he will become a stumbling block for them this very night. They expect one thing (especially Judas?) and they will receive something else. Instead of glory and honor he and they will receive pain and sorrow. They will stumble over what Jesus will become. The shepherd will be struck and the flock will scatter.

Jesus then promises a return where he began his ministry and where he called his first followers. In the conclusion of the gospel, Jesus appears after the resurrection in Galilee and gives them a mission to continue. The boast of Peter that Jesus will never become a stumbling block for him prepares for Peter's threefold denial before 3:00 a.m.!

Questions

294. Jesus seems in control. Did Jesus know everything?

295. What is so important about Passover and how does this relate to the Christian Eucharist?

296. What are your thoughts about Judas?

297. Jesus changed the meaning of the Passover meal. What does it mean for Christians?

298. Does the celebration of the Eucharist bring forgiveness of sins?

299. Was Jesus a stumbling block?

300. Peter returns as the impetuous and weak disciple. Does this make him appealing as a leader?

Conclusion

Throughout the passion Jesus seems to know beforehand what will happen, and often gives orders that are followed. Jesus certainly knew the Scriptures and probably came to the conclusion that not only would he be rejected by the religious authorities (this had already happened), but that he would die. How much of what Matthew portrays comes from the actual events and how much from an understanding after the events remains unknown. If Jesus "was like us in all things but sin" he would have had ordinary human knowledge. His knowledge of Scriptures as well as his ability to read people and events surely prepared him for his passion and death. Not much more can be said.

The Passover comes from the experience of the people of Israel in Egypt when the angel of death passed over the homes of the Israelites. The feast celebrates the freedom of the people from slavery. The ritual comes from a combination of farmers' and herdsmen's religious rituals. The lamb and the sacrifice and meal come from the herdsmen. The unleavened bread comes from the farmers. Passover in the time of Jesus meant a feast celebrated in Jerusalem concentrating on the Temple ritual. The city of Jerusalem would have swelled with pilgrims outnumbering inhabitants two to one. With this as a backdrop, Jesus would be arrested, sentenced, and crucified.

Passover took place in the spring and began at sundown on the fifteenth of Nissan. The lambs were slaughtered in the Temple the afternoon before (in the Gospel of John this is when Jesus died). Each gospel places the last days of Jesus in the context of Passover. Since it commemorates the Exodus, Passover remains the principal feast of Judaism. The Eucharist for Christians celebrates the presence of Jesus among them, recalling his death and resurrection by which Christianity began. Jews celebrated freedom from slavery and Christians celebrate liberation from evil, sin, and death. Whether Jesus celebrated the Passover meal or anticipated it (the Gospel of John) remains unclear. Either way, Jesus celebrated the Last Supper in the context of a Passover meal.

After the destruction of the Temple, Jews no longer could celebrate a sacrificial Passover meal. The rabbis then transformed it into a family Seder meal to commemorate the same events in the past. Christians joined the remembrance of Passover to the eucharistic meal. They could recognize in the sacred meal the fulfillment of the Old Testament Passover, finding favor with both Jewish Christians and Gentile Christians.

As the passion events unfold, Matthew speaks more of Judas. A tragic figure, he had received much and had failed. He had sinned as would Peter. It seems he was not present with Jesus for the celebration of the Eucharist, which promised forgiveness of sins. Throughout the ages Catholic theology has always taught the celebration of the Eucharist brings the forgiveness of sins. Judas was absent and Peter was present.

If the disciples expected honor and glory and fulfillment (as evidenced in the dialogue between Peter and Jesus in chapter 16), then pain and sorrow did not belong. When Jesus accepted his passion and upcoming death, he became a stumbling block for his disciples. Very often honor and glory includes pain and sorrow. When a person integrates pain into life, then the stumbling block becomes a building block.

Poor Peter! In this gospel he never seems to get things right. One moment he boasts of his loyalty only to be told of his coming denial. Is he any worse than Judas? Unlike Judas, he acknowledges his sins and experiences forgiveness. Peter can function as a good role model for all Christians, especially Christian leaders. The "rock" has become a "pebble."

Section Fifty:
The Arrest in the Garden,
26:36–56

Introduction

The death of Jesus the Messiah caused great consternation among his early followers and especially among Jewish Christians. Very early the church tried to deal with its meaning and offered explanations that created the passion accounts in the four gospels. Each gospel has a different perspective, depending on the theology of the evangelist and the needs of the community for which the account was written.

Matthew has, for the most part, taken over the account from Mark with certain Matthean characteristics—for example, in the opening verses Jesus wants to include his disciples in the whole experience and they fail to grasp its significance. Together they go to Gethsemane (Olive Press). Evidently a part of the Mount of Olives contained an olive press to make the oil. Traditionally it is located at the base of the hill across the Kidron Valley from Jerusalem.

Peter, James, and John join Jesus as he prays. These three had also been present with Jesus at the transfiguration. Jesus emphasizes the seriousness of the situation with his reference to "sadness unto death." Jesus prays and the disciples sleep. Falling to the ground calls to mind an attitude of serious prayer. Matthew echoes the Lord's Prayer in the prayer of Jesus in the garden. Either the early church shaped the prayer of Jesus in the garden by the Lord's Prayer or Jesus taught the disciples the Lord's Prayer here in the garden.

The "cup" refers to his death as already seen in Matthew 20:20–28. As Jesus accepted the cup offered, he calls to mind

215

"Thy will be done" from the Lord's Prayer. The warning to his disciples, "Lest you enter into temptation," also reminds the reader of the Lord's Prayer. It seems the disciples have gotten themselves into a situation that they cannot handle. The disciples are both faithful and of "little faith." This contrasts spirit and flesh. In the center of their being, they want to be faithful but they fail. The weakness of body and psyche brings on the failure to understand and accept.

Jesus prays again, accepting the will of God, and returns to find the disciples asleep again. For the third time Jesus prays and the disciples sleep. Now Jesus gives in with resignation to the weakness of his disciples. So frequently in this gospel the disciples frustrate Jesus. Now his hour of passion and death has arrived and they sleep on. Jesus, in control of the situation, acknowledges the one who will hand him over and thus begins the series of events that will lead to his death.

Judas arrives with a delegation of Temple police from the chief priests and elders (not a band of soldiers as in John 18:3) and addresses Jesus as "rabbi" as he did at the Last Supper. Tradition has maintained that James looked similar to Jesus. Large crowds would gather at the Mount of Olives during the Passover (many would have camped there). Thus, Judas devised a signal to make sure they arrested the right person. Judas does so with a kiss.

Jesus calls Judas "friend" and they arrest Jesus. Tradition evidently held that someone tried to defend Jesus by drawing a sword (John says it was Peter in John 18:10). Jesus remains faithful to his principles of nonviolence and love of enemies. Jesus refuses to turn his arrest into a conflict of angels and his enemies, although he claims he could do just that. The Scripture mentioned in Matthew 26:31 concerning the shepherd has been fulfilled, for the disciples flee.

Jesus speaks to those who have come to arrest him and accuses them of hypocrisy. Daily he taught them and they did nothing. Now under the cloak of darkness they treat him like a bandit or a revolutionary. They think one way and act another. Their actions do not flow from their values and beliefs.

Questions

301. Jesus wants company and his disciples fail. Is this still true today?

302. Is accepting the will of God painful?

303. Why is prayer important for Jesus and for Matthew?

304. Betrayal by a friend with a kiss is hard to accept. Do friends betray friends?

305. Jesus advocates nonviolence. How can this be accepted today?

306. Was Jesus arrested as a revolutionary?

Conclusion

The arrest in the garden has two divisions: the prayer of Jesus with the disciples asleep and the arrest. Jesus, aware of what is about to happen, looks for comfort with his band of followers and they fail him. Throughout the Gospel of Matthew (more so in Mark) the disciples lack understanding and fail in their commitment. Here they sleep, initiate a feeble attempt to defend Jesus, contrary to all that Jesus has taught, and then flee.

Throughout the history of Christianity disciples have done the same. Keeping Jesus company means to follow his teachings as outlined in the Sermon on the Mount. Sometimes disciples succeed and sometimes they fail. But having kept Jesus company once means a disciple can do it again. That alone gives comfort in the midst of human weakness and failure.

Jesus accepts the will of God. He knows what will follow since he knows the Scriptures. He accepts the pain and the sorrow, and his spirit remains committed to following what God wants. Living according to the will of God never destroys the person. Actually, Jesus grows in strength to face his lot because he follows God's will. Jesus allowed himself to be arrested. He could have gone to Bethany and avoided the whole episode, but he knew his arrest and death fit into the divine plan. He accepted it but not without apprehension. He prayed for the cup to pass. His pain

217

and sorrow never entered into the depth of his spirit. Jesus did what he knew God wanted and did it willingly.

Jesus has taught his disciples to pray. Now he exemplifies the attitude of the Lord's Prayer in his own experience in Gethsemane. When in distress people should pray, whether surrounded by the storms of life (Matt 8:25), when afraid (Matt 14:30), or when facing opposition and death.

Friends betray friends. Family members fail to live up to the hopes and expectations of other family members. Within the church, leaders betray the flock and the flock betrays leaders and each other. Judas, for whatever reason, failed to grasp the teachings of Jesus. He wanted Jesus to conform to his own ideas and thus slipped into betrayal. When a person considers only self, then betrayal is easy. It matters little when the one betrayed is a friend, a family member, a fellow believer, or a caregiver. Self-centeredness and self-concern make betrayal easy. Judas exemplifies this attitude and people follow his example.

Jesus advocated nonviolence. Here he refuses to use the sword, even to protect himself. He had taught the love of enemies, to accept insults, to stand up for justice but not to use violence in the defense of justice. In a violent world of war and terrorism and injustice, nonviolence does not work. But for some Christians to maintain a commitment to nonviolence stands as a critique of contemporary life. It is good that some Christians remind other Christians and all people what Jesus advocated. Perhaps someday nonviolence will take its rightful place in the global society.

Jesus was not a Zealot, anxious to overthrow Rome, but he was a revolutionary in his teachings. He advocated a different understanding of religion. He criticized the religious authorities. He caused unrest, for he not only taught different ideas but had the freedom and strength to live them. He was dangerous to religion and thus to civil authority. He had to die.

Section Fifty-one:
The Trial and Peter's Denial, 26:57–75

Introduction

The judicial proceedings against Jesus the night before he died raise several historical questions. Was it a regular session before the Jewish court? Could it be legal if held at night? Did it include a death sentence? What was the exact procedure? Most think something happened at the house of Caiphas, but an official trial at night before Passover seems unlikely.

Peter joins the servants wishing to "see the end" in the courtyard. He follows, but "from a distance." The brave Peter, if he was the one with the sword, seems less brave.

The religious leaders sought witnesses against Jesus. Mark refers to them as witnesses while Matthew calls them "false." Two witnesses were necessary for a death sentence. Matthew presents two witnesses. One accuses Jesus of an offense against the Temple, and the chief priest demands to know who he is. First, Jesus remains silent. The chief priest then adjures Jesus to tell him if he is the Messiah, the Son of God. Matthew had used both titles frequently and to this question with these titles Jesus answers.

Jesus responds with a Son of Man saying, implying that he is both Lord and Messiah. Another climax has taken place. In the presence of the religious authorities Jesus declares his identity. The chief priest accuses Jesus of blasphemy. The second charge has been leveled against him. The misuse of the divine name carries with it a penalty of death by stoning. Technically Jesus has not committed blasphemy and thus the sentence is unjust. The members of the Sanhedrin abuse Jesus and mock him by calling him "Messiah," not understanding how Jesus is truly Messiah.

Meanwhile Peter stands outside and displays his weakness. Jesus remains faithful to his beliefs and to his God while Peter denies Jesus three times. The denials of Peter intensify, the second with an oath that Jesus had forbidden and the third with a shout, cursing, and swearing: "I do not know the man!" Then the cock crows.

Questions

307. Does it make any difference if the procedures were illegal?
308. What is blasphemy? Was Jesus guilty of blasphemy?
309. Why does Jesus remain silent?
310. Do the religious leaders follow procedures? Should they?
311. Once again Peter the "rock" is a "pebble." Why?

Conclusion

Historically this episode has been seen as the Jewish trial of Jesus. It takes place at the beginning of Passover, which began at sundown, in the house of the high priest. It seems unlikely that at the time when families would be eating the Passover meal the whole Sanhedrin would be in the house of Caiaphas.

John seems to have a better scenario. Jesus was arrested the night before Passover began. The trial in John takes place with Pilate and thus the Jewish event may have been an investigative hearing. Matthew records the thinking of the early church. The Eucharist is closely associated with a Passover meal and the blame shifts from Romans to Jews. Matthew has changed the events in chronology and in meaning.

Did Jesus commit blasphemy? Speaking against the Temple could be understood as blasphemy since the Temple represented the presence of God. That Jesus cleansed the Temple and made remarks about its destruction seems historically accurate.

Moreover, since the Temple offered a serious foundation for the economy anyone who would talk about its destruction would not sit well with the local people. This could explain why the local people would oppose Jesus. Too often every event in life has an economic basis along with a religious purpose.

When the chief priest asked if Jesus was the Messiah he probably was asking if Jesus was a troublemaker like many others who claimed to be the Messiah. The chief priests and leaders probably viewed Jesus as one of a series of religious pretenders who caused trouble with the Romans. When Jesus responded positively to the question of the chief priest, they accuse him of blasphemy, for he has made himself equal to God. The accusations against Jesus were technically false but on a deeper level they were true: he could destroy the Temple and he was the true Messiah and the Son of God. When the chief priests join in the abuse, the trial becomes a sham. True judges do not engage in such treatment. Jesus remains silent since he need offer no defense against false accusations. He also knows that no matter what he would say, he would be condemned. All falls within the divine plan. Both religious leaders and civil leaders should follow legal procedures, but when the officials have made up their minds, they will do anything to execute their previous judgment. Procedures fall by the wayside. Thus it has always been and always will be.

Peter must truly have denied Jesus during the passion since no early church member would have invented the story. Placing Peter in the context of the faithful Jesus, as Matthew does, shows Jesus as the one to imitate and Peter as the one not to follow. Peter the "rock" fails just as most Christians fail in always professing faith in Jesus. The "pebble" returns.

Section Fifty-two:
Jesus and Judas and Barabbas, 27:1–26

Introduction

Whatever happened before Caiaphas, the scene shifts to Roman authorities and Pilate. Whether the Jewish Council had the authority to execute remains disputed. Many think that as long as the matter was religious the religious authorities did not need Roman approval. Here the religious authorities seek Roman approval, perhaps to ensure crucifixion rather than stoning.

The religious leaders had made their decision. In the morning all the chief priests and elders gathered and decided to put Jesus to death. What had been decided at Caiaphas's house now took on a more legal aspect with the decision to bring Jesus to Pilate. Pontius Pilate governed the Roman Province of Judea from AD 26 to 36. Proof of his rule has been unearthed in Caesarea. Although he resided in Caesarea he would have been in Jerusalem during Passover to oversee his troops and control any disturbance.

Meanwhile Judas changes his mind (Matthew does not use the ordinary word for repentance) and returns the blood money. When the religious leaders reject his offer, he throws the money down and leaves. The priests take the money and will not replace it in the Temple treasury; instead, they buy a field for burial of strangers. "Until this day" suggests that in the time of Matthew people still knew where the field was located.

Once again Matthew turns to the Old Testament for a fulfillment prophecy. Loosely, the saying in Matthew comes from

Zechariah with reference to thirty pieces of silver that the prophet cast into the treasury.

After his comments on the death of Judas, Matthew returns to Jesus and Pilate. The title King of the Jews loosely translated the Messiah of the Jews. To Pilate it would conjure up political trouble. Jesus agrees in an ironic way. To Pilate and the Jewish leaders the title meant one thing and Jesus and his followers, the church of Matthew, understood it to mean something else. Jesus acknowledges his identity but will not respond to any charges against him.

No one is sure of the practice of a release of a prisoner on Passover. Perhaps it happened occasionally. Barabbas means "son of the father." How ironic! The true Son of God the Father goes to death while Pilate gives Barabbas freedom. The Roman governor knew enough about the Jewish authorities to conclude that they envied Jesus and were jealous of his power. But that did not encourage Pilate to release Jesus.

Traditionally all this took place in the Fortress Antonia (now the convent of the Daughters of Sion) on the Via Dolorosa near the Temple area. Many today relocate the actual setting to the palace of Herod, where the Citadel now sits. Many ancient peoples believed in the preternatural meaning of dreams. The wife of Pilate has such a dream and informs him of her fear. Matthew alone records this event. The wife refers to Jesus as "just." Pilate pays more attention to the Jewish leaders who had encouraged the people to choose Barabbas and ask for Jesus to be destroyed. Pilate insists on a clear choice. The Jews not only choose Barabbas but declare that they want Jesus crucified. The weak Pilate tries to avoid the sentence by insisting on asking what evil Jesus has done. Knowing he faced a possible political disturbance, Pilate gives in, signified by the washing of his hands, which in Judaism meant he wanted nothing to do with the blood of an innocent man. Matthew now adds "all the people." They accept responsibility for their action and pass it on. Pilate acquiesces and has Jesus scourged to weaken him before crucifixion.

Questions

312. How much do you know about Judas? How much comes from the Old Testament rather than a historically true picture?

313. What do you think of Pilate?

314. Did you realize the meaning of Barabbas? What is Matthew trying to say?

315. The wife of Pilate calls Jesus "just." Why does Pilate not accept her judgment?

316. The people call for crucifixion. Was this the same crowd from Palm Sunday?

317. Does Pilate refuse to accept the consequences of his actions?

Conclusion

The death of Judas has no parallel in the other gospels. The only other account appears in Acts 1:18–19, which fills in some details. The tradition passed on includes a violent death and some relationship to a potter's field, a field of blood. According to Matthew, Judas committed suicide and the chief priests bought the field. According to Acts, Judas bought the field and probably died an accidental death there and thus it was called the field of blood. Both traditions are independent of each other and manifest the lack of accurate knowledge of the end of Judas.

Most of the elements in the story of Judas and his end come from the Old Testament. The thirty pieces of silver, the throwing of the money in the Temple, the idea of a field of blood all come from the Old Testament. Christians then and now know very little about Judas. Does the saying of Jesus in Luke, "Father, forgive them for they know not what they do" (Luke 23:34), apply also to Judas?

Pilate has always been depicted as weak as water. In the Coptic martyrology he is called a saint. Legally Pilate was responsible for the death of Jesus and not the Jews. Clearly, the Jewish leaders were involved and were responsible but so was Pilate. Matthew, writing from a Roman city, would have wished to lessen Roman guilt and since Jews in the city persecuted the community of Matthew naturally he would have included them more directly in the death of Jesus. The wife of Pilate, a Roman, declares Jesus to be just and Pilate feigns noninvolvement. The Romans say, "no," and the Jews call for his death.

Pilate's effort to release Jesus by referring to a tradition of releasing a prisoner during Passover may not be historically founded or maybe it was true but just not recorded. The play on the name of Barabbas and Jesus as the Son of the Father may account for the inclusion of the episode. People reject the true Son of the Father for a fake son of the father. People settle for the lesser because it suits their needs.

Not too much is actually known about Pilate. He reigned for a long time, which may mean Rome forgot about him since Judea was a backwater part of the empire and his ineptness caused no great trouble for Rome. He frequently clashed with the Jewish authorities, according to Josephus and Philo. He brought Roman standards into the city, took money from the Temple treasury, put down a disturbance of the Samaritans, and, according to Luke, mixed the blood of some Galileans with their sacrifices. These are not signs of a weak man. Philo says he liked to annoy the Jews and refers to him as "naturally inflexible, a blend of self-will and relentlessness." Yet Matthew portrays him as weak and unwilling to accept the consequences of his actions with regard to Jesus. He blames the Jews.

Matthew climaxes the whole episode with "all the people" accepting responsibility for the blood of Jesus to be passed on to future generations. For centuries Christian tradition has held the Jews responsible. Jews killed Jesus and are guilty of deicide. In truth, some Jews and some Romans were responsible for the death of Jesus. Of course, the Romans are no longer around but the Jews are. Christians can direct their anger against Jews today for killing Jesus. Although most Christians reject such guilt and the Second Vatican Council officially rejected inherited Jewish guilt for the death of Jesus, prejudice continues against the Jews of today. Jesus died because people tend to destroy what is good.

Anyone who destroys what is good, especially a good person, whether physically or psychologically, is guilty of the death of Jesus. People are fickle. One day they proclaim "Hosanna to the Son of David" and the next they call for crucifixion. Same people, different chant!

Section Fifty-three:
The Crucifixion and
Death, 27:27–56

Introduction

Matthew describes the mocking by the Roman soldiers more graphically than any other evangelist. Six hundred soldiers constituted a cohort. Here the word may mean only a large number. The mocking probably took place at Herod's palace, as already noted. The mocking presupposes the condemnation of Jesus as "King of the Jews." The soldiers place a scarlet military cloak around Jesus, a crown of thorns on his head, and a reed in his right hand as a scepter, with which they strike him. Mark has the soldiers place a purple cloak on Jesus. Purple designated royalty. Matthew changed purple to scarlet more in accord with the circumstances of soldiers since they wore scarlet. Whether the soldiers were true Romans or locals employed by Rome remains an unanswered question.

The image that people have of the crown of thorns does not fit reality. The purpose was mockery and not pain and cruelty. Western artists have often exaggerated the type of thorns and the pain. The soldiers tried to imitate the crown worn by the Roman emperors but, instead of laurel leaves, the soldiers used a bramble with thorns. Thus royally arrayed complete with his scepter, they acknowledged him as "King of the Jews."

Cyrene is present-day Libya. Simon may have been a pilgrim or a resident in Jerusalem who came from Cyrene. Unlike Mark, Matthew does not mention any family members. The condemned usually carried only the upper beam of the cross, again unlike most artistic depictions. Jesus was probably already weak and the soldiers pressed into service a bystander. In the Gospel of John (John 19:17) Jesus needs no help in carrying his cross.

The Latin translation of Golgotha is "Calvary." It means "skull" and may refer to a hill that looked like a skull or was called so because of executions there. The executions took place outside the city. To lessen the pain the condemned man was given a drug. Matthew says it was wine mixed with gall, which may refer to Psalm 69:21, or perhaps it was intended as a poison for Jesus to drink to avoid the pain completely. Jesus does not drink it. Matthew simply states the act of crucifixion with no details. The clothes of the condemned man become the property of the executioners.

Matthew alone introduces the presence of the guard to watch over him. This same guard will be present at the tomb. Matthew wants to clarify and discredit the claim that the disciples of Jesus stole the dead body. The Roman guards fulfilled this purpose.

Each evangelist narrates the official charge placed over the cross: "King of the Jews." John says it was written in three languages: Latin, Greek, and Hebrew. With Jesus two others were executed. They probably were guilty of political crimes. Seeing them as revolutionaries may be an exaggeration, whereas depicting them as robbers may be an understatement.

The passers-by also join in the mockery, echoing the charge in the courtyard of Caiaphas. Once again the crowd use the title Son of God, which for Matthew expressed the truth about Jesus. They use the title in mockery. The chief priests and elders join in and also include in the ridicule the good works that Jesus performed for the sake of others. They proclaim that they too will believe if the one who saved others will now save himself.

Questions

318. Jesus is mocked and ridiculed. Jesus told his followers to accept such ridicule (Matt 5:11). How do you deal with mockery?

319. Do you think the drink was meant to lessen the pain? Why did Jesus refuse it? Do people have to accept all pain or can they lessen it?

320. The title King of the Jews appears over the cross in each gospel. What are the different meanings of the title?

321. What are your images of the two crucified with Jesus?

322. Why did Jesus not come down from the cross?

323. Matthew continues to place the religious leaders in a bad light. Why?

Conclusion

Following Mark, Matthew divides the crucifixion into three scenes: first the mockery by the soldiers; then the actual crucifixion; and finally the mockery by the chief priests and bystanders. The middle scene nestles between the two scenes of mockery.

The mockery by the soldiers was personal. They treated Jesus as a joke, dressing him as the emperor and pretending to honor him. He was in truth the "King of the Jews," the Messiah, and yet accepted this mockery. In the Sermon on the Mount Jesus taught his disciples that they are blessed when they accept such mockery on account of their commitment to Jesus. He gives the example to follow. The best revenge is no revenge. When mocked and ridiculed, the best response is no response. That usually stops the mockery. Here, although Jesus does not respond, the mockery continues.

Usually the drug offered was meant to lessen the pain of crucifixion. Matthew adds the wine mixed with gall to relate to Psalm 69:21, "They gave me poison for food and in my thirst they gave me vinegar to drink." Jesus willingly endures the full pain of crucifixion. This does not mean that every follower should have to endure as much pain as possible in life. Today, with the prospect of painful diseases and deaths more prevalent, accepting pain killers, even if eventually lethal, falls well in accord with the teachings of Jesus.

To Romans "King of the Jews" meant a revolutionary anxious to overthrow Rome. To the Jewish religious leaders it meant that Jesus was a false messiah. To the members of the community of Matthew it meant Jesus was truly both the Messiah, the Son of God, the descendent of David, and the one true ruler of all

Judaism and the one who fulfilled all of the hopes and expectations of Judaism.

Romans used crucifixion as a deterrent. Jews saw it as an additional curse: "For a hanged man is cursed by God" (Deut 21:23). Romans crucified violent criminals and political rebels. The execution was public with much pain. Then the body was casually disposed of. No wonder the crucifixion became "a stumbling block to Jews and folly to Gentiles" (1 Cor 1:23). But for Christians the death of Jesus fulfilled the Scriptures and all took place as part of the divine plan.

Following the portrayal in Luke, most Christians think kindly on one of the two crucified with Jesus (Luke 23:40–43). The "good thief" sits well in Christian consciences. Matthew does not know the tradition and so both are portrayed in a negative manner. Thieves were usually not crucified, so they probably were more than just robbers. Jesus the King of the Jews was executed like a violent criminal although he was not. In Luke's version at least one of the thieves recognized the identity of Jesus.

Would people have accepted Jesus if he came down from the cross? In God's plan the tendency of human beings to destroy what is good, even people, reached a climax in the death of Jesus. But God would not allow human goodness to be destroyed. Karl Barth said that the crucifixion is man's no to goodness. The resurrection is God's yes.

The scene includes mockery by the chief priests and elders. They have what they wanted: the death of Jesus. They even mock God. Matthew has trouble with Jewish religious leaders not only in the time of Jesus but in his own time. He never misses an opportunity to present them in a bad light. Readers must always put Matthew and his gospel in context. The Jewish authorities persecuted early Christians. The Christians did not always follow the example of Jesus in accepting mockery, ridicule, and persecution for his sake. Even the gospels suffer from human limitations.

Section Fifty-four: Death and Burial, 27:45-66

Introduction

Matthew likes drama and so he portrays the death of Jesus with cosmic occurrences. With the death of Jesus, human history has reached a turning point. Although Jesus is mocked by humans, God justifies him and humans acknowledge him as "Son of God." People say "no" to goodness and God says "yes."

Darkness covers the earth as if the world mourns the death of Jesus. Over the centuries many have attempted to explain Jesus' cry of abandonment. The words echo the beginning of Psalm 22 and many think Jesus was actually praying this psalm. Even if this is true, the sense of divine abandonment should not be overlooked. Matthew has taken the verse from Mark and, in Mark, the family of Jesus thought he was crazy (Mark 3:21), the religious leaders accused him of being possessed by demons (Mark 3:22), and his disciples do not understand him (Mark 9:32). Why would he not feel abandoned by God?

The bystanders confuse "my God" (*El*, God, *I*, my) with the name of Elijah. In Jewish history Elijah became the patron saint of the helpless. Perhaps some sympathetic bystanders first wanted to help only to be rebuked by others. Jesus speaks again (continuing to pray Psalm 22?) and releases his spirit. In Matthew this should not be understood as the Holy Spirit. It means that Jesus died. In the Gospel of John, the author uses a different Greek word for handing over or releasing the spirit. Jesus handed over to Mary and the beloved disciple his own spirit (John 19:30).

A curtain shielded the Holy of Holies. Matthew may intend its tearing to prefigure the destruction of the Temple, which had already taken place by the time of writing, or perhaps it symbolized the end of traditional Jewish worship. The presence of God was no longer limited to a holy place but actually was in an unlikely holy person, the crucified one. The earthquake preceded the resurrection of the dead. The death of Jesus for Matthew makes possible the coming to life of those who had died. Paul has a similar teaching in 1 Corinthians 15. Finally, the centurion with others makes a confession of faith in Jesus.

The women had been part of the company of Jesus from the beginning, ministering to him. They watched from afar the crucifixion and death and would be able to go to the tomb after the Sabbath. All four gospels acknowledge Mary Magdalene. In this gospel she witnesses his death, his place of burial, and the empty tomb. In the Gospel of John she also proclaims his resurrection to his disciples (John 20:18). Matthew does not clearly state that Mary the mother of Jesus was present. It all depends on punctuation. Is there a comma after Mary, so that they are two distinct women?

Joseph of Arimathea, a disciple, wished to bury Jesus and Pilate agrees. The previously unknown disciple carefully wraps the body and places it in a new tomb. The large rock would prevent robbery. The two Marys watched.

The scene switches to the chief priests and Pharisees (not mentioned during the crucifixion scenes). They recall the claim of Jesus when he predicted his death (Matt 16:21; 17:9, 23; 20:19). They fear the disciples of Jesus will steal his body and claim resurrection. Whether the guard is the Temple police or a Roman guard that Pilate gave to the chief priests is unknown. Whoever they were, they sealed the tomb and set watch.

Questions

324. Do you think the earth visibly mourned at the death of Jesus?

325. Did God abandon Jesus?

326. People reacted differently. One seems more compassionate and the others mean. Has anything changed in life and in the church?

327. Did people really rise from the dead at the death of Jesus?

328. Non-Jews proclaim their faith. Why would Matthew want this to take place?

329. What role did women play? Mary Magdalene, sinner or saint?

330. Why the emphasis on the tomb and the guard?

Conclusion

Like the previous section, Matthew divides the telling of the death of Jesus into three scenes: the actual death, the cosmic omens, and the role of women. The cosmic events come from Ezekiel 37:10–14. The darkness at noon refers to Amos 8:9. Once again Matthew turns to the Old Testament to support his teaching on the fulfillment of prophecies through the ministry and death of Jesus. Just as the heavens rejoiced at the birth of Jesus with the star, so Matthew has the earth in mourning at his death. The images are meant to explain meaning and are not to be taken literally.

The Synoptic Gospels portray the pain and suffering of Jesus in his passion. Matthew throughout this gospel hints at the frustration of Jesus in dealing with his listeners and his disciples. If Jesus was "like us in all things but sin," he truly must have felt abandoned but did not give in to despair. He trusted God. He did not curse God nor did he curse those who brought him to this cruel death. He gave himself back to his God.

That someone in the crowd felt compassion should not cause surprise. That others mocked should also not cause surprise. The first gave up when ridiculed. People still ridicule Jesus and his followers today. Many might feel interested or compassionate but too many other influences impede a response. Compassion and ridicule exist in society and in the church. Actions follow values. Those who truly believe should manifest their faith in how they live, no matter what others think or how others may react.

The resurrection of the dead is yet to come. Jesus as the first-born from the dead promised resurrection for all. Matthew's community experienced persecution and possibly death. Other members had already died. He informs his community of hope for the future and for eternal life. Death was not the end for Jesus and will not be the end for his followers.

Mark has a centurion proclaiming faith. Matthew includes the others guarding Jesus. It seems they all were Gentiles. The chief priests and elders want him dead and the Gentiles proclaim him Son of God. A mixed community, Jewish Christian and Gentile Christian, would not miss the meaning.

Mary Magdalene has been portrayed as prostitute and sinner. She has received bad press. Nowhere in the gospels is she presented as such. Luke does have Jesus expel demons from her (Luke 8:2) but this need not be interpreted as possession by Satan or the devil. Evil spirits can be just sickness. The gospels do not give a name to the woman taken in adultery, or the woman who washed the feet of Jesus. John has Mary a witness to the resurrection (John 20:18). Matthew mentions her only in this chapter and the following chapter at the tomb. Mary Magdalene in Matthew is a faithful follower of Jesus to the end. Women played an important role in the ministry of Jesus and in the early church. The early Christian communities were communities of equals. With success and development of Christianity, very often this role was overlooked or forgotten.

Early stories about the disciples stealing the body of Jesus and thus proclaiming the resurrection must have influenced Matthew's description of the guards at the tomb. The tomb belonged to Joseph of Arimathea, a rich disciple, and thus it was a wealthy man's tomb. Although crucified as a violent criminal Jesus would not be buried as such. The tomb was large, designed for multiple burials, as were most such tombs at the time. After a period of decomposition the bones would be gathered and placed in a smaller niche to allow for more burials. The new tomb, the separate burial, befitted the "Messiah" and "Son of God."

Matthew wanted to emphasize the true death and the burial to prepare for the resurrection. All the details narrated would support the claim of the empty tomb. Jesus dies. The women disciples knew the place of the tomb as did the officials. Matthew is ready to declare that Jesus was raised from the dead.

THE RESURRECTION, 28:1–15

Section Fifty-five: The Empty Tomb and Resurrection, 28:1–15

Introduction

Matthew continues the drama. Instead of the young man at the tomb, as in Mark, Matthew has a powerful angel roll back the stone and sit on it. The evangelist describes the angel. He looked like lightning and his clothes were white as snow, which brought fear to the guards. Matthew likes earthquakes. In the episode of the storm at sea Matthew says an earthquake occurred (Matt 8:24). He referred to earthquakes in his apocalyptic discourse (Matt 24:7); another occurred at the death of Jesus (Matt 27:51) and finally at the resurrection.

The two Marys establish continuity to the death of Jesus. They arrive at the tomb at dawn and the angel assures them Jesus has been raised, as Jesus had said he would. Matthew joins the resurrection to the three predictions of the passion. The women have a duty to fulfill and they do so with fear and joy.

Jesus appears and greets them. The episode sounds like a variation on the scene in the Gospel of John (20:1–18). The women did him homage, another favorite theme of Matthew going back to the Magi. That both the angel and Jesus refer to Galilee points to the final scene of Jesus and his disciples in Galilee.

235

Matthew ends with the story of the bribed guards and once again the chief priests and elders enter the scene and lie. They seem confident that Pilate would agree since it would not help him politically if people began to believe that Jesus was raised from the dead. The rumor evidently still circulated in the time of Matthew that the disciples had stolen the body of Jesus. Matthew needs to discredit it.

Questions

331. The scene is dramatic. What appeals to you and why would Matthew make it so dramatic?

332. Mark has the women leave in "fear and trembling." Matthew adds "great joy." Why?

333. Why the relationship to John?

334. Jesus will appear only to those who believe in him. Would this further necessitate trying to disprove the stealing of the body story?

Conclusion

Matthew likes the dramatic. Earthquakes cause more than just ordinary drama. A powerful angel visibly moving the stone with an appearance that could only shock, fits well into the Matthean scheme. The death of Jesus was a dramatic moment in human history but the resurrection outclasses the death! Many people were crucified. For Jesus to be crucified meant nothing. For a crucified person to be raised was news. The drama should be evident and so Matthew supplies the images.

The original ending of Mark concluded with the women leaving in fear and trembling and telling no one (Mark 16:8). Such was not a happy ending to the story. Later scribes would offer many different endings to the Gospel of Mark. Matthew followed Mark up to the end but will conclude his gospel with a dramatic mission-giving appearance of Jesus in Galilee. The gospel should end in triumph and not in fear and confusion. Matthew will supply the triumph.

The relationship to John may come from similar oral traditions. Many stories of Jesus circulated orally long before someone began to gather them and write them down. Evidently many had resurrection appearance stories and they told them from one generation to another. Some have survived in the gospels and others have not. Paul recalls appearances to Peter and to James and to five hundred disciples that are not recorded in the New Testament (1 Cor 15:5–7). Matthew was not an eyewitness. He used Mark and "Q" and had his own traditions. Some of these evidently had something in common with the traditions behind the Gospel of John. Thus, the similarity to John.

Jesus appears only to believers. Opponents could easily deny the resurrection and make up stories to support their opinion. Matthew is convinced that Jesus was raised from the dead and he lives. He has heard of the rumors of body stealing and creates a scene with the guards to disavow such theories. Still, belief in the resurrected Lord is just that, belief. No one can prove it, not even an empty tomb.

THE FINALE, 28:16–20

Section Fifty-six:
The Dramatic Conclusion
of the Gospel of Matthew,
28:16–20

Introduction

Everyone likes a happy ending. Matthew supplies one for his community and for Christians of all times. Over the centuries many have tried to analyze these few verses as part of baptismal liturgy, or an example of an enthronement liturgy, or an episode similar to divine revelation in the Old Testament. All fail. Matthew created the scene to suit his own purpose, the time of the church. It all takes place on a mountain. The best image might be the Christ of the Andes towering over Rio de Janeiro.

Matthew refers to eleven disciples. Judas is gone and not replaced. Jesus had told them he would precede them to Galilee (Matt 26:32) and the angel and Jesus himself announced it at the tomb. The mountain in itself has meaning even if no mountain is specified.

Once again someone offers homage to Jesus. As Son of God and Messiah he deserved worship. Whether some worshiped and some doubted or all worshiped and all doubted or whether the verb *distazo* should be translated as "hesitate" remains disputed. Jesus approached them and gave them their mission.

Jesus has all power in heaven and earth and he gives to his disciples the mission to make disciples of all nations just as he made disciples. Does this refer only to Gentiles, as some think? Or does it include the Jews, as others think? Certainly the gospel was first addressed to Jews and then to Gentiles who eventually flocked into this new religion, leaving the Jews behind.

The baptismal formula comes from the early church. This signifies that the Matthean community was well organized with authority, structure (Matt 16:16), and liturgy. This saying of Jesus gave them a mission to perform. They would baptize and teach. The content of their teaching was what Jesus taught them and they should observe the Law as Jesus observed the Law. Jesus concludes with a promise of an abiding presence among his followers forever.

Questions

335. Do you like the dramatic ending of Matthew?
336. What are the signs of an institutional church?
337. Who has the authority in this gospel?
338. What is the relationship between preaching to Gentiles and to Jews?
339. How is the abiding presence of Jesus felt in the church?

Conclusion

Matthew alone ends with such a dramatic appearance of Jesus. Mark ends with confusion. Luke ends with the disciples at Emmaus. John ends with a frustration that all the books of the world could not contain the meaning of Jesus. Matthew ends the best! Matthew concludes the ministry of Jesus by thrusting a mission to his followers into the future, the responsibility especially of the eleven apostles. From the mountain Christianity may go from triumph to triumph until the end of human history.

An institutional church has a common bond: faith in Jesus. It has a purpose and a mission: to baptize and teach. It has clear lines of authority: Peter and the eleven. It meets regularly to celebrate baptism and Eucharist. To survive in an evil and sinful world, the church needs all of the above and Matthew provides them.

Authority in Matthew belongs to Jesus and then to Peter and to the eleven. It also must be remembered that the same authority given to Peter in chapter 16 is given to the church in chapter 18. No doubt Peter figures prominently in Matthew but he is not without his flaws. All leadership in Christianity has weakness and flaws and perhaps this is why Matthew composed chapter 18.

The earliest followers of Jesus preached first to Jews and the first followers were Jews. When fewer Jews joined the new movement and more Gentiles became converts, Matthew recognized the future of Christianity belonged to Gentiles and not Jews. He will not deny the origins of Jesus and his teachings in Judaism but is open to the new, a Gentile church. Paul deals with the relationship between Judaism and Christianity in Romans 9—11. Matthew leaves the door open to the Jews but knows the future lies elsewhere.

Matthew believed in and experienced the abiding presence of Jesus in the church. He supported the authority of Peter. If he did write his gospel in Antioch, this was the first city to have a monarchical episcopacy. Such would be the natural outcome of what Matthew proposed in his gospel. He also knew that Jesus remained with his church and not just with its leaders and ultimately it all comes down to how people treat each other.

241

Answers

Section One:
The Beginnings, 1:1–17

1. Genealogies offer support for legitimacy. Jesus inherited a blood line and a faith line going back to Abraham. Luke traces his genealogy to Adam. Both probably use popular genealogies of ancestors. Since they differ from each other and from some of the names in the Bible, they should not be considered to be historically accurate. They serve a theological purpose and not a historical one.

2. Since the Gospel of Matthew was addressed to a Jewish and Gentile Christian audience, the inclusion of Abraham would have pleased the Gentile audience and not have excluded the Jewish Christian members of the congregation.

3. Relating Jesus to the Jewish patriarchs certainly pleased Jewish Christians. For Christians today it binds Christianity irrevocably to Judaism. Christians are spiritual Jews.

4. Christianity was open to all peoples: Jews and Gentiles, men and women, saints and sinners. The inclusion of women who were Gentiles or married to a Gentile and who had a "shady" past emphasized the call to all. The women so named may also have prepared the audience for Mary, who probably gave birth to Jesus within the nine-month period after Joseph and Mary came to live together.

5. Numbers continue to fascinate. Matthew used a play on the number 14. Why some numbers are "lucky" and others are not has long interested people. Over the centuries many have tried to give explanations to such beliefs, all to no avail. Perhaps the answer can be found in human curiosity in how things work. After all, mathematicians claim the universe revolves around numbers.

Section Two:
The Birth of the Messiah, 1:18–25

6. Jews and early Gentile Christians would have found it difficult to believe that Jesus was divine. At the outset Matthew makes his claim and then throughout his gospel supports his claim. Belief in Matthew depends on a willingness to accept the divinity of Jesus and then recognize the consequences for personal life.

7. The virginity of Mary in the birth of Jesus has been a constant belief in Christianity. Throughout history Catholics have maintained a belief in the perpetual virginity while others have believed that Mary had other children with Joseph. The New Testament gives no firm answer. The meaning of the virginity certainly emphasizes that God gave Jesus as a gift to humanity. The virginity of Mary supports this belief. Whether God could have given Jesus to humanity through ordinary human conception remains a speculative question. Faith says that Mary remains a virgin in the conception of Jesus.

8. Joseph knew the Law and also that the Law does not fit every circumstance. He remained faithful to the Law while acknowledging the Law did not fit the actual situation of Mary.

9. Reasonable people may disagree with regard to the virginity of Mary. Meaning outweighs the physical reality but the physical reality supports the meaning. Thus, Christians believe in the virginity of Mary.

10. God acts through Jesus. Jesus is the human face of God. Jesus saves not from death or from evil and sin but from despair and hopelessness. Jesus saves people from the sins and faults of the past by giving them a future in which they can hope.

11. Many of the members of the Matthean community came from a Jewish background. The fulfillment of the Old Testament encouraged them to remain faithful to their newfound faith. Christianity continued what had begun with Abraham and Moses.

12. Jesus remains with his followers through his teachings, in their praying together, and in the celebration of the Eucharist.

Section Three:
The Magi and Egypt, 2:1–23

13. The Christmas story combining the details in Matthew with the account in Luke creates a wonderful, touching, and almost romantic explanation for the birth of Jesus. A couple looking for a place to stay, a manger, angels, shepherds, Magi, and the birth of a baby tug at the human heart every December 25.

14. The religious leaders should have recognized Jesus as the Messiah and they failed. Foreigners, Gentiles, saw in Jesus the coming of God. The same was true during the ministry of Jesus; the unlikely recognized him while those who should have seen him as God's Son closed their eyes. The same was true for the time of Matthew.

15. Ancient people always associated signs in the heavens with the birth of a great person. Perhaps when Jesus had been recognized as a great person, some might have remembered some strange heavenly phenomenon, for example, the juxtaposition of planets or a comet.

16. Matthew continues to make references to the Old Testament to show both fulfillment of the Old Testament

and encouragement for Jewish Christians as they were forced to rethink their religion and culture.

17. Since both Luke and Matthew are concerned more with theology than history, no effort to harmonize the actual details of both gospels will ever work. Be attentive to the story within the theology of each gospel and find the meaning there.

18. Human anthropology often recognizes or creates obstacles in the youth of great personages. How a person responds to the difficulties allows the greatness to shine forth. Evil will always try to destroy the good but always fails. Goodness ultimately triumphs.

19. Jesus is both like Moses and more than Moses. Likening him to Moses joins Christianity to Judaism. Making him more than Moses allows Christianity to be different from Judaism.

Section Four: John the Baptist and the Baptism of Jesus, 3:1–17

20. Both John and Jesus point out the presence and absence of God in their society and in their religion and culture. They both speak for God. People like it when a prophet points out the presence of God but rebel when the prophet highlights the absence of God, especially in religion and among religious leaders.

21. Rethinking how to live takes place daily or at least for Roman Catholics once a year in the celebration of Lent. In secular society the New Year's celebration encourages a rethinking of how one is living. The resolutions usually do not last long. Thus, yearly rethinking takes place. Joined to faith and religion the resolutions may last a bit longer.

22. Baptism is a washing, a cleansing, and a renewing. Since all life came from the water, the ritual of baptism symbolizes new life. For Jesus the baptism by John begins his new life of ministry for others. For Christians baptism means the beginning of new life in the church continuing the ministry of Jesus.

23. Becoming a member of the church and being joined to the body of Christ should bring changes in how a person lives. What a person does flows from beliefs and values. Baptism is completed only when a person has fulfilled his or her life.

24. Just talking values and beliefs means nothing unless they are lived. This is particularly true for any religious leader. Words can be empty. Actions demonstrate the meaning of the words.

25. At the time of Matthew some still believed that John was the Messiah. Constantly showing the superiority of Jesus to John would help these individuals to recognize John as the precursor of the Messiah, Jesus.

26. The new in the life of Jesus means his ministry. After the baptism and the time in the desert he begins his preaching of repentance, continuing the ministry of John and adding the power of the Spirit.

Section Five: The Desert and the Temptations, 4:1–11

27. Too often people fall back on blaming the devil for everything. Life brings its own temptations and people create temptations both for themselves and for others. Actions follow values and beliefs.

28. Jesus was a Jew and fulfilled Jewish law. He followed the traditions of his ancestors but also ignored some traditions

when they hindered the love of God and love of neighbor. When the traditions helped in the relationship to God, Jesus, like any pious Jew, observed hem.

29. Jesus wins because his quotes are superior in a rabbinic argument since they come from Deuteronomy. The rabbis considered any quote from Deuteronomy superior to other books in the Pentateuch. Jesus also adds nuances to the debate by his choice of quotations.

30. God supports people even when they do foolish things. God does not protect people from doing foolish things. Doing something foolish demands living with the consequences.

31. When power and wealth are used for the good of others, they no longer corrupt. When used for the self they tend to destroy the person. Worshiping God means caring for others.

32. The audience of Matthew was Jewish Christians as well as Gentile Christians. His constant reference to Israel and to the Old Testament encourages Jewish Christians and reminds Gentile Christians of their origin in Judaism.

33. "Q" was a collection of sayings of Jesus. Perhaps its author grouped these sayings to create a trilogy of the most common human temptations. Actually, no one can be sure how Jesus taught the temptations. But no doubt exists that he did teach about pleasure, power, wealth, and responsibility for one's actions.

34. Everyone should recognize in the temptations of Jesus what occurs in daily life. Most people have problems with at least some of these temptations. Jesus offers some help in dealing with them.

Section Six:
Ministry in Galilee, 4:12–25

35. Both John and Jesus challenged their religious culture and institutions. They also caused problems for secular administration. Both separated themselves from the ordinary and accepted authorities. Jesus in particular gave people too much religious freedom. He needed to be stopped.

36. Galilee was always considered "too pagan" by most Jews. True Judaism belonged in Jerusalem. Jesus, an "unlikely" prophet, began in an "unlikely" place. In Jerusalem, the center of Judaism, he would die.

37. Jewish Christians and Gentile Christians did not get along in the early church. Each group considered themselves superior to the other for various reasons. Matthew opts for a middle position, trying to keep both groups together by their common faith in Jesus. The problem eventually goes away when the church becomes predominantly Gentile. But then Christians and Jews become antagonists.

38. The sea remains the sea. No church is built over it. No dispute exists as to its location. People can sail on it using a boat similar to those used in the first century. The sea is beautiful and peaceful (except when a sudden storm arises!). No wonder Christians like to visit it.

39. If they had their own boats they were not destitute. They probably made a good living. They may not have been the ignorant peasants they are often depicted to be. Very often fishermen and farmers have a special wisdom learned from their closeness to the sea and to the land. They also seem to have suffered from the temptation of power and position. They were an unusual and gifted group.

40. Everyone needs friends. Jesus was like us in all things and so naturally he had his close friends. No doubt some were

251

comfortable with this and others were not. Enough evidence exists in the gospels to show that the disciples did not always get along with each other. Jesus had to deal with them as well.

41. Jesus accomplished victory but the ultimate sign of this victory remains for the future. Now his disciples continue the struggle, knowing that their future is God and thus the future is good.

Section Seven:
The Sermon on the Mount, 5:1–12

42. The Beatitudes, like the whole Sermon on the Mount and much of the commandments in the Bible, can seem to be too much. However, they are meant to remind people of what they have already done and encourage them to repeat their good works in the present and in the future.

43. People usually interpret "poor in spirit" as living the spirit of poverty while not actually being financially poor. Luke has a special predilection for the poor. Both Beatitudes mean fundamentally depending on God alone. The person with money usually has power and too easily relies on these for life and may forget about God.

44. Some things should be mourned. Some things and some people are worth living for and worth dying for. People who mourn know what is of value in life. Their comfort comes from appreciating that value and from their faith.

45. Usually the "meek" or "gentle" get walked on. Those who stomp through life miss its meaning. The gentle have their reward by enjoying life.

46. Standing up for justice usually means getting shot down. Doing the right thing is better than doing the thing right.

A good conscience allows a person to sleep well. If more stood up for justice, justice would prevail.

47. Forgetting is more difficult than forgiving. Sometimes all a person can do is "turn down the volume." It is easy to say "forgive and forget" but difficult to do, especially if one has been badly hurt.

48. People need to leave room in their lives for God. Filling up the nooks and crannies of the human personality with the presence of God takes a lifetime. Chastity is just one element to be integrated among many others.

49. Wishing everyone the best of everything is a fantasy: "how things might be even if they never are." People need fantasy to live. "Wouldn't it be nice if everyone wished everyone else the best of everything?" Fantasies can become real at least on a minor scale. That is why people exchange the sign of peace at Mass.

50. Being gentle, standing up for justice, making room for God, and the other Beatitudes can cause trouble. Ultimately they make the world better and then there will be peace. Actions follow values and beliefs.

Section Eight: Salt and Light, Law and Prophets, 5:13–20

51. Both images offer "food" for thought. Salt preserves and enhances taste but can cause problems as well. To be the salt of the earth demands knowing when to preserve and when to enhance and how much to use. Christians preserve what is good and add spice to life. Light means knowledge. Christians share with others their acquired wisdom.

52. Christians are spiritual Semites. No one can ever understand the New Testament without knowing the Old Testament.

Most if not all of the teachings of Jesus can also be found in the Old Testament. Even if Christians see Jesus as fulfilling the hope and expectations of Israel this does not mean that they overlook these hopes and expectations. The word of God remains in force forever. That understanding includes the law and the prophets.

53. Some laws are obsolete. Any law that supports the love of God and neighbor remains in force. All others can be forgotten. Jesus gives the example of how to respond to the laws of the Old Testament.

54. What a Christian believes should be expressed in personal activity. Otherwise the values and beliefs lie sterile. Jesus calls Christians to a life of service for others. That expects activity for the sake of others. This is particularly true for church leaders.

Section Nine: Six Antitheses, 5:21–48

55. Jesus often exaggerates to prove his point. Psychological murder can cause great pain. Physical murder, great evil in itself, passes quickly. The murder by word endures. Jesus wants his disciples to be careful of how they treat each other, even in conversation.

56. The images should remain that: images. Damnation means the deprivation of God's presence. Sometimes the Bible uses the image of eternal darkness and at other times everlasting flames. Both convey the meaning of pain and separation. The individual knows that one should find personal destiny in God and refuses to accept the relationship.

57. Any ritual should express another reality. A "goodbye kiss" should mean both an expression of love and sorrow for separation. A "hello kiss" means love and happiness for presence.

58. The desire for adultery is never the same as the actual adultery. However, when a person has the desire every effort will be made to find the opportunity. Dismissing the desire as neutral or of no consequence can lead to committing adultery. When desire and opportunity cross, chances are the person will give in to the temptation.

59. Jesus exaggerates. His point is clear. Make sure you establish the proper values in living and then follow through with them in actions.

60. Since the Bible knows of exceptions to divorce and remarriage and since life knows them, somehow as painful as divorce can be, it must be integrated into the Christian life. The Orthodox Church and the Protestant tradition follow Matthew and allow for divorce and remarriage. The Catholic Church follows Luke and Mark and does not accept divorce and remarriage except in the case of an annulment.

61. Some Christians take the words of Jesus in Matthew literally and will not swear even in court. Others recognize the meaning behind the words. No oath should ever be taken lightly.

62. Graciousness in human relationship means the acceptance of the other and not just the toleration of the other. Graciousness means appreciation of the other and a willingness to celebrate life together.

63. If "perfect" really means to be complete then to be compassionate fits in the sense of completion. A compassionate person enters into the experience of another. If the experience is joyful, it is doubly enjoyed; if painful, the presence of the compassionate person helps the person in pain to deal with it. A compassionate person is "whole" or "complete."

Section Ten: Charity, Prayer, and Fasting, 6:1–18

64. Charity relates one person to another. Prayer relates a person to God. Fasting helps a person deal with herself or himself by proper discipline in eating and drinking. All religions bind (the basic meaning of the word *religion*) people to God and to each other and all religions offer help in life by suggesting rules and regulations.

65. Anonymous donations always bring good to the person as well as the recipient. The emphasis moves from the giver to the one benefited. The reward flows from the good accomplished rather than the enhancement of one's name or reputation.

66. The Our Father functions as a model for all prayer. First the attitude of a child before God sets the scene. Praising and thanking God before asking for something acknowledges what one has already received. Promising to make a change in living and asking for continual support in living characterize all prayer. Each petition can be taken apart and amplified by fleshing out its meaning. In this way the common prayer takes on a personal meaning.

67. "Daily bread" means all a person needs to live: food, clothing, shelter, being loved, and having someone to love. Having a meaning and purpose in life and a sense of accomplishment adds to a full life and constitutes "our daily bread."

68. Everyone needs to be forgiven since no one ever lives up to the expectations of another. Most often a person does not live up to personal expectations. Failures characterize all of human life. Sinful activities, the lack of appropriate responses in situations, all contribute to missing the mark (the meaning of sinning in Greek). To be fully

human brings failure and thus the need to forgive and to be forgiven.

69. Fasting can cause weight loss, which is good since many Americans may be considered overweight. The motivation, however, differs from a diet. People fast to seek some control over the human need for pleasure. Discipline and moderation in all things bring about the sense of wholeness and completion already mentioned. Fasting contributes to balance and harmony.

Section Eleven: Further Teachings in the Sermon, 6:19—7:12

70. Most people do not think of heaven as a goal. Life offers too many other goals, which cause distractions. As time passes some people begin to think of heaven as a hoped-for possibility. Unfortunately, most do not see life as directed toward heaven. The final goal should influence the value judgments made in life. In dying the person ratifies how she or he has lived. Keeping an eye on the goal helps a person make the right decisions in life.

71. People are more important than things. In American culture the one with the most "toys" wins. Things are meant to enhance life and need to be used. Saving things for special occasions will ensure the special occasions will never come. Giving things away while alive seems to make more sense than waiting until after death. Surplus things need to find a new home.

72. Anxiety never helps anyone. Seeking only what is necessary and being satisfied with what one has overcome any anxiety about needs. Compared to the rest of the world, Americans have too many things. Paying more attention to people and less attention to things also lessens anxiety.

73. Judging someone else often exalts one's idea of self. Putting someone else down brings the hope of elevating the self. Pointing out the failures of others disguises one's personal faults. Thus, judging others comes easily.

74. However difficult, correcting another with love and for love strengthens a relationship. Too often people avoid the conflict and everyone suffers. Provided the motivation is love, all fraternal correction brings good to all parties involved.

75. Doing foolish things, doing inappropriate things, doing sinful things—all have consequences. Trying to hide or disguise the consequences only prolongs the pain. Recent civil and religious sexual scandals are good examples. Actions follow values and beliefs. If the values and beliefs are personal pleasure with no regard for others or for position in the community, such an attitude can only cause great damage to all.

76. God does listen and sometimes says, "no." God speaks if the person listens. Sometimes the response comes through others, or through events, or in a quiet moment. The answer is always there if one seeks it.

77. Both. Even if a person did not believe in God the Golden Rule helps in living. Every society has had some variation of it. Once two people existed the Golden Rule came into play. It remains ever more necessary as society becomes larger and more complex.

Section Twelve:
Judgment and Conclusion, 7:13–29

78. People usually begin to think about the final outcome of their lives when they age or when someone close to them

dies. The young think they are immortal. The middle-aged think they have centuries left. The old aged begin to wonder and when illness comes, they often go through the five stages of denial, anger, bargaining, depression, and finally acceptance. By the time many think of the outcome of their lives they are living at the end of their lives.

79. Sometimes following the teachings of Jesus is difficult because of self-concern. Whether God exists or whether Jesus existed and was the Son of God, his teachings offer help in living. Besides being religious they are humanistic. Difficulties arise when a person moves from self-centeredness (all are self-centered, otherwise they would not be human) to self-concern. Then everything revolves around the self. Then the teachings of Jesus about giving of oneself to others become annoying and even impossible.

80. The false prophecies seem to abound in many secular advertisements, especially when messages, promises, or offers of riches, beauty, pleasure, or power hide behind them. People often fall for the hope and end up disappointed. Drugs to stave off aging, drugs to enhance sexual enjoyment, cars to add to one's self-esteem, clothes to add to one's appeal— all offer a false hope since all passes and all people are destined to go to the grave. Living realistically and ignoring the ads make life more enjoyable.

81. Good works express what takes place in prayer. Knowing in prayer that God loves and cares helps a person care for others. Who a person is finds expression in how a person lives. "By their fruits you will know them."

82. A person can live only in the present. This does not mean that a person has no concern for the future. Looking to the future and planning accordingly brings the future into the present. But living in the future can only cause the person to miss the reality of the present. If the future is God, then

the future is good. The follower of Jesus has no anxiety over what is to come.

83. Jesus has a right to influence thought, opinion, and behavior since he speaks for God. Jesus is the human face of God. Yet, he does not force but invites and allows all to be free to accept or reject. "Will you also go away?" (John 6:67).

Section Thirteen: Jesus Heals, 8:1–17

84. The Law of the Lord was meant to help people in their relationship to God and to each other. Jesus ignores the Law when he wants to respond to the leper with a compassionate touch. Common sense and kindness come first for Jesus and then for his followers. This will cause problems with religious authorities.

85. Some people automatically think of Jesus as God or the Second Person of the Blessed Trinity or divine. Jesus also was very human. Usually people turn to the Gospel of Mark to notice the human Jesus. However powerful and divine as the Lord in Matthew he also lives and reacts humanly. To the human Jesus people can easily relate.

86. Evidently Jesus has two hometowns. He left Nazareth and moved to Capernaum. Today the remains of a synagogue can be found there going back to the first century. Probably Jesus visited this very place and read the scroll of Isaiah.

87. Both act with politeness. In a community of Jewish and Gentile Christians politeness may have been in short supply. Jesus is sensitive to the needs of the centurion in the illness of his servant and the centurion evidently knows the niceties of Jewish laws and traditions and seeks to avoid embarrassing Jesus by not expecting him to enter his house.

88. The faith of the Gentiles will run throughout this gospel beginning with the Magi in contrast to the Jewish authorities. The centurion, loyal to Rome, now becomes loyal to Jesus and presumably to his teachings. Gentiles had to shift their loyalty from paganism and Rome to Jesus and Christianity. The Jews had to switch their loyalty from Moses to Jesus.

89. Every religion claims to be the only true religion. Islam sees itself as superior to both Judaism and Christianity. Catholicism sees itself superior to other forms of Christianity. Today the better approach seems to concentrate more on what all religions have in common and what all the different Christian churches share in common. For Christianity, one Lord, one faith, one baptism, and one Father of all lays a good foundation for unity if never uniformity.

90. Jesus began a change in the role of women in society. Paul continued the change in Galatians 3:28. The change continues.

Section Fourteen: The Stilling of the Storm, 8:18–27

91. Sacrifice means to make "holy." To become holy demands an acceptance of the teachings of Jesus, which can at times prove to be painful. Following the Lord entails going beyond care and concern for self to include the service of others. It also expects devoting time and energy to prayer and fasting. Each moves the individual to think and act outside of ordinary human concerns.

92. People should always fulfill family obligations. However, if families interfere with one's calling from God, the person must first respond to God. In the instance narrated here it may have meant staying with parents until the parents have died. That would have been delaying a calling from God.

93. Matthew is the only gospel to use the word *church*. His community had become institutionalized, a necessary development for survival. The barque of Peter has always experienced storms caused by external forces as well as internal forces. Jesus remains with the church and eventually the storm subsides.

94. People usually pray when they are in trouble. "There are no atheists in a foxhole." It is better to pray all the time. God is present in good times and in bad. Prayer helps in the ups and downs of daily life.

95. Eventually all storms pass but sometimes they do not pass as quickly as one may wish. Trusting in God and praying help the person deal with the storms. Hope in the future, which is God, enables the person of faith to weather any storm.

Section Fifteen:
More Healings, 8:28—9:8

96. Jesus is the one who suffers, the one who will come in glory, the one who descended from heaven, the one who takes the place of God on earth. Anyone who has been in a small boat during a storm knows the water is out to get him. Of course, this makes no sense intellectually, but emotionally it seems as if that dark water below wants to destroy both boat and occupants. Even in a big boat water can be frightening. Certainly anyone in South Asia who experienced the tsunami knows the evil that water can cause. Emotionally, evil exists below the most tranquil body of water.

97. Theology is more important in the Bible than geography or even history. It is helpful to be attentive to the story and understand the teaching. This should apply to every book of the Bible. The Bible is without error when it teaches

what God wants people to learn. This does not necessarily include accuracy with regard to time or place.

98. Some people think all evil comes from the devil. Actually evil comes from the hearts of people and even from institutions. Greed exists both in people and in organizations. If the devil is involved, people have prepared the way and invited him in.

99. Some think the dietary laws evolved from the experience of what food is dangerous to eat. Perhaps the dietary laws existed to help people add discipline to this important part of human life. All may be clean but that does not mean that people should eat whatever and as much as they want.

100. Unfortunately, some people still associate sickness with sin. The first reaction to the AIDS crisis from some Christians was to see it as punishment from God for homosexuality. Sickness is part of the human experience. Too many innocent people get sick to claim that it is punishment for sin.

101. Sins are forgiven when people ask pardon and seek forgiveness. In the Catholic tradition, confession ritualizes both the asking for pardon and the actual forgiveness. In fact, sins are forgiven by God when people are sorry for their sins.

102. The Son of Man means many things in the gospels: the human Jesus is the one who suffers, the one who will come in glory, the one who descended from heaven, the one who takes the place of God on earth.

Section Sixteen:
Sinners and Eating, 9:9–17

103. Apart from Peter and Judas, the Bible gives little information about the apostles. In fact we have fourteen names. Thus Levi and Matthew are thought to be the same person as are Nathanael and Bartholomew. The Bible never says this. Most do not think the apostles John and Matthew wrote the gospels ascribed to them. Some apostles, such as Thomas, appear several times, but in reality we know very little about the majority of the Twelve.

104. Jesus does not exclude anyone. The marginalized belong as much as the privileged.

105. Everyone needs Jesus. Sometimes piety can cloak hypocrisy. Jesus evidently had a problem with false piety. In this gospel Jesus frequently criticizes religious leaders for their hypocrisy.

106. Traditionally Christians fast during Lent. Any day is a good day to fast and any day is a good day to celebrate. Christians know the proper time.

107. People are not used to seeing leather wineskins but the story makes sense. Do not put an old head on a young body. Do not put a young head on an old body. It does not work.

108. Religious communities include anyone who has faith. Some avoid external signs of piety; others surround themselves with signs of piety. All belong since all share a common faith and charity covers a multitude of sins.

109. Only individuals can decide which pious practices help faith. For some a charismatic experience should be a part of the life of all Christians. This need not be so. Some like novenas and eucharistic devotions. Others prefer the prayerful reading of

the Bible. Individuals alone can decide what helps them in their life of faith and what does not.

Section Seventeen:
The Healings Continue, 9:18–38

110. Matthew has his own understanding of Jesus and a particular community for which the gospel is written. This enables him to use sources, including the Gospel of Mark. He will include from Mark what he finds helpful for this community.

111. Magic still exists in religion. Depending on how they are used, the nine first Fridays or the nine first Saturdays may be perceived by some as an attempt to control God. Superstition has always been part of human anthropology. All religions should be careful to help people to avoid it.

112. Faith can move mountains and so faith can heal. No one knows exactly the complete interaction of the spiritual with the physical. If doctors can claim psychosomatic illness, the same can be true for healings. The best of theology can mean nothing when the spiritual affects the physical. Faith knows more answers than theology.

113. People will dispute this forever. Were they actually dead or only seemed to be dead? What is death? If death includes a final and irrevocable acceptance or rejection of God, could a person die and come back to life? If Jesus is divine, certainly God can raise from the dead. This answer needs more thought.

114. Why not? Faith can work miracles. Opening eyes spiritually at times can be more of a miracle than opening eyes physically.

115. Recognizing the goodness in others often forces a person to examine his or her own life. Better to ignore the goodness and be content with oneself. Even better, pick out the

fault in the other who appears to be good. People have subtle ways of not dealing with themselves.

116. The future should affect the present. Matthew wants his community to think about the future with God so that they will make the right decisions in the present.

Section Eighteen:
The Twelve and Their Mission, 10:1–15

117. Jesus chose twelve for his new community. Just as the Israel of old had twelve tribes, so the new Israel will have twelve leaders. Their mission continues in the college of bishops who have a concern for the worldwide church.

118. Usually people like certain apostles more than others. It all depends on what one knows about them. Some of the legends, about Thomas in India or James in Spain, will affect a devotion to the individual apostles.

119. Just as Jesus preached a mission of love of God and neighbor, a life renewed in the Spirit of God, so the apostles did the same. We know more about the apostle Paul than the other apostles precisely because of his many letters. His theology expressed in his letters continues the teachings of Jesus with an emphasis on faith.

120. The Jews first received the revelation of God through Moses. To them belongs first the proclamation of Jesus as Messiah. Only when the majority of the Jews rejected Jesus as the Messiah did the followers of Jesus turn to the Gentiles. In all probability, however, Jesus would have had many interactions with Gentiles in his ministry, as is evident in the gospels.

121. Depending on free will offerings of the faithful is good. It may seem impractical in a world of high finance and invest-

ment but also might help the church leaders to live more simply and to be more accountable. In fact, most parishes and clergy live on what the people offer every Sunday.

122. Peace should mean wishing others the best of everything. Sometimes even the faithful followers of Jesus have to settle for a cessation of hostility.

Section Nineteen: Missionary Instructions, 10:16–42

123. The church has always experienced persecution. "The blood of martyrs is the seed of Christians." Christians today experience persecution in parts of Africa and Asia. People in Western countries can experience persecution by ridicule and derision. Sometimes it is not so easy to follow all of the teaching of Jesus, especially with regard to justice for all.

124. Ancient people often paid close attention to animals to learn from them. Pick out the positive qualities of the animals named and imitate them.

125. Where people differ with regard to the fundamental questions of life, conflict will arise. Jesus wanted people to rethink radically how they were living. Religion will always cause disputes, especially if one tries to impose one religion on another person. Christianity demands a rethinking but always done freely.

126. The Holy Spirit remains with the church and with each individual believer. Paying attention to church teaching and trusting the guidance of one's conscience will never lead a person astray.

127. Probably the early Christians thought Jesus would return in their lifetimes. With the death of many of the earliest fol-

lowers, the early church had to rethink the second coming. Some thought Jesus had already returned through the resurrection while others pushed the second coming into the distant future.

128. The church can always learn from the Bible. Being open and transparent can only add to the glory of Christianity. Trying to hide faults and failures and sins never works. Only when people recognize the failures in Christianity can they also see the glory that God has bestowed on the church.

129. Trusting in God as the future of the human race should wipe out all fear. Seeing the future of the human race as just itself should cause great fear. God cares for all and supports all, good times or bad.

130. Following Jesus demands a continual change of living. Repentance does not happen just once but daily. As life changes for an individual so should living the Christian faith adapt to new circumstances.

131. Those who point out the presence or absence of God in contemporary life both in society and in the church usually are not accepted. This is especially true when they point out the absence of God. What Jesus experienced his followers will as well.

Section Twenty:
Jesus and John the Baptist, 11:1–19

132. Luke alone says that Jesus and John were cousins. Yet the gospels apart from the infancy narrative of Luke give no such evidence. Who knows?

133. The people wanted a political messiah who would restore the lost glory of Israel. Some in the Qumran community

envisioned a spiritual messiah, but the majority of people wanted someone to throw off the yoke of Rome and bring back the glory of David and Solomon.

134. When someone points out the presence and especially the absence of God, they should expect trouble. People like to live comfortably and they do not wish to be disturbed by someone who tells them they are not honoring their commitment or are not fulfilling their obligations to God.

135. Whenever authority is questioned, those in authority will centralize and reaffirm their power. Jesus questioned the authority of the Jewish religious leaders. They responded by claiming that they alone spoke for Moses and thus for God. Eventually anyone who challenges authority must be destroyed one way or another.

136. John pointed out Jesus. He announced another, did not pretend to be someone he was not, and told the truth. He has always been a great saint for Christians to imitate.

137. Asceticism may or may not be a part of a prophet's life. Provided the prophet fulfills his or her mission to announce the presence or absence of God, lifestyle may vary. "By their fruits you will know them."

Section Twenty-one: Reactions to the Preaching of Jesus, 11:20–30

138. The Germans have a proverb, "For every gift there is a corresponding responsibility." Actually the proverb involves a play on words since *Gabe* in German means gift and *Aufgabe* (based on the same word) means responsibility. Jesus teaches the same.

139. Since repentance means a continual rethinking, sometimes using discipline can help in controlling the physical

demands of life. Pleasure can be a controlling appetite. Fasting and sackcloth can help to control the desire for pleasure.

140. The wise are those who learn from life and change their way of living. The "little ones" are those who do not depend on power or wealth but on God alone. Twelve-step programs recognize both the need to depend on God and the need to learn from past experiences.

141. God cares for all. Since many of the marginalized and less gifted people often need more care than others, God wants the gifted to act in the name of God and care for the less fortunate. At times God does seem to intervene for the sake of the "little ones."

142. Jesus is the Word of God incarnate. He alone can speak the word of God humanly in a complete fashion. He gives to his followers to continue to speak this word even if imperfectly and incompletely.

143. Most people add to their own burdens. Some people like to burden others. Some people allow others to burden them. Life brings its own burdens. At least people should not add to their own problems and should try not to overburden others. "Being of good cheer" (John 16:33) can lessen any burden.

144. The kind person emphasizes the positive. The mean person always picks out the negative. The gentle person walks or strides through life; the harsh person stomps through life.

145. Rest and refreshment have come. People have to recognize them and enjoy them. Living in a kind and gentle fashion and not burdening self or others bring refreshment and rest.

Section Twenty-two:
The Servant Causes Problems with the
Sabbath Law, 12:12–21

146. In Judaism only religious leaders can interpret the Law. Jesus gives this right to everyone.

147. The fulfillment of the Law means knowing the purpose of the Law and honoring it. It does not mean that the Law obliges in every time and place. Jesus interprets the Law of God to include what is good for the neighbor.

148. Jesus says so. Making holy (sacrifice) demands forgiveness and compassion more than the acting out of a ritual. The ritual is supposed to express the reality already present, which would include mercy and compassion.

149. Giving people freedom always has caused problems whether in civil or religious life. Yet Jesus seems to do just that. In the long run, living freely and acting freely add to the human spirit while seeking to control behavior by force or fear may bring compliance but not conviction.

150. Jesus challenged the religious authority of the scribes. They had to react to protect their power and position. First they tried to discredit Jesus and when this did not work, they sought to destroy him.

151. People who live according to the Spirit usually are gentle people. But sometimes the Spirit brings a fierceness that expects a stronger reaction. In both cases when the person "feels at peace," then the person can presume the Spirit works within.

152. Balance and harmony have been the sought-after ideal of all peoples and all civilizations. Sometimes it has been present but too often it has been lost. Just as repentance is an

ongoing task so the seeking of balance and harmony in every aspect of life remains the goal for individuals and society and the church.

Section Twenty-three: This Evil Generation, 12:22–50

153. The Jews expected a political messiah. Jesus was not. Often when he healed he did so on the Sabbath and thus violated the Sabbath law. He acted as if he were God and thus blasphemed. To the pious Jew, Jesus would have been an abomination even if he did good. To religious leaders he undermined their authority. He had to go.

154. Some who rejected Jesus probably were more concerned about their own position than anything else. Often they used and abused their power. But not everyone who rejected Jesus did so with wrongful motives. For the one who tried to observe the Law, Jesus would have caused great concern. Paul, for example, rejected Jesus and his teachings until he had his religious experience of Jesus.

155. Jesus was the divine Son of God. To attribute to him evil motivations and evil bases for his actions contradicted the very being of Jesus. Such denied who Jesus was.

156. Every sin can be forgiven if the person is truly sorry. To deny the divinity of Jesus precludes any part in the life of Jesus. To claim that Jesus was evil excludes the person from participating in the healing ministry of Jesus. Denying the source of salvation means no salvation.

157. Individuals must continually examine what they believe and what values are parts of their lives. For Jesus the religious leaders did not live what they proclaimed. They were

"fakes." Today all followers of Jesus must ask themselves if they are "fakes." Actions follow values and beliefs.

158. In American culture people like to blame others. "I am a miserable person because I had a terrible childhood." "I failed the test because I had a bad teacher." People need to accept the consequences of their action or nonactions. Religious leaders, including the Pharisees, had to learn to accept responsibility and not try to blame others. Many did not, as do many religious leaders today.

159. The true family of Jesus is those who believe in him. We may never know the true history of his biological family.

160. Some accept the brothers and sisters of Jesus as half brothers and half sisters. They are followers of the Lord and should be accepted as such. At the same time Protestants and others who accept true brothers and sisters of Jesus should respect the Catholic tradition of the perpetual virginity of Mary.

Section Twenty-four: The Parable of the Sower, 13:1–23

161. Some parables are easier to understand than others. Usually the parables have one point. Sometimes when they have been adapted to the needs of the early church, that one point can get lost. Some people like poetry and figurative speech while others prefer prose. The Bible contains both types of literature.

162. "Teasing the mind into active thought" challenges the mind. People have to think about the meaning of a parable. The whole Bible does just that. The word of God gives people something to think about. Once people think, they might even pray and might even change how they are living.

163. The gospels give us more than the words of Jesus. They have been crafted by later generations for a particular time and place. Actually Jesus did speak simply. Some of the parables are better understood by a particular audience and some have been changed by the early church. The basic message of Jesus, however, remains simple and plain. "Since God cares for you, you can care for each other. Your future is God no matter what."

164. Jesus wanted people to understand but that depended on a willingness on the part of the listeners. Some did not want to hear and understand. The same is true today. People hear what they want to hear.

165. God predestines people to salvation. People have to accept this offer. Luck often seems fickle. Life does seem to have favorites but all are called to experience eternally the saving presence of God.

166. There is a lawn. Some parts are sparse and others are full. Some days are 60 percent and some days are 10 percent. Rocks and thorns inhibit the lawn from growing, but it is growing.

Section Twenty-five: More Parables and Rejection, 13:24–58

167. Too often people use mystery as if they understood nothing. "It's a mystery" is meant to end the discussion. Just as the human person is a "mystery" to the self, never understanding everything but growing in understanding of the self, so the same is true for God, for Jesus, for life, and for other people.

168. Weeds grow in every human heart along with good plants. Weeds live in the body of the church as well as the sanctu-

ary. Weeds grow in business offices and in the offices of politicians. Weeds will never destroy the crop but need to be controlled. Just as the person has patience with his or her own weeds, so all should have patience with the weeds of others. Some weeds, however, because they are pernicious need to be uprooted lest they harm the crop.

169. God remains God. God must have other plans for billions of other peoples. In the meantime Christians should live their lives as examples for non-Christians and concentrate on what they can share with those who believe differently.

170. Most people do not think of the reign of God. Yet, it has begun in the death and resurrection of Jesus. Love, truth, justice, peace, and freedom exist even if not perfectly. Be attentive to what already is while awaiting the fulfillment.

171. When people get older they begin to think about death and judgment. In fact, people who have come to the light, who believe, are already judged (John 5:24). They have nothing to fear. The final decision in life in death depends upon the intervening decisions. People will die how they lived. A person of faith lives and dies by faith.

172. Most people find it difficult to hold a middle position. Too many hold on to too much while others discard too much. The follower of Jesus is like salt: preserving the good of the past while adding the spice of the new to enhance life.

173. People judge people because it makes them feel superior. When a person can't wait to talk, then that person hears nothing of what the other has to say. Beginning with "Don't you think…" already tells what the speaker thinks and precludes an ability to listen to what someone else thinks.

Section Twenty-six:
The Death of John the Baptist, 14:1–12

174. Curiosity can both help and hinder religion. The curious
will seek more information about religion but then when
the information does not agree with preset notions, then
the religion and the information are discarded. Some religious leaders were curious about both John and Jesus.
They learned something but it did not fit what they wanted
to hear and so they dismissed it. Other curious people
learned and changed their way of living.

175. Telling the truth is always dangerous because some people
do not want to know the truth. Denial seems easier.
Knowing when to tell the whole truth can be tricky. When
Leo XIII opened the Vatican archives, he said there would
be two rules: no one will lie and no one will be afraid to
tell the whole truth. Who or what institution has lived up
to these rules?

176. Human beings can change their minds. Even the Supreme
Court can reverse itself. One foolish action following
another does no good. Admit the mistake and correct it
makes sense.

177. John arrived, preached, was handed over, and died. Jesus
arrived, preached, was handed over, and died. The early
followers preached, were handed over, and died. Thus has
always been the history of Christianity.

Section Twenty-seven: The Feeding and
the Walking on the Water, 14:13–36

178. People usually refer to the multiplication of the loaves and
yet nowhere does the gospel say that Jesus multiplied
loaves and fish. Certainly as the divine Son of God Jesus

could have done just that, but perhaps the miracle he performed was having people share with others what they had. The gospels do not make clear exactly what he did.

179. Bread and circuses still please and still blind people. Looking at a miracle only as a work of magic never brings faith. Seeing beyond the miracle to recognize the presence of God fulfills the purpose of the actions of Jesus. Giving people what they want either through church or society can prevent people from seeing what is most important in life. Tastefully done liturgies that never deal with controversies such as justice for all can be modern bread and circuses.

180. Feeding is important in life. Eating socializes. Breaking bread together unites people. Jesus knew all of this and made sure he and his followers enjoyed each other's company as well as the company of thousands.

181. God comes in human form. The human face of God seems like any other. He is from Nazareth, has a family. How unlikely that Jesus could be God's human face. But God always seems to do the unlikely.

182. The Greek preposition could mean "by" the water. It all depends on what one accepts as proper activity of Jesus and whether one believes in miracles.

183. Peter made a fool of himself. He does it more than once in the gospels. He is so brave and so cowardly. Yet, Jesus chose him to be the foundation for the church.

184. Everyone's faith can be "little" and in need of support. Faith needs nourishment and no better way than by the lives and example of other believers.

185. Jesus appeals immediately to some people. Others need more time or encouragement. Some who have a religious personality beat a path to Jesus. Others step out of the way even if they meet Jesus on the road. Different people react

differently and people respond differently as the circumstances of their lives change.

Section Twenty-eight:
Jewish Traditions, 15:1–20

186. Every family, every society, every culture needs to preserve
traditions. Traditions keep the beliefs and values alive.
With the change in time and place, however, some traditions must fall by the wayside. The wise person knows what
to hold on to and what to discard. The wise group knows
the same. Holding on to too much prevents future growth.
Holding on to too little kills the roots.

187. Accepting personal responsibility makes demands.
Acknowledging that gifts are meant to be used for others
(*Gabe* and *Aufgabe*) can take too much time and energy.
With limited time and energy people can often concentrate
only on themselves.

188. Hypocrisy needs to be exposed to the light of day.
Everyone knows it exists and trying to hide it only makes
matters worse. No one ever lives completely according to
values and principles but when failure happens, the failure
needs to be acknowledged and corrected. Pretending only
adds to the hypocrisy.

189. People do what they like. Very often people pay lip service
to the law of God and ignore it. Going to church on
Sunday should affect the rest of the week but often it does
not. Sunday becomes leisuretime activity. Not hearing the
word of God (coming to church after the word has been
read) or not listening even while in church, and settling for
the ritual can be the temptation of both religious leaders
and people. Actions depend on beliefs and beliefs rest on
the word of God.

190. Not performing the ritual as demanded or expected can be an expression of moral defilement. Mocking the ritual by the actions of minister or people means that the reality that should be present is absent.

191. As human, Jesus experienced all the frustrations of trying to interact with others, even those closest to him. Misunderstanding, lack of appreciation, being ignored, can all add to human frustration. Jesus knew them all.

192. The wise person discovers what works and what does not work in life. Once learned the wise person does not repeat the mistakes of the past. God has established an order in life that the wise discover. Unfortunately, too many fail to discover the order or, even if they do, fail to follow through by learning from their mistakes.

Section Twenty-nine: More Healings, 15:21–31

193. Although sent to the lost sheep of Israel Jesus continues the minor tradition in the Bible of including all nations, Gentiles. As already noted, once the large number of Jews rejected Jesus as the Messiah, the early Jewish preachers of Jesus turned to the Gentiles. The Gospel of Matthew, written for both Jewish and Gentile Christians, always leaves room for Gentile participation while holding on to the Jewish roots of Christianity.

194. The gospel contains more than just actual history. Sometimes the gospels contain more information than would have been available within the historical period of Jesus. Or, his reputation had spread even among non-Jews.

195. It seems harsh but then some groups always put down other groups. Was this Jesus speaking, his disciples, or the

people of the time of Matthew? Putting the remark on the lips of Jesus strengthens the impact of the final remark.

196. Throughout this gospel Gentiles pay Jesus homage beginning with the Magi. Here homage is joined to faith explicitly. Too often in the gospel, Jews pay him no homage and have no faith, especially the Jewish leaders. The Gentile woman stands as a model to imitate.

197. Although hard to accept coming from Jesus, how often does the term come from the lips of Christians referring to others who are different? How often a woman is called a female dog, even in cultured and Christian society!

Section Thirty: The Second Feeding Miracle, 15:32–39

198. Some think the change in numbers signifies a change from a Jewish to a Gentile crowd. Since Matthew used Mark and Mark had two miracles of feeding, Matthew, unlike Luke, includes both. If it took place in Gentile territory Matthew subtly leaves room for Gentiles being part of the ministry of Jesus.

199. By the end of the first century Christians regularly celebrated the Eucharist. Probably they began its celebration shortly after the resurrection because of the words of Jesus. The need for ritual sacred meals has long been part of religious anthropology. Christians followed the example of the Jews in their sacred meal and Matthew would have emphasized the presence of Jesus in the celebration of the Eucharist.

200. The Gentile theme continues throughout this gospel because of the nature of the community of Matthew.

201. The two feeding miracles emphasize the importance for followers of Jesus to eat together and enjoy each other's company. This fittingly would prepare for the celebration of the Eucharist.

Section Thirty-one: Further Controversies, 16:1–12

202. Pharisees attempted a strict observance of the Law. They devoted themselves to its meaning and application. They exhibited their piety by their actions and demeanor. The Sadducees came from the priestly order within Judaism. They both competed for power. With the destruction of the Temple in AD 70, the role of the Pharisees increased. The community of Matthew may have had continued problems with the Pharisees.

203. Matthew will build up the drama of his gospel leading to the death of Jesus. He has to increase the opposition to explain the ultimate condemnation of Jesus and his crucifixion.

204. Neither the Jewish leaders nor his disciples understood Jesus. They all seem to have been looking for power. One group did not want to give it up and the other group wanted it. Some things never change.

205. Everyone can influence others for good or ill. Those with authority usually have more influence and thus carry the greater responsibility. "Heavy is the mantle on him who wears the crown." When religious authorities fail in their responsibility the pain seems greater. In fact, every Christian bears responsibility when one fails in helping others by word and example.

Section Thirty-two: Peter and the Passion Prediction, 16:13–28

206. Matthew continues to stress Old Testament continuity because of the nature of his community: Jewish and Gentile Christians. As a centrist he wanted to hold on to the best of the past while being open to the new.

207. Peter was a "rock" with imperfection. He became a "pebble" during the passion but then repented and boldly preached Jesus crucified. Later he would be strong in his willingness to die for his Master.

208. Peter's authority continues in the church today through the role of the bishop of Rome. Like Peter and the Twelve, the pope functions with his fellow bishops, working for the good of the whole church.

209. Some successors of Peter have caused great suffering for the church while others were willing to die as Peter did for their Master. The church has had both saints and sinners in leadership roles.

210. Carrying one's cross means accepting the ups and downs of daily life. No need to look for pain or trouble; it will find everyone. How a person integrates the sorrow and difficulties of life into one's person develops Christian character. Perhaps the greatest cross is the knowledge of human failure and sin.

Section Thirty-three: The Transfiguration and the Disciples' "Little Faith," 17:1–20

211. The material always manifests the spiritual. It begins with the human body. The person, the spiritual reality,

finds expression only through the bodily. Artists best recognize the presence of the spiritual in the physical. No matter exists that is not a sign of the spiritual from the smallest rock, to plants, to humans, and to all that humans create.

212. Mystical experiences occur when a person goes beyond space and time. It can happen on a ski slope or on a sail-boat or while listening to music. It happens in the birth of a child and in moments of prayer. The experiences abound. People have only to be aware of them.

213. The earliest followers of Jesus did not understand him completely. They often were lost in their own needs and concerns. The same has always been true in the church. Jesus had patience with Peter and his earliest followers and continues to have patience with his followers today.

214. Once again, Matthew turns to the Old Testament and shows the superiority of Jesus. Moses and Elijah are the companions of Jesus, not the other way around. Jesus controls the scene, uniting the old with the new.

215. Jesus often seems frustrated by the lack of understanding of his followers and audience. People should trust God and be loyal to God's commandments. When people rely only on themselves, they will find no comfort and relief. Relying on God brings a sense of peace. No one can ever record all that faith has accomplished in human history.

216. Prayer and fasting manifest a trust in God and trusting in God brings miracles. Even if the desired effect is not always present, the prayer and fasting will bring reconciliation and acceptance. Sometimes God says, "No."

Section Thirty-four:
The Temple Tax and the Second Passion Prediction, 17:22–27

217. Some Jews and some Romans actually killed Jesus. Anyone who destroys what is good participates. Sin, which entered the world through Adam and Eve, reaches its culmination in the death of Jesus. Jesus was good and people who have the tendency to destroy the good destroyed Jesus. His death lies heavy on the hearts of all people.

218. Jesus did not want to cause unnecessary problems for himself or others. In some circumstances where little is at stake, it is better to go along. Everyone can learn from this lesson.

219. Peter again is a spokesperson and again lacks understanding. With patience Jesus continues to teach Peter.

220. Many similar legends exist in the ancient world. A fisherman put his wedding ring around the beak of a swordfish after experiencing a painful divorce. Years later he caught the same fish.

Section Thirty-five:
The Church Sermon, 18:1–35

221. Status in the church rests on baptism. All followers of Jesus are equal in dignity through baptism. Within the community of equals, some have been called to serve the larger community by ministering the word and sacraments. Clergy, bishop, priest, and deacon ordained through the sacrament of holy orders assume a role to serve the other members of the church. However, everyone shares in the one priesthood of Jesus through baptism. The priesthood of all believers founds the church.

222. Any member of the church can cause a scandal, a "stumbling block," to others. The block must be removed and always with the hope of redemption to the one causing the scandal. Causing a scandal does not mean the person has no value, worth, or dignity in the eyes of God and so retains this value and worth in the church. Sometimes the scandals seem worse when caused by church leaders but in reality the church will suffer from the scandals caused by any member.

223. Too often attention is paid, even in the church, to those in power and authority and the "little ones" are neglected. Jesus would not be pleased. Every baptized person has worth and value and should be treated accordingly.

224. When a person is ordained through holy orders he accepts a responsibility to serve the church, especially those in most need. Just as Jesus paid attention to the poor and marginalized, so clergy should do likewise. Clergy lead by example and not just by words.

225. Dissenters have always existed in the church. In the early centuries the church dialogued and met and discussed and sought some solution. Augustine believed that heresy pointed out some lack in teaching and helped to clarify teaching. The church should welcome discussion and eventually the whole church should decide on how to proceed. Councils performed this function for centuries.

226. Jesus is present wherever Christians gather. Jesus is present in a meal celebrated by a Christian family in which prayer forms an important part. Theologians and canonists will argue forever with regard to the validity of the Eucharist in Protestant churches. No one, however, can deny the words of Jesus promising his presence when Christians gather in prayer.

227. Since everyone sins, everyone needs forgiveness. Asking God for forgiveness in the Lord's Prayer carries with it a

promise to forgive others. Pope John Paul II frequently asked pardon for the past sins of the church. All members should do likewise.

Section Thirty-six: Marriage, Divorce, Celibacy, Children, and Wealth, 19:1–30

228. Evidently for Matthew, like today, divorce was a problem. He was a centrist and although he knew the teaching of Jesus he seems to admit an exception. He would have been opposed to divorce but realized that, in some instances, it might be the best solution for a bad situation. Paul also acknowledges an exception (1 Cor 7:10–16). Divorce, however painful, is accepted in both the Orthodox and Protestant traditions.

229. Celibacy can always make sense if accepted as a special gift from God to serve others. Historically more than Catholic priests lived a celibate life (religious communities of men and women, for example) in order to respond to the needs of others. Whether celibacy should always be joined to priesthood is another question. Certainly having married clergy will not solve all of the problems of the contemporary church but it is worth discussion given the history in the Orthodox tradition.

230. Being like a child does not mean innocence since only infants are innocent. Children learn guile quickly and usually the first word they learn after *mom* and *dad* is *no*! But children are dependent. They need the care and love and support of parents. In the presence of God all people are dependent. God supports and loves even when people do not respond, much like parents who continue to love even when rejected by their offspring.

231. Wealth brings two temptations: people are never satisfied with what they have and want to protect what they have. What can a person do of value with five million dollars that an individual cannot do with one million dollars? Yet the millionaire wants to be a multimillionaire. Wealth also brings power. Who needs God when one has money and power?

Section Thirty-seven:
The Parable No One Likes, 20:1–16

232. Everyone thinks the master is unfair. Yet, reading the agreement shows he is not. That makes little difference. Everyone who hears this parable does not like the outcome. It is unfair to give to the ones who worked the shortest the same pay as the ones who bore the heat of the day and worked all day.

233. People like to be rewarded for their labor and do not like others to be put on the same level unless they deserved it. The ones who worked the shortest do not deserve equal pay. Such practices go against all the traditions of American fairness and work experience.

234. No explanation ever seems to satisfy everyone. People will still say it is unfair. But then, is God unfair? At times it seems that way. "If I were God, I would treat all people in a fairer manner!"

235. The parables are similar in outcome. The elder brother cannot rejoice in the good fortune of the younger brother who has returned. Those who worked the hardest cannot rejoice in the good fortune of those who received the same pay for unequal work. No one likes to identify with the elder brother, but no one likes to be one of those who worked the longest and the hardest.

Section Thirty-eight:
The Passion, Discipleship, and the Blind Man, 20:17–34

236. Jesus had to die because he was human like us in all things but sin. Jesus suffered in life because that is part of the human condition. Some of the particular pain he suffered came from others who did not understand him or who rejected him. Eventually having failed to destroy him by derision and innuendo, they destroyed him by crucifixion.

237. Glory and power are always better than pain. The problem is how to get the power and glory. Jesus says people will receive power and glory by serving others. Blessed Mother Teresa of Calcutta is a good contemporary example.

238. Too often in the history of Christianity those in authority, unlike Jesus, "lord" it over others. They failed to recognize that they, like Jesus, came to serve and not to be served.

239. In the church clergy are supposed to serve the faithful. In universities faculty is supposed to serve students and administrators are supposed to serve the faculty. In business workers are supposed to serve their clients by their good products or service and administration is supposed to serve workers, their clients, and stockholders. Unfortunately, too often clergy and administrators receive the service and the others are forgotten.

240. Many people remain spiritually blind to Jesus and his teachings. He tries to open their eyes but they remain shut. Some claim to see and are blind and some who were blind by birth come to see through the eyes of faith. The spiritually blind exist today in society and in the church. The multiple healings of blind people in the gospels emphasize the need for all followers of Jesus to open their eyes to see

all those in need: physically and economically, mentally and psychologically, and, especially, spiritually.

Section Thirty-nine: Jerusalem, 21:1–17

241. Jerusalem is a city of three faiths: Judaism, Christianity, and Islam. Eastern Jerusalem is the old city and has three quarters: Armenian Christian, Christian, Jewish and Arab. The platform on which the Temple was built now has the Dome of the Rock, an Islamic mosque. The Western Wall, one of the walls that supported the Temple platform, is the only part of the Jewish Temple area that remains and is sacred to Jews. A church covers the traditional place of the crucifixion and burial of Jesus.

242. Jerusalem was the center of Jewish worship from the time of David. Here was the Temple in which the high priest once a year spoke the sacred name. Here priests offered sacrifice. Here Jews celebrated Passover.

243. People are fickle. Miracles, bread, and circuses are good but only for a time. Jesus demanded too much. He caused trouble for the clergy and possibly for the Romans. Better to go along with the status quo. He did not deliver the people from the Romans and was causing more trouble. The priests want to get rid of him, so why not?

244. With the destruction of the Temple in AD 70 Judaism lost its place of worship, its priesthood, and its sacrifices. The cleansing of the Temple symbolizes this eventual loss for Judaism.

245. Jesus challenged the authority and power of the religious leaders. He gave people the freedom to interpret the Law and actually lived what he taught. He was dangerous for

both religious society and secular society. Since he could not be discredited, he had to be destroyed.

Section Forty: The Fig Tree and the Authority of Jesus, 21:18–28

246. The story seems out of character for Jesus. Why pick on a poor fig tree? If the original story was a parable, then the early church quickly saw its implications after the destruction of the Temple in AD 70. The fig tree symbolized Israel and its religious traditions. With Jesus all of this would change and Judaism and the world would never be the same.

247. Matthew portrays Jesus moving from frustration to anger. Whether this was Jesus or Matthew is unknown. No doubt Jesus became frustrated frequently. He also became angry enough to drive money changers from the Temple. Jesus, if like us in all things, probably did get angry but in this instance it may be more Matthew than Jesus.

248. People did not expect the type of Messiah that Jesus demonstrated. Faith in him was a gift and people did not want to accept the gift. Jesus was an unlikely prophet and Messiah and thus people did not recognize him as God's human face.

249. Jesus did what he wanted to do and acted in a way to draw people to himself. It is always easier to be a "Monday morning quarterback" or to think anyone today could have done a better job of convincing people. The gospels give us the bare elements. We know something of what Jesus said and did but not everything.

Section Forty-one:
The Parables Return, 21:28—22:1-14

250. Matthew more than the other gospels seems to like parables. By the time of its writing many of the parables had been told and retold and in all probability additions came naturally. It is always helpful to concentrate on the fundamental meaning of a parable, paying attention to the classic definition already studied.

251. Most people have found themselves in the position of both brothers. The ability to change one's mind belongs to being human. Unfortunately, sometimes the decision to change is the wrong one. Better to do the right thing whether the decision to do so is first or second in the thought process.

252. Sometimes the allegorical elements obscure the original meaning. In later church history much attention was paid to seeing allegories in every aspect of the parables of Jesus. Augustine, for example, could find meaning in almost every detail of every parable. Better to try to first see the original meaning intended by Jesus and then limit the allegorical elements unless they seem to be part of the original thought of Jesus. The parable of the wicked vinedressers, although clearly allegorical, probably goes back to the thought of Jesus.

253. The meaning of the wedding garment has intrigued people for years. Some think that the garment would have been supplied but then why did the person not choose to wear it? Why should the host be concerned about what people were wearing, if called at the last minute? The parable probably developed in the early church and so the wedding garment would have signified that some people, although invited, did not belong. This would be understood in relationship to some Jews who refused to accept Jesus as the

Messiah. Later church history would see the lack of a wedding garment signifying improper dispositions.

254. Matthew probably had problems with some Jewish religious leaders. He recognizes that Jesus had similar problems. Throughout his gospel he will build up the opposition to Jesus by these religious leaders. What was true for the Master will be true for the followers.

Section Forty-two: Four Questions: Taxes, the Resurrection, the Greatest Commandment, David's Son, 22:15–46

255. The coin has nothing to do with the separation of church and state although frequently used for this purpose. People have obligations to both institutions and sometimes they are separate and sometimes they overlap. Jesus does not solve the question of when they should be joined and when they should function separately.

256. The resurrection may mean different things to different people. For the child it can mean that Jesus lives. For the philosopher it may mean that Jesus enters into his definitive mode of existence. For the theologian it may mean that Jesus passes out of space and time now able to be present in the church, especially in the Eucharist. For the student of the Bible resurrection means that God has made Jesus both Lord and Christ. To the poet and theologian the crucifixion was the human "no" to goodness and the resurrection was the divine "yes" to goodness.

257. The one commandment in John fulfills the twofold commandment in the Synoptics and the twofold commandment in the Synoptics fulfills the hundreds of commandments of the Old Testament.

258. Scripture can always confuse people. The Old Testament was written over a period of a thousand years covering a longer period of time. The New Testament, while written in under a hundred years, came from diverse communities with different needs. The Bible often seems to contradict itself and readers can find many images of God or Jesus. The more a person studies the whole Bible the better the understanding.

Section Forty-three:
The Pharisees, 23:1–39

259. This chapter contains the most scathing attack on the Pharisees in any gospel. Certainly some Pharisees were sincere followers of the Law of Moses. What seems to annoy Jesus the most is hypocrisy. Their actions do not flow from their beliefs. They profess to uphold the Law of God and yet fail to take care of those in need. They pay more attention to observance than to human pain and suffering. They place burdens on people's back that people cannot carry. They separate themselves from the toils of daily life and maintain a piety that masks infidelity.

260. How much of the criticism of the Pharisees goes back to Jesus and how much was added by Matthew because of his problems with the Pharisees and his community's problems with these same religious leaders remains unknown. Jesus does seem to be too harsh. After all, Jesus said and did things that were against the Law and yet he claimed to honor the Law. The sincere Pharisees may have been caught in a "no win" situation. They wanted to observe the Law and saw in Jesus a good man who did not always honor the Law. What should they do? Some no doubt accepted Jesus in spite of their concerns and others rejected him. When the final break came with Judaism and Christianity became a separate religious tradition, the differences between the

teachings of Jesus and that of the Pharisees became evident. Then Christianity was on its own.

261. "Whitewashed sepulchers" seems very strong. "Blind guides" is a harsh title for a religious leader. Calling a person a "hypocrite" always hurts. "Serpents and brood of vipers" only adds to the harshness. No wonder any Pharisee or any Jew who reads this chapter would be offended. Could religious leaders ever be that bad?

262. What Jesus says about the Pharisees can apply to any religious leader, whether Jewish, Christian, or Islam, or from any other religious tradition. Power can corrupt and too often religious leaders have absolute power, which corrupts absolutely. Any religious leader should regularly read this chapter of Matthew, especially Christians. Any Christian can read this chapter and examine his or her conscience.

263. Hypocrisy remains in the church and in society. People do not always live what they profess to believe. Living two lives has characterized both Christian leaders and ordinary believers for two thousand years. Saying one thing and doing another have plagued the clergy and the laity. Of course when the clergy fall, it always seems worse because of the high expectations clergy engender in people.

264. Surely not all Pharisees were that bad. Even today no one likes to be called a Pharisee since in Christianity it implies hypocrisy. The gospels contain more than the words and actions of Jesus. They also contain aspects of the life of the community for which they were written. Evidently the community of Matthew had severe problems with Pharisees.

265. Many times a commentator finds it difficult to separate what comes from the ministry of Jesus and what comes from the context within which the gospel was written. Certainly Jesus had problems with some religious leaders

of Judaism, as did the community of Matthew. The situations probably became intertwined within the community of Matthew. The author may well have wanted to use the opportunity to warn Christian leaders to avoid falling into the same trap that the Jewish religious fell into in their exercise of authority.

Section Forty-four: The Final Sermon: The Temple and the Signs, 24:1–14

266. Most people do not know the word *eschatological*. Some have heard of the word and know it has something to do with the end of history. Others know it deals with the "last things"—death, judgment, heaven, or hell. Still, most people do not know much about the "eschatological," especially when Scripture scholars use it in conjunction with the apocalyptic. However, people know that whatever apocalyptic means, it is bad.

267. Jesus really does not respond clearly to the questions of the apostles. He uses images and symbols that offer more darkness than light. Matthew probably joined the words of Jesus with other Jewish apocalyptic images, especially after the Temple had been destroyed. Matthew does not make clear exactly what Jesus is trying to say, other than it is bad.

268. Some ages are very apocalyptic. People think things will get worse before they get better. In an age of worldwide terrorism and insecurity, people find it hard to think things will improve. The world will never return to the security of the time after the Second World War. Yet, even then people lived under the threat of nuclear annihilation. The United States used to think it was beyond the reach of terrorism. That myth died on September 11, 2001. Insecurity, anxiety, and fear affect everyone, even small children. Many think the end of the world is near. Yet, no one can be sure.

People may have to learn to live with these negatives for a long period of time.

269. Some prophets predict the imminent return of Jesus and the end of human history. They offer times and dates and yet nothing has happened so far. The popular series of books on the "rapture and those left behind" appeal to many. Some see the failure of great institutions such as the church or Wall Street or the failure in education to educate as clear signs of the end. Others recognize the decline in morality as signs of the final age of destruction. Human cloning, euthanasia, abortion, the so-called homosexual agenda, the lack of morality in Hollywood, the strange change in the climate with massive hurricanes and tsunami for many show the decline in human beings and the anger of God. Many wish the whole thing was over. Yet, Christians have to continue to live. Is this age more apocalyptic than others? It seems so.

270. Persecution has always existed. In certain parts of Asia and Africa, as already noted, persecution continues for all Christians. Even in so-called Christian countries, followers of Christ experience ridicule or are ignored. But always, even in the worst of times, Jesus offers hope, for God remains the future of the human race.

Section Forty-five: The Coming of the Son of Man, 24:15–31

271. As already noted, people know something of the meaning of apocalyptic through the movie *Apocalypse Now*. The time period, the Vietnam War, along with the death, destruction, and the violent reactions in this country, all pointed to a bad period for everyone. People may not have related apocalyptic to theology but they had some sense of its meaning. A final violent intervention by God to destroy

all that is evil could give hope to followers who were discouraged by wholesale abandonment of Christian morality.

272. Some will proclaim an apocalyptic age has begun. As already noted, it is hard to say this age is more apocalyptic than others but some think so. The Black Plague was apocalyptic. For Jews in the 1940s the Holocaust was apocalyptic.

273. Some want each gospel to narrate exactly what Jesus said and did. Some people think the gospels do just that. But the gospels often cannot be harmonized. Bible research for decades has demonstrated that the gospels are books of faith and not of accurate history. Yet, people continue to be troubled when someone will say that an author added to the words of Jesus, or changed some of the sequence of events, or even included events from the evangelist's period and added them to the time of Jesus. Seeing the gospels as accurate historical documents may have offered more security but not much reality. Faith documents use history but are never slaves to history.

274. Some do and will continue to do so. Often a literal interpretation loses the true meaning. Paying attention to the story rather than the details makes more sense. Such is how people live.

275. People may fear this passage because of its implications. For faithful followers of Jesus the return of Jesus will be a triumphal parade. God will create a new heaven and a new earth and every tear will be wiped away and death shall be no more (Rev 21:1–4).

276. Most people prefer the eschatological to the apocalyptic. The former is more positive. God as the future of the human race could not be more positive. People are redeemed; the world is redeemed. People and the universe contain a value and worth and dignity that can never be

destroyed in spite of the power of evil. The future has already begun even if incomplete and imperfect. The apocalyptic may offer hope in a time of near hopelessness, but the eschatological focuses on the goodness of God, people, and creation.

Section Forty-six:
More Parables: Watchfulness, Maidens, and Talents, 24:32—25:30

277. Matthew evidently wants people to pay attention to watchfulness. Probably Jesus frequently wanted people to take seriously his teachings and used many parables to explain his concern. Following Jesus meant making a decision and time is passing. Matthew combines the various parables to create a tapestry of teachings on watchfulness.

278. In the church some leaders think plenty of time remains just as many people in the pews share this belief. But God alone knows when a person's time on earth has ended. People are supposed to live each day as if it were the last because one day it will be the last. Failing to honor commitments and to live up to responsibilities can bring only heartache for all.

279. The generous person would have shared some oil. That seems to be the general outlook as someone reads the parable. They seem selfish. Christians are not selfish. But then all would have failed to meet the bridegroom. Sometimes paying attention to one's obligations, even when it adversely affects others, is the right thing to do.

280. It seems the punishment does not fit the crime. After all, they did not plan for contingencies. Why is that such a crime? Pay attention to a basic theme of Matthew going back to the temptations of Jesus. People have to learn to

accept the consequences of their actions. Rather than trying to take apart the parable, one should learn its meaning.

281. Once again, the punishment seems not to fit the crime. In this parable Jesus wants people to be prudent and take a chance. Security may not be the best answer if the easiest. "Put out into the deep" (Luke 5:4). Followers of Jesus do not just settle for security.

282. Fear, anxiety, lack of self-esteem or human respect can affect a person's inability to accept the consequences of her or his actions. Blaming others is always easier. Hiding the truth seems the prudent decision but nothing works other than acknowledging fault and moving on after correction.

Section Forty-seven: The Judgment, 25:31–46

283. More than any other gospel Matthew pays attention to law. No doubt he expected his listeners to understand the demands of law and the benefits of law. Yet, throughout the gospel he seems to go beyond the Law. Joseph the "just" man did not follow the Law. Jesus, who came not to destroy but to fulfill the Law, changed the Law. Matthew knows the law of the love of the neighbor also expresses the love of God. In the Gospel of John there is no twofold commandment but only the law of the love of the brethren (John 13:34).

284. Since Christians make up little more than a quarter of the world's population, the plan of God for universal salvation must go beyond Christianity. But perhaps not. The criteria for Christians surely can be applied to all people.

285. Matthew came from an institutional church with a clear purpose, rules, and authority. Evidently this is not enough. Christians do not fulfill their commitment to the Lord by

institutions but by how they treat each other and then all others.

286. Conservatives in general like law and order and rules. Liberals often overlook the rules and pay attention to human needs. Reducing all law and all criteria for the fullness of salvation to responding to human needs sounds more liberal than conservative.

287. People are usually afraid of judgment and do not look forward to the general judgment when the tradition teaches that all sins will be publicly revealed. The Gospel of John says that judgment has already taken place with the decision to come to the light and follow Jesus in faith (John 5:24). Matthew has a final judgment when those who have responded to the needs of the "little ones" are welcomed into heaven. People will die and will be judged as they have lived.

288. Many early church fathers, especially Eastern church fathers and theologians, could not reconcile eternal damnation with a merciful God. They could not conceive anything that a human being could do that would outweigh the love of God. Western theologians thought differently. Some early Eastern theologians believed in eventual universal salvation. They did not explain how other than the love of God overcomes all evil and sin. Western theologians taught the possibility of eternal damnation but never taught that the possibility ever became a reality even for a single person. God alone knows who are saved and who refuse salvation.

Section Forty-eight: The Plot, 26:1–16

289. As already noted, some Jews and some Romans were guilty of the physical death of Jesus by crucifixion. Any person who has tried to destroy what is good, especially another person, participates in the crucifixion since it was the human "no" to the power of goodness.

290. Anonymity happens frequently in the Bible. Most of the authors are anonymous. Even when names are given to books, very little is known about them. Most of the followers of Jesus other than the Twelve are anonymous. That the good deed remains in the telling is enough.

291. Many times people make terrible mistakes by not paying attention to the right time. Qoheleth says there is a time for everything (Eccl 3:1–9). A time to live and a time to die; a time to fast and a time to celebrate; a time to laugh and a time to cry; a time to speak and a time to be silent. The wise person picks the right time for the right activity.

292. Judas could not have been completely evil. Jesus chose him and he responded. Jesus must have loved him and he must have loved Jesus. Judas is a tragic figure to whom much was given. Unfortunately, he had a major flaw that he did nothing about until it was too late. Perhaps he wanted Jesus to be the political Messiah everyone wanted and tried to set things up to force Jesus to act. His plan backfired and Jesus died. Surely the words of Jesus on the cross, "Father, forgive them, for they know not what they do" (Luke 23:34), apply to Judas.

293. Money makes people forget about everything else. Money entices people to seek more and more. Money tells people to do anything to protect it. Too many people will do anything for money.

Section Forty-nine: The Passover and Last Supper, 26:17–35

294. No one will ever know exactly what Jesus knew in his ministry and what the gospel writers added to make Jesus appear as if he knew everything. In the Gospel of John Jesus knows everything throughout his ministry. In Mark

he does not know the day of judgment (Mark 13:32). Some will go immediately to the being of Jesus, the Second Person of the Blessed Trinity, and conclude he knew everything. Others will suppose he grew in knowledge just like any other human.

295. The Passover commemorated the Exodus, which created Judaism. God rescued a people in slavery and promised them land and prosperity. God was good to the people of Israel in the past, in the Exodus, and in Passover they expressed their hope God would continue to be good to the people of Israel in the present and in the future. In the Eucharist Christians proclaim the death and resurrection of the Lord, which created Christianity. God was good to them in the past through Jesus; God will continue to be good to them in the present and in the future because of the presence of Jesus.

296. Judas was a flawed disciple who suffered probably because of power rather than money. He gives followers of Jesus something to contemplate.

297. Jesus offered his sacrifice once for all (Heb 10:12–14). Offering creates the heart of sacrifice. Christians offer themselves daily and join their offering to the one eternal offering of the Lord. God sees the offering of Jesus and Christians share in the benefits.

298. Medieval theologians taught that the celebration of the Eucharist forgives sins since the perfect offering remains that of Jesus. The Eucharist usually begins with a confession of sins. When people ask pardon for their sins, God forgives the sins.

299. For many Jews, Jesus was a stumbling block, a scandal. He did not always observe the Law as prescribed by the religious authorities. How he died was a scandal (Deut 21:23). Paul says he was a stumbling block to the Jews (1 Cor

1:23). He remains a stumbling block to anyone without faith.

300. Peter appeals precisely because he was imperfect. He eventually recognizes his weakness and becomes strong in dying for the Lord and for the followers of the Lord. One of the strange coincidences of fate is that he may have been betrayed by one of the members of the Christian community at Rome. He followed the footsteps of his Master to the end.

Section Fifty:
The Arrest in the Garden, 26:36–56

301. Everyone desires company in life. The journey of life needs companions. In this regard Jesus was no different than anyone else. In his time of celebration he enjoyed the company of his disciples. In his time of sorrow and need he counted on them to be present but they failed. Christians today are the hands and heart of Jesus in the world. He needs them to continue his ministry to others, yet sometimes they sleep.

302. Giving one's will to another is always difficult. Giving to God is problematic, since who knows what God wants of a person? Allowing God to fill up the many nooks and crannies of the human personality takes time. God has patience and followers of Jesus should have patience. In their hearts people know what God desires. It just takes time for it to sink in.

303. Prayer allows God to enter into a person's life. Prayer allows the person to listen to God. Prayer helps in the filling of the nooks and crannies.

304. Friends always betray friends. No one ever lives up completely to the expectations of another. True friendship

remains in spite of betrayal since forgiveness can fill up the hole caused by betrayal. However, it may take time.

305. Some Christians proclaim and live nonviolence. They stand in tribute to the teachings of Jesus and remind all other Christians of the ideal to be pursued. In a violent world, not all can bear testimony to nonviolence.

306. Jesus may have been arrested as a revolutionary although he was not. He did disturb the peace by disturbing the religious authorities. Rome would not want any trouble and so the Roman authorities went along. He was no threat to Rome, as became evident only after several hundred years.

Section Fifty-one:
The Trial and Peter's Denial, 26:57–75

307. The religious authorities wanted Jesus dead. The Romans would cooperate. They knew that. Whether the trial was legal or not made no difference. Any organization, when threatened, will do anything to protect itself. If legal means cannot be used, then illegal will do just as well. This is especially true if the leaders are accountable only to themselves. The religious authorities knew that the Romans would not interfere and the people were incapable of countermanding the decision of their religious leaders. Legal or not made no difference.

308. Blasphemy was cursing or reviling God or anything associated with God or claiming the attributes of God. Speaking against the Temple for a pious Jew was blasphemy. Making oneself equal to God was blasphemy. For many pious Jews, Jesus was guilty. For Christians he was innocent since they believed he was the divine Son of God.

309. Sometimes silence is the best defense. Jesus knew when to speak and when to remain silent. He knew when to say "yes" and when to say "no" and that was sufficient. His followers can learn from his example.

310. Sometimes religious leaders, like those in authority, follow procedures but often when the procedures do not fit the occasion they are abandoned. Sometimes not following procedures is good and sometimes it is bad. Wisdom makes the difference.

311. Each gospel presents Peter as a spokesperson. Matthew alone has the episode in which Jesus gives him the keys (Matt 16:16). Peter appears frequently in this gospel. Perhaps Matthew wants to acknowledge that the leader, the "rock," sometimes can be a weak "pebble."

Section Fifty-two:
Jesus and Judas and Barabbas, 27:1–26

312. Much of what we know about Judas and his treachery has roots in the Old Testament. Each gospel refers to him as the one who betrayed Jesus, but only Matthew and the Acts add any details after the betrayal. With the death of Jesus, the early followers used Judas to explain just how Jesus fell into the hands of his enemies. It seems the early church did not have many details about the later life of Judas and so took some details from the Old Testament and applied them to Judas. If his problem was power, perhaps eventually he was able to deal with it before he died. No one really knows.

313. Pilate was weak. The finding of a memorial stone with his name on it near Caesarea is the only nonbiblical reference to him. Thus he never progressed in the Roman hierarchy. Legally he was responsible for the death of Jesus. He could have dismissed the charges but for political reasons he

complied. As the representative of Rome in a backwater part of the empire, he probably had ambitions and would do nothing to impede advancement. He saw no advantage in not giving in to the demands of the religious leaders. Although Pilate is a saint in the Coptic martyrology, most Christians remember him with indifference if not disdain. Evidently he did not advance politically.

314. The Jews should have chosen the Son of the true Father in heaven. Instead, they chose Barabbas, whoever he was. Matthew does not often use irony or a play on words. He does so here. Too often Christians make other choices in which they reject the Son of the Father for some trite and momentary earthly need.

315. Women are often in the background of the gospels. Yet, if one pays attention to when they appear and what they do, it seems they played significant roles in the ministry of Jesus and in early Christianity. This is a subtle case of Matthean irony: the woman recognizes Jesus as "just," the same word Matthew used in referring to Joseph in chapter 1. The woman sees and the political leader is blind.

316. People are fickle. Bread and circuses please. When they stop, people are less interested. Jesus has ceased to be a charming performer and has become a condemned man. At least crucifixion is something to watch.

317. Frequently people in this gospel refuse to accept the consequences of their actions. In the temptations of Jesus, Matthew picks out this temptation as fundamental in human existence. It remains so. Pilate blames the Jews and will not accept his role in the condemnation and death of Jesus although legally he was responsible.

Section Fifty-three:
The Crucifixion and Death,
27:27–56

318. Usually people strike back when mocked. Jesus does not. When someone makes fun of another, the victim wants to retaliate. If clever, the victim will think of some cutting remark or will wait for an opportunity to get even. Jesus ignores the mockery, which often is the best revenge.

319. Some think the drink was drugged, as it was customary to give the crucified a drink that would lessen the pain. Of course, the reference to the psalm adds another dimension. Instead of lessening the pain, the jeerers wanted to increase it. Jesus refuses, or at least that was the tradition. He did not need to run from his fate. He accepted crucifixion as part of his destiny. Some may want to model themselves after Jesus and refuse any effort to lessen pain. Others rightfully will accept any relief possible. Life brings pain and modern medicine can alleviate some pain. Christians are surely able to avail themselves of what medicine offers.

320. Some feared a political meaning. Some wanted a political king of the Jews. For most it probably means the Messiah but as already noted, different people had different understandings of the Messiah. If Jesus is king, he is king of hearts and not of any earthly kingdom.

321. Most people like the good thief and despise the other. Some prisons have chapels dedicated to Dismas, the good thief. Redemption is always possible. The good thief took advantage of his situation and received salvation.

322. Faith does not depend on miracles. Jesus, like the prophets of old, pointed out the presence and absence of God in history. Some accepted him as speaking in the name of God and others did not. Jesus would not be used to perform.

For a person of faith, God was present in the death of Jesus, even the cruel death of crucifixion.

323. Matthew had trouble with religious leaders, as did Jesus. Matthew never seems to miss an opportunity to present them in an unfavorable light. This may be indicative of Matthew and his community.

Section Fifty-four:
Death and Burial, 27:45–66

324. If not, it should have. Just as the heavens declared the birth of a great person by some unusual sign (the star of Bethlehem), earlier peoples believed that the earth would mourn the death of a great person. Maybe there was an earthquake. Whatever the history, the meaning is clear: creation mourned the death of the Son of God.

325. Jesus had to experience the darkness of separation in death as every human must. Otherwise he would not have been like us in all things but sin. In dying every person has to trust that God is present in the dying process. Just as God may seem to be absent in life, and God is not absent, so the same may be true in death. Some like to think Jesus is reciting the psalm and does not experience the darkness of separation. If people have to face this darkness, Jesus did it as well.

326. Some can enter into the experience of another and help bear the pain. Others increase the pain by their actions or lack of action. What was true two thousand years ago is true today. How much more pleasant life is when one is surrounded by compassionate people.

327. The imagery expresses the release of those good people, though dead, from any pain or even separation from God.

They too would enjoy the benefits of Jesus. His death affected all whether people are aware of it or not.

328. This would have pleased his Gentile Christian community. The unexpected came to faith and the expected did not. Sometimes the most unlikely people are people of great faith.

329. Women always played a significant role in the ministry of Jesus. Mary Magdalene is not a prostitute. Although Luke 8:2 refers to Jesus driving out demons, this need not refer to devils. She was not the woman taken in adultery. She was at the foot of the cross (Matt 27:56; Mark 15:40; John 19:25) and Jesus appeared to her first after his resurrection (John 20:1–18). She is portrayed more a saint than a sinner.

330. The enemies of Jesus and his followers could always claim that his disciples stole the body. Matthew wanted to deal with this claim firsthand.

Section Fifty-five: The Empty Tomb and Resurrection, 28:1–15

331. Drama can help faith if faith is already present. Drama cannot create faith. Matthew will end with power and triumph. Jesus conquers death. His enemies do not win. The "no" of people to goodness turns to the "yes" of God. Jesus lives a Messiah in power.

332. The ending of Mark has long been disputed. Over the centuries many added longer endings. Perhaps Mark wanted his listeners to find the resurrected Christ on their own. He had no resurrection appearances. Matthew wants to end in triumph.

333. Oral traditions live longer than many think. Especially in an age of limited literacy people memorized long stories

and epics. Many stories of Jesus must have circulated during the first century into the second century. Matthew would have learned of some of these and included them in his account. The Gospel of John probably came from an eyewitness, at least from the times of Jesus in Jerusalem. Some of those stories would have circulated independently from the gospel and could explain how the two gospels are similar in some details.

334. All of the appearance stories of Jesus after the resurrection involve people who already believe, however weakly. The only exception is Paul. Since Jesus did not appear to his enemies, either religious or civil leaders, the story of the stolen body could circulate with little difficulty. However, people believe in the resurrected Lord and not in an empty tomb, which makes the difference.

Section Fifty-six: The Dramatic Conclusion of the Gospel of Matthew, 28:16–20

335. Matthew has the best ending of all the gospels. Mark ends with confusion, Luke concludes with the story of the two disciples on the road to Emmaus, and John has two endings that sound literary. Only Matthew ends with a flair. The all-powerful Lord sets the scene for the church and promises his abiding presence. Just think how Hollywood in film would create this wonderful ending!

336. The institutional church has a common bond, a purpose and authority and rules. Matthew includes all of these in his ending to his gospel. The bond is faith in Jesus, the purpose is making disciples, the authority is Jesus and the eleven, and the rules are obeying the eleven.

337. In this gospel alone Jesus gives Peter the authority to bind and loose (16:16). Peter and the Twelve have authority and in chapter 18 the whole community has the power to bind and loose.

338. Matthew's community is composed of both groups. Matthew ends with preaching to all nations. Matthew includes everyone.

339. Jesus remains in church leaders, in the Eucharist, and wherever his faithful followers gather in prayer.

Bibliography

Betz, Hans Dieter. *The Sermon on the Mount*. Minneapolis: Fortress, 1995.

Hare, Douglas. *Matthew. Interpretation*. Louisville: John Knox, 1993.

Harrington, Daniel. *The Gospel of Matthew. Sacra Pagina*. Collegeville: Liturgical Press, 1991.

Kingsbury, Jack Dean. *Matthew*. Philadelphia: Fortress, 1986.

———. *Matthew as Story*. Philadelphia: Fortress, 1989.

Luz, Ulrich. *Matthew 8—20*. Minneapolis: Fortress, 2001.

Meier, John. *Matthew*. Wilmington: Michael Glazier, 1980.

Morris, Leon. *The Gospel According to Matthew*. Grand Rapids: Eerdmans, 1992.

Schnackenburg, Rudolf. *The Gospel of Matthew*. Grand Rapids: Eerdmans, 2002.

Schweizer, Eduard. *The Good News According to Matthew*. Atlanta: John Knox, 1975.

Senior, Donald, *The Gospel of Matthew*. Nashville: Abingdon, 1997.

———. *Matthew*. Nashville: Abingdon, 1998.